C000171974

BACKING BLETCHLEY

BACKING BLETCHLEY

The Codebreaking Outstations,
from Eastcote to GCHQ

Ronald Koorm

AMBERLEY

First published 2020

Amberley Publishing
The Hill, Stroud
Gloucestershire, GL5 4EP

www.amberley-books.com

Copyright © Ronald Koorm, 2020

The right of Ronald Koorm to be identified as
the Author of this work has been asserted in
accordance with the Copyrights, Designs and
Patents Act 1988.

ISBN 978 1 4456 9652 2 (hardback)
ISBN 978 1 4456 9653 9 (ebook)

All rights reserved. No part of this book may
be reprinted or reproduced or utilised in any
form or by any electronic, mechanical or other
means, now known or hereafter invented,
including photocopying and recording, or in any
information storage or retrieval system, without
the permission in writing from the Publishers.

British Library Cataloguing in Publication Data.
A catalogue record for this book is available
from the British Library.

Typesetting by Aura Technology and Software
Services, India. Printed in the UK.

CONTENTS

This book is dedicated to my good friend David Plummer, who inspired me to start giving talks on Eastcote and the codebreaking outstations, and to further research the subject.

I also thank my wife Susan for supporting me in this venture, encouraging me to share my knowledge with others, for not complaining when I bury my head in specialist books, for keeping my lecture appointments diary up to date, and for making those cups of refreshing Earl Grey tea.

INTRODUCTION

Few people are aware of the significant contribution the outstations made to the British intelligence effort in the Second World War. By outstations, we generally mean the codebreaking outstations that deciphered German military intelligence messages. But 'outstation' has also a more expansive meaning too, being the wider infrastructure supporting the renowned Bletchley Park, and enabling it to do its job efficiently. Indeed, without the outstations, Bletchley Park's work would have had a limited impact on the outcome of the war.

This extensive infrastructure made Allied codebreaking possible. Although there are snippets of information in many books out there as regards the outstations, they are fragmented. This book, then, is an attempt to bring that information together in one place. The subject is part of the wider story of both military codebreaking history and the later development of the Government Communication Headquarters (GCHQ), which still exists today. The role of GCHQ has expanded in terms of challenges and resources, to fight terrorism and cyber-attacks. The next war may well avoid guns and armies, and concentrate on intercepting and disabling government infrastructure through those cyber-attacks.

The development of this support mechanism evolved over time, originating in Room 40 in Whitehall, many years before Hitler was elected Chancellor of Germany. Some sections were developed via trial and error, as this was an age of innovation, challenges and 'can-do' attitudes, which made Britain a force to be reckoned with. A problem was identified, and with teamwork, ideas were tabled and worked through to arrive at a pragmatic solution. Inevitably there were disagreements, arguments and fallings-out among senior personnel at times. After all, the stakes were high. Get it wrong, and Hitler would be occupying the United Kingdom. The British had to be robust in their methods, coordinating ideas and plans and helping the best ones to flourish.

Alan Turing is the name that most people know in relation to this work, and he is remembered for his forward-thinking use of machines to help with codebreaking. But there were so many others, less well known, who also made major contributions to victory and the post-war development of intelligence gathering and decoding. In studying and researching this subject, the core information on codebreaking outstations and infrastructure can be considered as the central part of a large jigsaw puzzle. I have those key pieces in place in the centre of the puzzle, and have

Room 40, June 1919.

been working my way out, picking up more and more detailed information. The big picture became clearer as more detail was found in the National Archives at Kew, through reading widely on the subject, visiting some of the wartime bases, reviewing various maps and diagrams, and talking to people who were involved, or whose parents were, all those years ago.

Where the people were at the time of the incident, the dates, the times, the activities performed, the options available, the choices made, the mistakes made, and of course the outcome, all clarify the situation. Occasionally, one comes across 'facts' which are reported differently in various places, and one has to make a judgement as to which of the accounts is accurate. Many of the people who have the answers are, sadly, no longer with us. Some answers are lost forever.

I am grateful to those who have taken the time to discuss elements of this subject with me and have passed on information and I thank those who have attended my talks on the subject. There has been considerable local interest when I have spoken in Eastcote, Ruislip and Northwood, as the largest codebreaking base is just down the road from the venue – or would be if it hadn't been flattened for a modern housing estate. But even if you live at the other end of the country, you should celebrate the innovation, determination and work of many thousands of people from all walks of life who contributed to this success story through their codebreaking and intelligence-gathering activities.

It is even more important to enable the younger generation to learn from what happened, and to see the crucial role played by teamwork. This was one huge coordinated and managed process, with a common cause. From the motorcycle dispatch riders travelling in all weather with little sleep or rest to the mathematicians at Bletchley Park, from the listening stations to the WRNS personnel (Wrens) who operated the codebreaking machines, from the designers and builders of the machines to those who had to maintain them and repair them when they failed, all played a vital part.

One of the most fascinating aspects of this subject for me is the social interaction during this period, with Wrens and others of different social classes having to get on with the job together, sleeping in the same barracks and doing similar jobs day after day. It was a sort of extended social experiment, as the class system was deeply entrenched at this time. It was demonstrated that anything is achievable with a common cause, which can overcome class, gender, race, creed and ethnic background. Though prejudice against using women for certain tasks did arise at Bletchley Park, it was soon quashed when the women proved themselves capable. The use of women also released men to fight. It was a 'win-win' situation.

In researching the subject matter, I was in awe of handling the actual Bombe Registers, which detailed all the Bombe codebreaking machines in some detail. I had part of British and Allied history in my hands. To be allowed access to such documents, and many others besides, was a privilege and an honour. To see the abbreviations 'O.S.E.' or 'O.S.S.' against a Bombe codebreaking machine's name or identity, representing Eastcote or Stanmore as the identity of the site it was based at. was fascinating; these abbreviations conceal part of our history.

An old school friend of mine emigrated to the US, and now lives in San Francisco. I emailed him a little summary of what went on at Eastcote. I mentioned that it was the British, and not the Americans, who later designed and built the world's first electronic computer during the war. He promptly emailed back that, well, it all depends how you define 'computer'. But as he had grown up for part of his childhood in Willesden, London, he was pleased that Willesden was only down the road from the place where the computer was designed and constructed. He now probably tells his friends and family that he grew up close to a historically important base in London. The Wrens, many quite young, were operating this new machine, albeit with a degree of technical supervision. There was trust in these people, who had worked on other sensitive technical aspects of the codebreaking process.

At Bletchley Park, a visiting couple asked me to take their photograph. It transpired that the lady's late mother worked at Chicksands, one of the many listening stations during the war. However, she had given away very little even to her daughter as to what she did, as security fears were instilled in the workers by the government at the time. This has resulted in many people's stories going with them to their graves. Churchill famously expressed his gratitude after the war for 'the geese that laid the golden eggs but would not cackle'.

There was a price to pay for that secrecy. Sons and daughters would sometimes feel awkward, and perhaps hurt, that their mother or father would not tell them exactly what they did in wartime. The nation would fall behind America and other countries who raced ahead in the early part of the computer age and flourished economically through companies like IBM. Perhaps, in hindsight, being more flexible and open after the war would not have made any real impact on our national security and indeed might have helped the UK enter the computer age more successfully.

Some, like Gordon Welchman, a key player at Bletchley Park, were effectively destroyed in the late 1970s and early 1980s. Welchman was prevented from contributing to the overall security of the West after he published *The Hut Six Story: Breaking the Enigma Codes* in 1982. The government abhorred his openness and he was fortunate not to end up in jail. He and his family were very bitter about this. They, and many others, felt he had done nothing wrong in writing his book. It was withdrawn on government and security agency advice, and most of the copies were destroyed. First published with approval in 1997, reissued in 2011, revised and reprinted in 2018 and with some parts removed, it is now available in bookshops, including the one at Bletchley Park.

I decided to the chapter 'Codebreaking For and Against the Russians' early on in the book as it helps to put into context the reasons why the Allies were comfortable with providing certain intelligence to help the Russians but not so keen to provide the source or sources of that intelligence – i.e. Enigma/Bombe or Lorenz/Colossus. A breach of security due to the Russians or others being careless could potentially set the Allied war effort back by months at a critical time. The background here is highly complex, and often overlooked in articles on the Internet. The World Wide Web is a wonderful resource, but one does have to be extremely selective and careful in using it for historical research. It is too easy to absorb things that later turn out to be mere hearsay. This is why, in some cases, I cannot guarantee that certain persons visited Eastcote after the war, but all indications point to the high probability that they did visit that base, particularly when one finds multiple references to them.

Although 'Eastcote' is in the title, clearly there were a number of other important outstations, and they all had their crucial part to play. There are two specific types of outstations: (a) Those which had actual codebreaking equipment, and operated it under the instructions of the HQ or codebreaking hub; and (b) Those which provided a key support role to Bletchley Park, but did not carry out codebreaking operations themselves.

This overall picture is difficult to convey in films about Enigma, as the interaction between all the relevant places is quite complex. Some may come away from the film *The Imitation Game* assuming everything was done at Bletchley Park during the war. Of course, that film was about Alan Turing, but you will find no reference to Eastcote, or indeed any of the outstations, the places of manufacture for codebreaking machines, the development of the devices that challenged the more advanced German encoding machines, the operators of the codebreaking 'Bombes', etc. It must be borne in mind that the film is not a documentary.

I found the 2001 film *Enigma* had far more tension than the later film, but it must be admitted the plot was fictional. Perhaps John Barry's last beautiful soundtrack made the difference. There was one mention of the complex mathematical permutations of Enigma in the latter, as the mathematicians at Bletchley walked between the huts one night, but the dialogue was such that one could easily miss the reference. This latter film did not obtain anywhere near the prominence that it deserved, but at least it was a film about Enigma.

There have been some excellent documentaries over the years about Bletchley Park and some of the individuals who worked there, such as Captain Jerry Roberts and Gordon Welchman. Let there be more of those.

Some of the content of this book may seem to veer from the subject of outstations at times, and to go into broader areas, which may initially appear unrelated. However, I always intend for there to be a link back to the outstations and codebreaking somewhere along the line.

Eastcote was the largest codebreaking outstation and later became GCHQ, which is why it features so prominently. But the other outstations were just as effective. They employed the same calibre of Wrens, engineers and personnel as at Eastcote, and had similar codebreaking machines, but in smaller quantities.

Chapter 20, 'Colossus, Michie and A.I.', explores the contributions of Alan Turing, Donald Michie, Max Newman, Tommy Flowers and others to the development of artificial intelligence. I have discussed the subject with a person who actually worked with Donald Michie, and while I do not pretend to be an expert on this subject, I do believe there is a significant link between codebreaking in the Second World War and artificial intelligence.

The unforgettable beginning of Stanley Kubrick's film *2001: A Space Odyssey* shows early man discovering that an animal bone can be used as a tool before the scene leaps thousands of years into the future to a space station.[1] Similarly, the Turing Bombe and Colossus were relatively primitive but important 'tools', the 'bones' in our quest towards artificial intelligence. This was not known at the time; the development of Colossus was as a weapon of war, and nothing to do with A.I. Nonetheless, it was an important rung in that ladder of opportunity to make machines work for mankind. In the short term, the consequences of its success were arguably to save millions of lives and avoid further suffering on both sides of the war. People began to learn from those systems, designs and processes.

If you have never been to the National Archives in Kew, I do advise a visit. The range of subject matter and information available is mind-boggling, and there will be something for everyone to investigate further. It's about our history and our heritage, so please do use it, and encourage your older children to do so. Wherever you are based in the UK, you can do some basic research of your own, to discover what role your local area played in contributing to the outcome of the war. You may well be surprised at what you find.

I

ARTHUR SCHERBIUS

It is 1918, and the First World War is at an end. This is the year
when Arthur Scherbius, a German engineer, patented his new
'Enigma' machine. Enigma was not the first rotary-based security
encoding machine, as the Dutch had got there first. But the Dutch
were slow in organising their patents, and Scherbius registered
his patent promptly. The original machine was cumbersome and
inefficient, but it was soon to be developed into something that
caught the attention of many different sectors of industry. Enigma
was a technically advanced security encoding machine, allowing
messages to be sent under secret code using a cipher system which
relied on the use of rotating wheels, electrical circuits and wiring.
It was developed from a rotary-based writing machine which had
been invented by Dutchman Hugo Koch.[2]

Scherbius was an inventor and engineer. He was born in
Frankfurt and, having studied in Munich and Hanover, had a
PhD and several patents to his name, including one for an electric
pillow and advanced work on electrical asynchronous motors.
His first company was called Scherbius & Ritter and was based
in Berlin, with a factory for the manufacturing of the machine.

'Enigma' is the Greek word for 'riddle', or puzzle, which it certainly proved to be.

Scherbius exhibited Enigma at an exhibition for postal services in 1923 and it soon started to attract attention, partly because of its unique claims in the promotional literature. Telegrams and cables were the standard mode of communication at the time, and sometimes one needed to safeguard sensitive information from prying eyes. Enigma was marketed as a commercial business machine, and its advertising targeted finance houses and the banking industry, who wanted to transmit confidential messages. Scherbius claimed in his literature that Enigma was unbreakable as a security cipher device, mainly due to the removable rotor wheels, which introduced many millions of permutations in the settings.

The German military were approached but did not seem interested at the time. Even the British were invited to look at Enigma, and they considered it too cumbersome to use in the field. By 1925, production of Enigma had reached an industrial scale, and by the next year Enigma had many different clients, with interest growing. In 1927, British patents were applied for and received for the device.

A man called Edward Travis, an important individual within part of the Government Code and Cipher School (GC&CS) in London, investigated further. Travis would later take over the role of running Bletchley Park intelligence operations. GC&CS was formed out of an intelligence division in October 1914 from an area known as Room 40 (Old Building) at the Admiralty in London. Intelligence had proved essential to winning battles during the First World War, and it would become more sophisticated over time.

Travis was deputy to Alastair Denniston, who would go down in history as the enabler of Bletchley Park as an intelligence and decoding base. At this time Denniston was second in command of the Room 40 intelligence base at the Admiralty. Curious by nature, Travis acquired an Enigma from Germany. After all, anyone could go to the factory and purchase one, as initially it was a commercially available machine. Travis asked some of his staff to further investigate Enigma, to check the claims made in the sales literature in respect of the level of security claimed. The sales brochure was headed 'The Glowlamp Ciphering and Deciphering machine "Enigma"'.

It would not be long before Enigma would be adopted by the German armed forces and the German railways, and produced in vast numbers for the country, of which more later. Interest also came from Italy and Switzerland. A special version was made for the Swiss early on. We will look later at the position of the neutral Swiss. One could ask, if they were neutral, why would they need an Enigma machine, and what did they have to hide? But Enigma could be used for so many purposes, and as Switzerland was a major finance centre for Europe, having a secure means of communication between banks and financiers would be simply prudent and forward-looking.

Enigma machines were now in a wooden box with folding top and front, a portable machine looking like a common typewriter but with no means of printing letters. Enigma Models 'B' and 'C' were still in need of further development but now incorporated an illuminated lampboard, where encoded letters could be seen as one typed the message to be encoded on the keys. This would be a significant common element in the design of all future Enigma machines. A plugboard, or *steckerboard*, was added at the front, to enhance the complexity and permutations of encoded letters, and that had a sort of mini-telephone exchange appearance, with many sockets and plugs and cables. The workings of the Enigma in 1927 were clearly described in the British patent, so everyone interested could see the principles of the design. It was not a secret.

But just because one had the machine and the patent description and sales literature did not mean that one could break Enigma, any more than describing the vault at Fort Knox and looking at plans enables you to successfully break in. What you needed to do was reverse-engineer the code settings, rotor sequence, the plugboard

The Enigma machine. (Photograph reproduced with permission of the Bletchley Park Trust)

connections and the electrical circuit routing. Enigma was quite advanced for its time, and arguably the most secure encoding machine in the world.

Scherbius made a big deal of the relevance and importance of the three rotors in Enigma, and the fact that one could change the sequence of them and add additional ones in their place. These rotors would have letters of the alphabet inscribed around them. Scherbius also made the point that if you removed the wheel rotors your adversaries would be none the wiser if they captured your machine, as it would be rendered effectively useless. The rotors were a key part of the system, and future cryptographers would spend a good part of their time trying to analyse those wheels and their sequencing. The investigation by the British resulted in a detailed technical report in 1928, describing how the machine was constructed and its strengths and weaknesses.

Scherbius had realized his Enigma had not sold well initially, and that he needed to upgrade and improve the machine so it was less expensive, more portable, simpler to use, and could reach a wider market. He reorganised the company to make it more efficient and reduce costs in manufacturing. He managed to bring the cost down to around one-eighth of the original, also reducing the weight considerably for easier portability. The plugboard made a huge difference to the permutations of letters for encoding. Now it was starting to gain momentum, and a version was made for the German railway. The German Navy, the *Kriegsmarine*, soon realised this machine had potential to be utilised on a large scale. It was not long before Scherbius started to get orders from them and other branches of the German armed forces, but only when it was made clear that commercial availability to the public had to stop. But by this time, the British and the Poles had already acquired Enigma machines to investigate, not knowing how significant they would become over the next few years.

Scherbius was delighted with the renewed interest in Enigma, and continued to make further models and improvements. The early years would have been tough, when frequent knockbacks from unimpressed clients would have left him frustrated. But he persevered. Over the years at least fifteen different versions or models of Enigma were made, and variations on some of those too.[3] The encoding became more advanced as modifications were made. Between 50,000 and 100,000 Enigmas were built eventually, principally for Germany, although the Italians, Hungarians, Dutch and Swiss also had them specifically made to suit their needs.

Sadly, Arthur Scherbius failed to live long enough to see his Enigma used on a large scale, as he died at the age of fifty in a horse-and-carriage accident in 1929. Before his death, Scherbius had bought Koch's patents in 1927 for rotary encoding machines. Scherbius's death was most inconvenient, coming at a time when Engima was gaining appreciation among the armed forces for its innovative design. Had he lived longer he would have been astonished, and possibly flattered, by the significant resources of men, women, materials, buildings, factories and infrastructure that would have to be organised by the Allies in order to penetrate and break the codes of his machines.

Codebreaking outstations such as Wavendon, Eastcote and Stanmore might not have existed had it not been for Arthur Scherbius and his Enigma machine. However, if Enigma had not been invented at that time, something else probably would have taken its place for the enhancement of German military security and encoding operations. Rotary encoding machines were being produced by others; Arthur Scherbius simply got there before them with his patents.

It would have been an interesting scenario if the British had ordered Enigma machines on a large scale for their own armed forces, but they were not convinced of Enigma's worth as a practical machine on the battlefield. As you would require two or even three people to make use of an Enigma machine, the British had a point. There would be various stages of error-free operational procedure which slowed down the process of converting a confidential text message to transmit it to a receiving station; fine in an office, but it would not be quite so easy in a bomb crater or trench. Some of these problems would be overcome through practice and familiarisation with the machine, but it was not straightforward. What if you were installing the special wheel rotors quickly, according to the codebook supplied, and you accidentally got them stuck so they wouldn't rotate properly, and had to un-jam them? Or dropped a rotor in the mud or a trench, and had to find it and clean it before you could insert it back in the machine? Perhaps these situations might be rare, but any machine with loose components would be potentially vulnerable to damage. At least the machine was largely self-contained, and didn't need lots of loose, lengthy cables to a power supply, as it could run on an integral battery.

Production of machines had to be ramped up, special versions made, new rotors designed, reflector wheels added to reverse the encoding circuit process, and of course it all had to be tested. Enigma had to be even more unbreakable as an enciphering machine than before. The volume of machines, spares and codebooks would have to meet the demands of the armed services and a manual of instructions and training would have to support it.

Enigma began to see use in military operations around 1935. The British had to get up to speed quickly to take this machine seriously. Koch, the Dutchman, became involved in further development of Enigma after Scherbius died. The *Abwehr*, or German secret service, headed by Admiral Canaris, insisted upon their own unique version of Enigma; the model 'G' Enigma would have no plugboard facility at the front of the machine, but would have four rotor wheels, which made cracking the code much more difficult. Enigma in its many different versions would become the main security device for the German armed forces and secret services, and it would be carried in the field by soldiers, sailors, U-boat commanders, the Luftwaffe and the Panzer divisions. It would be used by their Italian allies and by sympathisers in Spain and elsewhere.

The Enigma, and its transcribed Morse communication, would be in constant and frequent use in the field: recording the continual movement of troops and supplies and planning of attacks and counter-attacks; reporting Allied positions for their 88mm guns to target; telling tank commanders at which grid reference on the map to meet up with other tanks and infantry before making an assault; transmitting information about the location of pockets of resistance. Enigma also confirmed the transport arrangements for sending Jews, and others, to concentration camps.

The British had been intercepting encoded Enigma messages from around 1926, but with no simple, practical, repeatable way of decoding them. They needed the input of the Poles, who were advanced in cryptographic techniques. Three Polish mathematicians eventually broke the Enigma code in 1933. One of these, Henryk Zygalski, would later become known for his method of inventing a process of overlaying many sheets of paper with permutations of letters with a light or lightbox shining through various holes to show patterns of letters to aid the decoding process. Zygalski sheets would be used and adapted by Bletchley Park for at least some of the decoding.

Around 1928, a package from Germany ended up at Warsaw's customs office. It was supposed to contain radio equipment, and the Germans had sent it to Poland by mistake and wanted it back. They were most insistent on having it returned immediately. The Polish customs officials were suspicious, and carefully opened the package to find an Enigma machine inside. They carefully studied it, and after disassembling it took copious notes and made diagrams before reassembling it, putting it back in its box and wrapping it up again. This was a real coup for the Poles, who had the opportunity to have a close look at the latest Enigma machine and would capitalise on that crucial information, the Germans being none the wiser. This incident gave them a head start as to the version of Enigma that was to be used by the German military, even though it would change and develop further over time.

The Wehrmacht, Luftwaffe and *Kriegsmarine* would each require their own versions from about 1932. The *Kriegsmarine* would require additional levels of security. These versions, particularly around 1942, would cause the Allies headaches, with many months of failed attempts to break the codes.[4] This was due to the additional rotors provided in those machines, plus the enhanced codebooks (short weather codebook and short signals codebook), and complex protocols adopted by officers to decode messages.

Arthur Scherbius, never lived to hear of Bletchley Park or Eastcote. But he would have still maintained that Enigma was unbreakable – after all, it said so in his sales literature.

2

THE ENIGMA CHALLENGE

In 1908 a middle-aged gentleman and his new wife spent part of their honeymoon in Eastcote, Middlesex. That gentleman was Winston Churchill, and his new wife was Clementine. They were in Highgrove House, located near Eastcote High Road. A family friend had a connection and offered the use of Highgrove until they moved to central London.⁵ Churchill had always been interested in military intelligence, and in future years would become more fascinated and deeply involved in the subject.

An old footpath nearby dated back to the sixteenth century. We don't know if Churchill wandered across that footpath from Highgrove House to stand at the five-bar gate overlooking a large field with cattle grazing and a cattle-trough near the gate; if he had done, he would not have been aware that in thirty-five years' time there would be many buildings and structures on that site, housing the largest codebreaking intelligence outstation in the country. He was literally a stone's throw from what was to become 'Outstation Eastcote' and GCHQ, post-war.

Churchill was a military man. He had been First Lord of the Admiralty from 1911 to 1915, and realised more than most the

Churchill on his wedding day.

importance of military intelligence, knowing more about your enemy's intentions, and far more than the enemy knew about you. Given the choice of extra tanks and troops or finding out in advance what your enemy was planning, Churchill would have chosen the latter. That was part of the key to military success in battle. As Prime Minister, Churchill insisted on being in the loop as regarded reports from Bletchley Park, the hub of the codebreaking process. He wanted to be aware of what the Germans were up to, as well as the Russians.

Churchill wanted every intelligence message on his desk, but the volume of intercepts would make that impossible. Instead, he accepted a summary of the most interesting decoded communications. That kept him busy, but also made him aware of what the Bletchley Park staff were up against. Churchill would later restrict access to decoded intelligence to a select few, cutting the numbers down from a much larger group, to avoid leaks. That would prove to be a wise decision.

The key difference between the First and Second World Wars, as regards military codebreaking, revolved around the mathematics and logic analysis needed to detect patterns and sequences in enemy messages. Coding and decoding in the first war relied on 'wordsmiths'. Whilst there was an element of that in the war against Hitler, one would not be able to make much progress without an understanding of mathematics, probability, sequences and mathematical patterns; hence the recruitment of British mathematics scholars. It is why the core of the codebreaking team had to be able to think logically, and sometimes 'out of the box', to make real progress. Being good at crosswords might be considered a help, but would not be enough to penetrate the modern encoding machines. One needed to spot mathematical sequences within those revolving rotors, and calculate probabilities of fitting various patterns using multiples of numbers, which were linked to the encoded message.

Unless you were in this clique of specialists, who thought in mathematical terms and applied mathematical logic, you would probably not get anywhere in decoding enemy intelligence. Even if you were qualified to do so, there would be few short-cuts in probing Enigma and other later advanced encoding machines, with many failures and frustration along the way. The Germans would be constantly updating and improving Enigma, making it more secure over time, modifying it, making specialist versions for different parts of the armed forces, and even other countries who wished to procure Enigma machines for themselves, like the Swiss and Italians. Bletchley Park may have had the odd replica Enigma machine acquired pre-war, and could investigate the design and mechanism in some detail, but that did not mean they could automatically decode the messages. At the time of the acquisitions, in the late twenties and early thirties, no one could have foreseen how widespread the Enigma machine would become for the German armed forces, the Italians and, later, the Japanese.[6]

It was the Poles who first cracked Enigma, manually, and with the help of three determined mathematicians. They would later assist the French and the British to understand the German cipher system and Enigma machine. The Poles would rely on their specialist codebreaking machine, the 'Bomba', to help them save time in deciphering the intelligence. But when the *Steckerboard* or plugboard was added at the front of the Enigma machine, this design change effectively made the 'Bomba' codebreaking machine obsolete overnight.[7] By mid-1928 the German Army had their own Enigma version, the model G. By 1930, the plugboard was incorporated into army machines.

The modified version 'G' Enigma became the model 'I', and this German Wehrmacht army version of the Enigma was a very different animal to the original. However, it would require at least two, and often three people to operate it in accordance with an encoding and transmitting process of secure messages. It would have keys only for letters, and no numbers or punctuation keys. It would take up valuable time to write in text-form numbers and map references via Enigma. The plugboard at the front of the machine was behind a hinged wooden door-flap, where you could connect with short cables and plugs up to twelve pairs of letters at the front, to improve the permutations of encoding, although in practice only ten pairs of letters were 'steckered' or linked with connecting cables. That would have left six remaining letters unconnected. It gave a significant boost to the level of security.

The job of typing out the entire number was also open to errors. One of the operators would have to set up the wheels, or rotors, at the top of the machine, note down the encoded letters that lit up on the display board, and then convert them into Morse code (in the relevant language, of course), and send them over the radio. That meant that encoded letters could sometimes be written down incorrectly, as it was a manual process, and that there was a second chance of an error when converting the encoded letters into Morse code for transmission. The errors would add some confusion later, particularly for the Allies trying to break the codes. Once the decoded letters were noted they had to be written down individually, and transferred to a sheet to be passed on to a person in authority. So many opportunities for errors, but it had one great advantage: it was a portable machine and could be taken into the

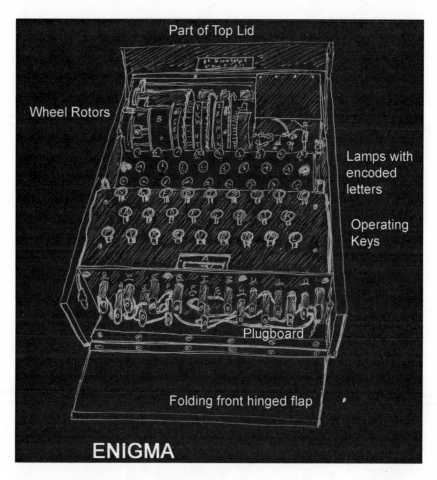

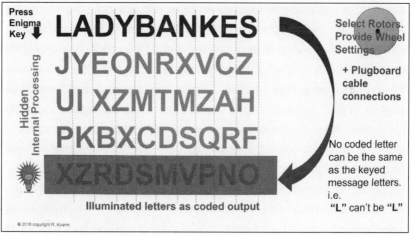

Enigma simplified processing diagram encoding letters.

battlefield. It could be unpacked, the wooden covers hinged down and the machine set up relatively quickly.

The unique selling point of Enigma was that it could be used in a trench with shells flying overhead, in an office, in a field station tent, on a ship or submarine, almost anywhere. At the receiving end the process was reversed, but the pre-start settings had to be set up exactly the same as at the transmission end. The encoded letters would need conversion into Morse code, and would be received and taken down by a radio-receiver-operator with a set of headphones. The Morse code letters would be typed into the Enigma machine by an operator, and the illuminated letters written down to provide, in groups of four or five batches of letters, the decoded message, it being of course in German.

The wheels incorporated the twenty-six letters of the alphabet around them. The internal structure of the machine, the wiring, the plugboard and position of the wheels encoded the letters pressed on the keyboard. The settings were changed by the Germans every twenty-four hours to add to the layer of security, usually at one minute past midnight. Hitler was told the Enigma was completely unbreakable. It wasn't, but it was a complex piece of equipment. Rotors could be changed in their sequence by an operator in accordance with codebooks and strict instructions. Scherbius made a point of telling everyone that the changing of wheel rotors would add significantly to the security level of the device.

Just three setting wheels resulted in 17,576 different permutations.[8] More wheel rotors would be added with newer advanced models, and the more rotors were provided the more the sequence of rotors became difficult to establish for those who tried to 'crack' the machine. The naval version of Enigma had three additional rotors, amounting to eight in total. That meant 336 different ways of setting just the rotor sequence,[9] compared with 60 different ways for the Enigmas of the other armed services.[10]

The development of Enigma and addition of the *Steckerboard* resulted in almost 159,000,000,000,000,000,000 permutations. Some models and other types of German encoding machines had many more permutations than this. It could be broken using a process of logic, mathematics and clues called 'cribs'. But it would be a laborious task, and speed in intelligence gathering is everything; no point having decoded an enemy's message 'Attacking at 0600 tomorrow' if you decode it thirty-six hours later. That would be too late to gain the intelligence advantage, and the Germans knew it, so it was part of their protocol to change the Enigma settings daily. One minute past midnight and the settings would change, frustrating the Allies.

Enigma had more than one weakness in its design. It would never encode a letter exactly the same as the entered keyed letter. A 'P', for instance, would never become an encoded 'P'. A letter 'J' would likewise never be coded as a 'J'. Only the remaining twenty-five letters of the alphabet could be used. This weakness eventually helped the British to break Enigma, but it would not be an easy task, and they would have many failures and disappointments. If Bletchley Park thought they had decoded an Enigma message, and any of the decoded letters were the same as the coded letters in the same word sequence, they then knew that decoded result was erroneous, and they had to review their approach and possibly start again. Enigma also had a reciprocal design: press a letter 'N', and say it was encoded as 'K', then if you pressed 'K' instead, it would be encoded as 'N'. This was down to the internal design and circuitry. This too would provide Bletchley Park with more clues as to how to penetrate it eventually. But press a letter many times and the encoded letters illuminated on the top of the machine would be different each time. It gave an appearance of randomness, but those who studied it in depth would eventually realise that it was not quite as random as it first appeared.

Every time the operator would press a key, the internal circuitry based on the setting of rotors, sequence of rotors, and *steckerboard* connections would help determine the encoded letter illuminated on the top of the machine. Pressing the same letter over and over again would produce different letters. One German Enigma operator made the mistake of pressing the same letter continuously as a test, as in KKKKKKKKKKK, and when the encoded version was transmitted and intercepted, the British were then able to work out what he had done. The codebreaker at Bletchley Park realized that there was an absence in a section of text of the letter 'K,' and put two and two together. Such mistakes would give the Allies opportunities to probe Enigma. Mavis Lever, one of the female codebreakers, was instrumental in exposing such weaknesses of the German and Italian Enigma operators.

The more deviation from the operational procedure of Enigma, the easier it would be for the British to find those weaknesses. It was highly unlikely that the manufacturers of the Enigma decoding machine, Hitler, or any senior officers knew of those breaches of operational protocols. If they had, they would have rammed home the importance of following the official manual and instructions, and not deviating from them in any way.

Another issue would be the wiring of the rotors to the letters and contacts. The wiring was simplified such that a rotor letter was wired in a simple sequence to the contacts, as described in the Enigma patent, but no one had thought to check that aspect of the design. It was wired alphabetically. Letter 'A' was connected to the first contact, and 'B' to the second contact, and so on. Arguably, if Bletchley Park had tried this sequence earlier, they might have been able to break Enigma earlier than before. Hindsight, they say, is a wonderful thing.

The Enigma machine gave the impression to those who were unfamiliar with it that the coded letter output was based on randomness. If this were true, then it surely was then be unbreakable. But it was not truly random, and no-one would be able to make an electro-mechanical machine with a completely random output. At best, it might be considered to be 'pseudo-random', which meant those trying to crack Enigma could look for those hidden patterns in the design which might be microscopically small, but could still be found, if one looked hard enough and spent the time. The concept of 'randomness' is explored later, as it can make a significant difference to the robustness of the cipher and encoding system.

As the Germans changed the key settings every twenty-four hours, one had to work quickly, to ensure information would not be out of date and useless as you decoded the messages. Mistakes made operationally in the field by the Germans would help the Allies to find the 'cribs' or clues to penetrate the Enigma cipher. Some of those mathematicians at Bletchley would become expert in the longer-term at decoding Enigma. However, there would be many disappointments, failures, arguments and intense frustration, in between the successes. Not all Enigma messages would be of important military use to the Allies, some would even be trivia, or not make sense even when decoded.

Many intelligence sources would need to be connected to make up the bigger picture of the enemy's intentions. Those at the top would gather as much information as they could from agents in occupied territories, from French resistance sources, from aerial photographs, and from recovered Nazi papers, codebooks, and equipment following military skirmishes and battles. The Germans knew that if retreating with little time, or under severe threat, or their U-boat was sinking, they would have to destroy their Enigma codebooks, remove Enigma rotor wheels, even destroy Enigma machines, to prevent them falling into enemy hands. Some had no problem with the Allies capturing an Enigma, but only if minus the rotor wheels, and minus the codebooks. This was because Enigma was seen by the Nazis as 'unbreakable', like an incredibly strong safe within a bank vault. Without the rotors it was like not having the combination of the safe, or the tools or equipment to penetrate it.

Communication in the German army was based on a 'Star' system. There would be a central controller, and communications sent out to the points of the star. The Control wouldn't themselves have a call sign. They would call outstations. Transmission and receiving would be for a lengthy time, so the Allies could find them without two much trouble, subject to weather conditions, of course. But the frequency would not in itself, identify any particular outstation. The call signs were mainly three symbols, and the aim was to try to establish which call sign represented which outstation on the 'star'. When the call signs were changing each day, based on their instructional codebooks, this made identifying the outstations a real problem. Y-stations and listeners to the Morse transmissions would record not only the messages, but the chatter which preceded the message, as that could be extremely useful.

Chicksands and Harpenden were two of these listening outposts. All the recorded logs were analysed after being sent to London to try and work out the relevance of the call signs, and who was sending and receiving them. Remarkably, over time, a 'map' or block diagram of the entire German Army was established through this complex and lengthy listening process. This framework became extremely useful for Generals and senior officers to identify which army section was where, and for what purpose. A similar 'map' or diagram was produced of the Luftwaffe.

This breakthrough was possible, in part, owing to the capture of German call-sign codebooks containing many thousands of call-signs. This began to outline in some depth the German chain of command for various arms of the services; extremely valuable information for the Allies. Practical problems encountered by Y-stations included overlapping frequencies confusing the listeners at times, and mistakes made when the amplitude and level faded. Messages would sometimes be passed to Bletchley Park which were incomplete and in some cases useless to process further. Captured call-sign books would prove invaluable over time, so long as the enemy remained unaware.

While each of the German armed forces had their own version of Enigma, the codebooks and settings allowed limited access to specific areas of command. As an example, let us say that you can send Enigma messages to companies and divisions in the county of Gloucestershire, based on the settings of the supplied codebook, but if you try to send messages to divisions in Lancashire, you need special authorisation before you can do it. You were going beyond your designated area for communication, and that might have an added security risk, so had to be controlled. It was not so much about geography as about what the purpose and objective of various divisions was, and how they might interact with other divisions. Information was passed to sections on a need-to-know basis, for reasons of security. The modern equivalent might be a type of password protection, where the codebooks provided for the armed services allowed communication between divisions but was strictly controlled. This system would provide a degree of added security. Of course, German generals would have the highest security clearance, and before long they would have the advanced S40, S42 and T52 encoding machines, which would only be available to the most senior officers, and the Führer.[11] These would be far more sophisticated than the Enigma machine, and would be a major a challenge to penetrate.

The challenge for the Allies was:

(a) To intercept the radio transmissions of the Enigma Morse code messages accurately.

(b) To establish the Enigma settings used that day and the order, ie sequence and position of wheel rotors

(c) To decode the messages relatively quickly using clues or 'cribs' and to obtain the 'depth' of information required to analyse their usefulness.

(d) To filter those decoded messages so they could be sent to the relevant parties.

(e) To pass the intelligence to the decision-makers quickly, so they could act on the information effectively and promptly.

There would be a degree of sophisticated trial and error involved, but pure guesswork would get you nowhere. Any trial-and-error basis would have to be structured to avoid time-wasting. Looking out for clues, or 'cribs', was going to be a part of the process, and fortunately the Germans would often insert predictable words of phrases in Enigma transmissions. 'Nothing to Report' was common, at or near the start of the message. The call sign of the division might be another, or weather conditions, and 'Heil Hitler' was also frequently inserted at the end of the message.

Hand-deciphering of coded messages at Bletchley Park was used initially, and had some considerable success, as well as periods of frustration, particularly deciphering 'Shark', naval codes used by U-Boats. For a period of nine months, no progress was made in decoding the naval codes, resulting in enormous losses of shipping and resources. It was quickly seen that a faster way of decoding the messages would be needed, particularly as the volume of enemy messages was increasing. Alan Turing developed the concept of a machine to help break Enigma, and his codebreaking 'Bombe', whilst similar in name to the Polish 'Bomba', was a very different machine in design and scale. It used rotating wheels approximately 125 mm (5 in) in diameter as part of the mechanism to emulate Enigma, and was built on a bronzed metal frame, 2 metres high and almost 2 metres wide.

It would weigh around a ton, and be assembled as a series of modular components, with numerous cables, wires and moving parts. The rear was a mass of cables, plugs and sockets, the front gave access to the wheel-drums, thirty-six of them, with an additional three on the right-hand side for taking readings. Each three-wheel-based Bombe had 111 wheel-drums, and had to be meticulously maintained. Around 11 miles of wiring and cables and a million soldered connections were in a Bombe machine. A lot could go wrong if there was a loose, or 'dry', soldered joint.

The decoded message needed to go through several more stages before it could be read in German and then be translated into English. Bletchley Park read the messages, irrespective of whether the Bombe machine used to decode it was at Bletchley Park or one of the supporting codebreaking outstations. The Bombe operators would not see the decoded messages, and this added to the monotony and frustration of the secret work.

Somewhere would have to be found to assemble a prototype Bombe machine, test it thoroughly, and then manufacture them in sufficient quantity. Engineers would be needed to support Turing and his team to build something that had not been attempted before, at least not of such complexity or scale. Gordon Welchman, another mathematician with a practical ability, assisted Turing on the Bombe machine development, and came up with some ideas of his own to improve the machine dramatically. This included his famous 'diagonal board' circuit, which helped reduce the need for elimination of certain wheel-drum settings, saving valuable time in processing 'menus' on the Bombes. Shorter menus were needed as compared with previously.[12]

Assembling the Bombes of course needed to be done under the utmost secrecy. It would take up considerable resources at a time when many materials and components were ending up on the bottom of the Atlantic. Ingenuity would be needed, and a dogged determination to achieve the objective quickly. This decoding process would give the Allies many sleepless nights and cause many disagreements among the codebreaking team along the way. It would engage numerous people from different backgrounds and social classes, from university mathematicians to engineers and Wrens. Some Wrens at Bletchley worked under the famous codebreaker Dilwyn Knox, who, sadly, would not live to see the end of the war.[13]

There was an urgent need for training and induction programmes in codebreaking and processing data, the establishment of outstations and manufacturing bases for codebreaking machines, and WRNS, WAAF, ATS, RAF Naval and other personnel would all have to be coordinated. This would be the groundwork for the next important stage after the Bombe machine: the development of the world's first semi-programmable electronic computer, 'Colossus'. Colossus would be needed to tackle more advanced encoding machines that were far more complex even than Enigma.

Several Polish mathematicians with a knowledge of codebreaking went to Bletchley Park in the early part of the war, fleeing from Poland via Romania and France. They were initially not employed on the most suitable type of work at Bletchley, even though they had experience of decoding Enigma many years before the British. There may have been a degree of reluctance to let them into the inner circle of codebreakers, at least initially. But the knowledge of the Polish mathematicians helped to accelerate the complex analysis of the structure of Enigma, at least until new improvements and additional rotor wheels were introduced. Their contribution to the war effort should not be overlooked. Some had passed information across to the British and French which proved invaluable in helping to crack Enigma. Polish mathematicians had spent many hours considering how to resolve the encoding and decoding process long before the British effort began.

In September 1939, the Poles provided the British with a replica Enigma machine as a gift. They had to flee from Poland rapidly as the Nazis occupied the country, and the cryptological team escaped via Romania just in the nick of time. Three key pioneering Polish mathematicians – Marian Rejewski, Henryk Zygalski and Jerzy Rozycki – would greatly assist the Allies. Their information saved the British valuable time. The process of breaking Enigma was largely a process of elimination; that is, eliminating, as far as possible, the irrelevant settings and non-message code letters, to leave just the original decoded letters and message remaining. The Poles had contributed significantly to this process.

Modern computers can process this sort of problem more or less instantly, but at the time one had to rely on decoding 'by hand', using logic, mathematics, probability, charts and tables, and determination. A cipher changes the individual letters in the system using an algorithm. A code is stored in a codebook. For example, a three-letter code such as 'XLU' might indicate in a codebook that it represents a message to say that an attack of infantry on an objective will happen within twenty-four hours of the time of transmission. The encoding of the three letters via Enigma, or into other apparent random letters, depends on the cipher system that is within the design, plus the sequence and type of rotor wheels, the plugboard settings, the wheel settings, etc.

Originally, all cipher systems would have been manually calculated, until machines came along. The manual decoding, which was used at Bletchley Park for some of the time, was a sort of reverse-engineering of the cipher, using clues and 'cribs', and mistakes made by the Germans and Italians.

Think of your password for an online account or similar. If there are just four digits you must enter, and no letters, then there would be 10,000 different possible permutations available to set up that password. Your bank phones you up and asks for two of those digits 'for security' purposes. Congratulations! You have just helped someone reduce the permutations down to 100, from the original 10,000. With three chances to enter a PIN on a credit card or debit card machine, I will have a one in 33.3 chance of guessing your PIN.

Now introduce to the password lots of upper- and lower-case letters, plus symbols and numbers. Say the password has to be exactly ten characters long. It would take even a fast computer a good while to break such a key, as there are just too many permutations of the arrangement of those characters, aided by the combination of upper and lower case, and the special symbols. Each character could be a lower-case letter, an upper-case letter, a number from nought to nine, a punctuation mark or other symbol. To work this out by hand is not impossible, if you have the time. But if you are including the Christian name of your partner in that password, or the name of your pet, then I might guess that, and with enough trial and error I just might get some of that password correct. The name is what we might call a 'crib' or clue. That is why it is not a good idea to put personal names into passwords. Make it as difficult as you can. Insert lots of symbols as well as upper case and lower case text, and numbers too. The trouble is, with a complex password you might forget it and then be tempted to write it down somewhere. Not recommended.

Enigma rotors. (Courtesy The National Archives)

Cipher encoding of messages was largely about having a robust cipher system that introduced such high levels of possible permutations of letters and numbers that it was going to be outside the reach of the enemy to eliminate all the probable characters in the correct sequence to arrive at the deciphered message. There would be far too many permutations available to break the cipher by hand, and even machines would not be fast enough or complex enough in design to discover the encoded message. Add to this that the enemy changed settings at one minute past midnight and had codebooks which changed frequently, and it would be even more challenging to penetrate it – until, that is, mistakes and errors were made by Enigma operators, allowing a possible way in.

Gordon Welchman commented after the war that if the German operators had used Enigma exactly as intended and instructed, then it probably would have remained unbreakable. Fortunately for the Allies, things turned out rather differently. For all their ruthlessness, German soldiers were human, and made mistakes like the rest of us. Through erring in their setting up Enigma, forgetting to change settings or just being too lazy, they played into the hands of the British.

The listening stations, or Y-stations, such as Chicksands, Sandridge, Flowerdown and Beaumanor, were spread throughout Britain and abroad, in Europe and North Africa. The signal reception at times would have been dire, with fade-in and fade-out, often due to varying atmospheric conditions. Writing down the Morse code took great skill and experience when the signal was fading and fluctuating in amplitude and clarity. Some messages would reach Bletchley Park incomplete, so it would be even more tricky to decode them and make sense of a disjointed message.

*Gordon
Welchman.*

Even if you managed to decode it, the missing part may well have been crucial to the intelligence. If part of a map grid reference was missing, it could be the critical portion of the intelligence. Some guesswork, creative thought, and trial and error would be necessary.

Not all intelligence could be intercepted by radio, and not all of it would be via Morse code, although most was. The select few landline connections in France, Holland, Belgium, Poland and Germany for transmitting German intelligence messages via Lorenz, 'Secret Writer' and other advanced encoding methods would prove too difficult for the Allies to intercept. One therefore had to concentrate on radio-listening stations, and with experience the listeners – WRNS, ATS and RAF staff – would be able to detect the signature of the Morse code operator if they listened for long enough. In this way they could identify and then listen out for the idiosyncrasies and peculiarities of the German operator sending the Morse transmission.

Eventually there would be a need for many more Y-stations, including some specialist versions in places like Denmark Hill, south London, and Knockholt in Kent. Those special listening stations would tackle the next generation of encoding machines sending non-Morse messages. Ralph Tester set up a specialist section at Bletchley to process and decrypt these advanced non-Morse messages.

Tester knew the German language well, as he had lived abroad in Germany for years. His background was accountancy, so numbers and mathematics were already of interest. He had worked alongside John Tiltman, one of Bletchley's key players. Tester had worked on other teams listening to German broadcasts and collecting useful information to be pieced together with intelligence from other sources. Tester's team at Bletchley specialised in analysing and decoding German Secret Writer ciphers, the 'Lorenz' teleprinter cipher attachment machines, and similar advanced equipment. All the founder members of this team, including Captain Jerry Roberts, one of the last codebreaking experts to survive into the twenty-first century, spoke fluent German. They success they enjoyed in infiltrating the more advanced and highly complex 'Tunny' intelligence with 'hand-methods' was phenomenal, with around 1.5 million messages analysed, and the team would grow to more than a hundred members. The vast bulk of messages would still be Enigma-encoded. All coded messages were initially filtered via Bletchley Park and many were then distributed around the codebreaking outstations to be processed via the 'Bombes' designed by Alan Turing.

In May 1940, Bletchley would decipher the German Luftwaffe key cipher, and have access to the military information exchanged between the Luftwaffe and the German Army on matters such as Allied targets and fuel supplies and general logistics. In June, information gleaned whilst the British retreated towards the sea at Dunkirk gained valuable time.

Churchill and his senior military officers could clearly see the advantage of the Enigma cipher being broken, providing the intelligence could be promptly conveyed to them to take advantage of it. However, breaking the naval *Kriegsmarine* codes would be a much more challenging proposition, even for the clever mathematicians based at Bletchley. A long period of frustration ensued with a multitude of methods being used in attempts to penetrate the 'Shark' naval intelligence, mostly without success.

As mentioned, the *Kriegsmarine* Enigma operation was a bit special in that it had an extra wheel rotor and several advanced codebooks, as well as maintaining a specific level of discipline in the use of the machine and operational protocols. 'Shark' Naval intelligence would frustrate Turing as much as the others in Hut 6 at Bletchley, but he knew it would only be a matter of time before the codes were broken. It was about using a combination of hand-deciphering methods and a secret weapon in their arsenal. Turing had taken perforated sheets, an aid to manual codebreaking, over to France to help the Poles. These sheets were one way help locate patterns of letters and exposing weaknesses, but purely manually, and that would be a slow process. What was needed was an electro-mechanical machine, the Bombe, to assist in the elimination of the letters in the encoded message to come up with a result more speedily. This was data-processing at the start of computational history, and would soon develop to a massive scale of processing as the war developed, and the Nazi threat increased.

Turing would be remembered for his work on the Bombe codebreaking machine, and for his papers on 'universal machines'. His 'universal machine' was described in a paper, in principle, but never built. He would discuss the concept of intelligent and universal machines with others he met at Bletchley, and strive to make them a reality using the Bombe as a stepping stone in the process. But the Bombe was far from intelligent. It needed mathematicians and others to use it effectively.

Like many specialist devices, the Bombe was improved and developed over time and high-speed versions were made. The Bombe needed instructions. By putting plugs into selected sockets at the rear of the machines, 'menus' would be followed by the Wrens, created by the clever people at Bletchley Park to make a meaningful attempt to eliminate many millions of permutations of letters. The main issue was that unlike a computer, which can do lots of different things through programmes, the Bombe was not able to carry out different tasks in the same way. It was basically a one-trick pony. Whilst it was possible to connect it in such a way that it eliminated lots of permutations of encoded lettering, it was limited technologically in what it could achieve. It was far from Alan Turing's 'Universal Machine'. But as a complex, electro-mechanical tool for data processing, it came into the war just at the right time.

Churchill was anxious about the number of people who had access to some of the Enigma-decrypted intelligence. It was accepted that there would be no purpose to Bletchley Park and its team of experts unless the information was communicated to the most senior politicians, and particularly to military senior officers, but Churchill considered the list far too extensive. Each additional person on the list was a potential risk to Britain and the Allies.

In October 1940, Churchill acted. The decrypt intelligence list would be reduced down to no more than thirty-one people, the majority being very senior military officers. The fewer people who knew about Enigma, the better. Churchill knew that it the hard-won penetration of Enigma could be exposed to the enemy in an instant, which meant back to square one. Keeping to the revised list would become a high priority, even though it upset a few in its implementation. Churchill didn't care about that. He was there to lead the country against Hitler and would use all methods and resources at his disposal.

3

BLETCHLEY PARK, GC&CS

Bletchley Park was established in 1939 as the GC&CS or Government Code and Cipher School, a new hub of military intelligence. As mentioned previously, its roots were in 1914 and Room 40 in the Old Building at the Admiralty. Alfred Ewing was technically in charge of Room 40, being an engineer by training. This room, about 17 feet by 24 feet in size, was the birthplace of the British Signals intelligence operations, or 'SIGINT'. Nine further rooms were added as the section grew. Herbert Hope was head of the division. Some reports state that in excess of 15,000 German intelligence intercepts were successfully decoded from Room 40 during the First World War. Ewing had previously been Director of Naval Intelligence in April 1903. Alastair Denniston was second in command at Room 40, and would later go on to make a name for himself at Bletchley Park.

From Room 40 this group moved to Watergate House near Charing Cross, before again relocating to Queen's Gate in Kensington in 1921.[14] That site now proudly displays a plaque to commemorate a hundred years of GCHQ from 1919, acknowledging that it was then known as GC&CS. Unveiled by HM The Queen in

February 2019, it is positioned to the right-hand side of the front porch. (For those cryptographers out there needing a challenge, the plaque even contains two sets of codes.) Watergate House is one of the few remaining structures in London boasting important historical connections with codebreaking prior to and during the Second World War. Located a short walk from The Strand, it now houses a finance company, and at the time of the author's visit it had a special edition of the Monopoly board game on the window sill: the Alan Turing edition.

GC&CS as a concept was being discussed in late 1918. The 'S' in GC&CS of course stood for 'School'; it was recognised that the area of cryptography and codes and ciphers was rapidly expanding, and this required development of techniques to make, and break, ciphers for military intelligence. It was a gradual

Plaque for GCHQ at Watergate House, off the Strand, London.

learning process. People would have to be a lot more shrewd in their work than before. Machines would play a big part. The British needed a new, better-coordinated intelligence structure that would apply specialized decoding systems, and this meant learning new methods and sharing those with likeminded people – mathematicians and others.

In February 1919, the combination of the Foreign Office, Admiralty, War Office and Air Ministry agreed on a practical 'School' for cipher and code-breaking specialist personnel. Around twenty-five staff and a limited budget would get them started – but where? And who should run it? Alastair Denniston was chosen as the director. The location was to be Watergate House, Adelphi, London, WC1 and operations would commence on 1 November 1919. The staff also included personnel from MI1(b) and Room 40.

The role of GC&CS would be quite broad and varied. It would be responsible for printing codes and ciphers for the government, ascertaining their security levels and liaising with government departments using ciphers, and would be under the Director of Naval Intelligence. Its workers would give opinions on when a British cipher or code was considered to be effective, or perhaps past its sell-by date and therefore potentially insecure. This would not be as straightforward as it might first appear. Instruction manuals, operational procedure systems and protocols were needed to ensure cyphers and codes were handled in an efficient way. Of course, one of its principal roles was to investigate and evaluate cyphers of foreign countries: Germany, Switzerland, Austria, Russia, Japan, Norway, Spain, Argentina, amongst others.

Denniston's team would later move to Queen's Gate in London in 1921 after various interdepartmental changes. Not all politicians and civil servants were happy with the relocation. Somewhere more permanent had to be found, but that would take almost twenty years. This would entail a major evolution of the original department, moving many miles out of London to the countryside, giving the staff more 'breathing space' and flexibility in working methods, with war once again on the horizon. In 1939, Denniston was put in charge of Bletchley Park. He was to transform and mould it into a complex, part-human, and part-mechanized decoding machine, supported eventually by numerous satellite stations or outstations. The location – Bletchley Park – had been Denniston's choice.

In February 1942, Edward Travis (Commander Travis) took over from Denniston, and developed the codebreaking activities and infrastructure further still.

Bletchley Park in Buckinghamshire is near the new town of Milton Keynes. Now an important military and computer museum (each as separate entities), it came close to being flattened after the war and redeveloped, but thankfully was saved in time. It was an ornate mansion house with many acres of landscaped grounds, a lake, and a degree of seclusion and anonymity. It was far enough away from cities and large towns not to attract attention and avoided radio aerials of any size, to keep the Luftwaffe guessing. From a small staff of around two hundred people, it grew into a mammoth codebreaking and intelligence 'city', with around 10,000–11,000 personnel at the end of the war, all of different backgrounds and abilities.

Staffed by both military personnel and civilians, it had a slightly more informal ethos compared with many of the outstations, such as Eastcote and Outstation Stanmore, which were later run as onshore naval bases with permanently uniformed naval and other military personnel. Some of those Bletchley people were eventually sent down to Eastcote in Middlesex after the war, to work at the new GCHQ. Several of these had made a name for themselves in progressing the war effort to a significant degree in codebreaking activities or support roles in intelligence. There are numerous publications on the detailed workings of Bletchley for the reader, so that is not the purpose of this book. However, it is appropriate to mention Alan Turing, Gordon Welchman, John Tiltman, Bill Tutte, Max Newman, Hugh Alexander and others, who formed the core of a processing hub, many seconded from the top universities at the time. Newman was Turing's tutor at university, so they knew each other well.

Turing is seen by many as an icon, and indeed he contributed greatly to the development of cryptography and codebreaking, understanding that much of the mathematical processing and hard work could be done by machines. But there were others who in the author's opinion were as forward-thinking as Turing, and contributed significantly to the outcome of the Second World War in Europe and elsewhere.

GC&CS had an interest in Turing and his universal machine theory. He was billeted in a pub a few miles away, within cycling distance. He was eccentric, chaining his tea mug to the radiator pipework near his desk in case it went missing and cycling to and from work in his war-issue gas mask.

Churchill and his advisers realised that the volume of messages coming through the 'Y' stations was increasing at an exponential rate, and that the initial processing needed to be spread beyond the Bletchley hub. Furthermore, Churchill knew that if the Germans had even a whiff of what was going on at Bletchley, the Luftwaffe would surely would flatten the site, resulting in the loss of Britain's only codebreaking base, and potentially all its intelligence experts. That would have given the Allies a very serious problem. It would have exposed them in a way that would have resulted in far greater casualties and losses at the very least.

Three local satellite bases were established at Wavendon, Adstock and Gayhurst Manor, all country houses and relatively close to Bletchley, chosen to house the codebreaking machinery: the Bombes. More outstations would come later, in 1942 and 1943, as the messages increased in volume, complexity and importance. They would need much larger sites in time. The outstations and the Bombe rooms at Bletchley would become data-processing production sites, relying on initial collection of encoded messages via listening Y-stations at home and abroad. Beaumanor, Cheadle, Chicksands, Sandridge, Hawklaw, Flowerdown and others were intercept stations with round-the-clock listeners, trained to identify Morse code at high speed and write it down quickly on log sheets. These messages would form part of the 'Ultra' intelligence that Bletchley Park processed for the most senior officers of the British armed forces, the most senior politicians and, later, the Americans.

The dispatch riders would take the messages across the country to Bletchley day and night, in all weathers. A mistake during the multiple stages from radio interception, transcribing Morse code, dispatching to Bletchley Park, decoding, and translation to English from German was always possible, the system was complex in nature and fraught with challenges. A mistake might mean ships being sunk by U-boats, rather than being diverted away from the danger area. Many lives were at stake. The pressure, particularly on those in the codebreaking huts at Bletchley, was immense. In the outstations, the stress was not that much less, but in a different way, coping with intense peaks of workload and breakdowns,

Gayhurst Manor. (Courtesy Philip Jeffrey)

Bombe wheel drums.

maintaining the accuracy of the Bombe machine settings, or 'menus', before the Bombe 'runs' could take place.

Add to this the fact that almost all operators of the machines had close friends and relatives in the armed forces, often abroad. The stress of not knowing about their safety and even their whereabouts was bound to affect morale and state of mind. But concentration on setting the machines and operating them was paramount, whether you were operating a Bombe, a 'Typex' machine, a checking machine, or just entering a log of messages.

Typex would be the British equivalent of Enigma, containing several wheel rotors (i.e. more than most early Enigma machines), and prove to be invaluable in testing decoded messages after machine-processing at the Bombe outstations. It would hopefully print out, at Bletchley Park, German text on a strip of paper on a backing of wider paper, providing the operator had the correct settings for the cipher. Once the decoded message had been analysed, either by hand or via 'Turing Bombe' codebreaking machines, the output of Typex would confirm the German text to be translated to give the English text. There would be rows of Typex operators at Bletchley Park HQ, doing nothing but typing the decoded text into machines to give the German text. There would also be Typex machines at some of the Y-stations, such as those abroad. It is highly likely that they would have been based on a copy of some of the German Enigma designs, but in a different form. Copyright breaches of design in wartime, would, of course, be ignored. The Typex machines did the same job as Enigma, even though they looked very different. Electrical contacts in the Typex machines were arguably more robust than in Enigma. If German text did not come out on the Typex, the settings had been incorrectly set.

The name Typex derived from 'RAF Enigma with Type "X" attachments'. The machine was bulkier than the Enigma, and not really meant to be portable due to the large weight (about the same as two bags of cement), but a more compact portable version was later made. Some models had a motor drive, although many were hand-operated to turn the rotor drums. Note that Typex was *not* the same machine as the checking machines used in the codebreaking outstations, and those 'checkers' would have a completely different role and purpose, related to the front plugboard connections of Enigma machines. The initial Typex model was produced around 1935, and the British were using them before the start of the war.

According to postwar reports, 'Typex' was probably never broken by the Germans. A rotorless Typex was captured in France by the Nazis, but they did not seem too concerned at its potential. The Germans realised it was based on Enigma, but they felt Enigma was completely secure. The contacts inside Typex were improved so they had double the contact area for passing electrical signals, making it more robust. The three wheel rotors would rotate as the keys were depressed by the operator, similar to Enigma. There were a number of Typex versions produced over time, and some did have plugboards from 1941. There would also be significant security improvements made, which meant it was more robust and less vulnerable than many models of the Enigma. With practice, operators of Typex might achieve twenty words per minute. Information was printed on a paper tape, and if the unit was decoding German intelligence, then the decoded message would need translating into English. Rotating the wheel rotors could be a problem, as the rotors could be stiff. Some Typex operators, mostly women, brought wooden sticks to help move the wheels around, and make the process less painful on their fingers. The reports indicate there was a shortage of engineers to maintain the large number of complex Typex machines at Bletchley Park.

There were of course teams at Bletchley with a good knowledge of German, who would concentrate on the translation aspect of the process. Thousands of Typex machines were made and used by the British, but the maximum number was around one tenth of the

Typex machine. (Photograph reproduced with permission of the Bletchley Park Trust)

quantity of Enigma machines. Some were used in the 1950s, and it is quite possible that Eastcote might have ended up with one or two after the war, in its new role as GCHQ.

Bletchley needed some sort of searchable database to help categorise the messages coming in and all the decodes. That was organised using cards, later punched cards using an American Hollerith machine.

Communication links had to be robust and reliable. Information pulled together by the team, when added to other intercepts, could make up a much bigger part of the intelligence jigsaw puzzle, and help the Allies in making strategic decisions.

Most people have never heard of Hollerith machines. However, they were not only useful in processing and bringing together important data to support Allied intelligence, during the war. They would later form part of a punched-card revolution in early computer development as a data-processing system, before digital tape and advanced memory storage took over. The Hollerith machines were supplied via BTM, a factory in Letchworth, Hertfordshire, who had the licence to market and sell them across Britain and abroad. The American suppliers and owners of Hollerith would charge BTM heavy royalties on the sales of their machines, so profits for BTM were limited. This meant they had to sell or hire out a large quantity each year to make money. But their market would be as wide as the British Empire, so they were in with a sporting chance.

The early first models were called 'Hollerith Pin Box Tabulators', and soon evolved into more sophisticated processing machines. Finding space to locate the additional Bombe codebreaking machines was not going to be easy, let alone the cards they were producing.

This was creating a large database of information; bits of intel which might be useful to piece together later, about a German officer's background, or tactical details of his unit, or his approach to transporting his artillery section. If a German officer mentioned in a received message he had a girlfriend and gave her name, even that information might be stored away as data which might help elsewhere later on. It was a sort of early search engine, an early Google but with punched cards to manage the information. It also had important indexes of 'Good Groups' and 'Differences', which would be very useful with the actual practical codebreaking at times. Storing these was a serious problem at Bletchley, and some photographs at the time showed them stacked in rows of cabinets, on shelves, on tables and large areas across the floors. The volume of cards being processed was enormous, approximately 2 million per week at one stage. They were first in Hut 7, then in Block 'C' at Bletchley. They had to go elsewhere.

A new base was found on a farm near Drayton Parslow, a few miles from Bletchley Park, and here they were relocated. In charge was Freddie Freeborn, who had been seconded from BTM in Letchworth, Hertfordshire. This was an intensive area of work during daytime and evenings, with eight-hour shifts, to get through the enormous quantities of data and provide feedback to Bletchley cryptographers. Many thousands of cipher text characters had to be processed, to find the groups required to help with the 'cribs', which were needed to help break the Enigma codes. The operators of such equipment were civilian women, ATS members, and Wrens. This was an early form of data filtering or data processing, and few people would be aware that it commenced just after the turn of the twentieth century. Punched cards would later develop into a support tool for the post-war business industry. BTM's licence from the American company for marketing and selling the machines in the UK was the link to release Freeborn at BTM Letchworth to support Bletchley Park.

In summary, the Hollerith punched cards largely fell into one of two groups: those which recorded specific and sometimes personal information, such as a German or Italian officer's wife's name, which might be of later use when putting other decoded intelligence messages together; and essential statistical and cryptographic data, which helped in making the codebreaking process more efficient, and enabled the analysts to eliminate more of the options and settings to help arrive at the decoded message.

Freeborn had two close relatives who were section heads in the department. It was almost run like a family. There were many women operating the machines and filing the punched cards. A high proportion of them were women from an upper-class background. One woman, Joan, had been a Hollerith operator. She was singled out and quickly made a team leader, but probably did not get extra pay for this role. The Hollerith section would have engineers on call to maintain and repair the machines, which of course had many moving mechanical parts. They were in operation constantly, and the wear on the mechanical components needed frequent attention.

Managed by Wrens and ATS staff, the cards would become an essential cog in the wheel of the complex codebreaking process. If there had been enough space at Bletchley, they would have remained there, as it was convenient. But space was at a premium, so Drayton Parslow became another outstation. It continued to be an important support to Bletchley, and the outstation manager, Freeborn, contributed greatly to its success. Towards the end, in 1945, they had accumulated over five hundred staff.

The block diagram on page 58 shows the basic arrangement of outstations/support bases, which enabled the secret codebreaking processes to evolve and deliver results. It would have been possible to expand the diagram further, adding more and more blocks to the network chart, but essentially the layout diagram as shown is sufficient to convey the range of facilities which were necessary to provide the overall picture. Some of the other secret bases not shown were for specialist activities, such as designing a speech-encoding machine, and similar research – not really codebreaking bases, but more like an annex to assist communications. If one added codebreaking bases and factories over in the US, then the graphics and place names would spill over onto a huge diagram.

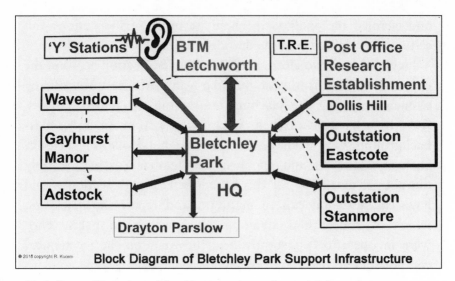

Block diagram of Bletchley Park Support Infrastructure

Block diagram illustrating codebreaking outstations and support infrastructure.

So this was the basic setup. The Y-stations gathered in the Morse code transmissions. Dispatch riders on military motor bikes would deliver the messages to Bletchley Park where they would be sorted. The messages would be allocated to the various sites for data-processing using the Bombes, and Bletchley mathematicians would provide the all-important instructional 'menu' to aid those setting up the Bombes. The partly decoded output was checked on a Typex machine back at Bletchley Park, and if it made good German reading, it needed translating into English promptly by those with the special linguist skills. This is a simplistic overview of the process, so the reader needs to refer to the diagrams provided.

It is important to remember there were nine months of failure to decode the *Kriegsmarine* Enigma. The continuing loss of Allied shipping to U-boats was Churchill's biggest concern of the war. At their peak success, the U-boats were sinking in excess of 800,000 tons of Allied shipping per month, a rate which was clearly not sustainable. Grain, aviation fuel, milk powder, steel, aircraft, trucks, timber and armaments would go to the bottom of the Atlantic on a regular basis. The period was known by the German U-boat commanders as 'The Happy Time'. A solution had to be found to end the U-boat menace and allow the convoys to replenish Britain.

Progress came in stages. In May 1940, U-boat *U110* was captured by HMS *Bulldog*, and codebooks acquired. The U-boat had been targeting Allied ships in the North Atlantic, and a corvette using ASDIC sonar tracking was able to locate her and fire depth charges. She was damaged and forced to the surface; a number of crew were killed. The codebooks were invaluable.

A German trawler was also boarded by the British at sea, and found to have important codebooks of interest. But this success was considered to be short-term, as regards penetration of Enigma.

Eventually, in October 1942, the British acquired Enigma codebooks through the bravery of some British sailors boarding a sinking U-boat from a British destroyer, HMS *Petard*. Additionally, progress was made through the introduction of improved 'sighting' of U-boats by the Allies via centrimetric radar. Those two sailors from HMS *Petard* looking for intelligence would sadly drown in their determination to obtain the intelligence, but not before they recovered Enigma naval codebooks, which went quickly to Bletchley Park for analysis.[15] This change in fortune for the Allies wouldn't come a moment too soon. The naval codebooks were written in water-soluble ink, so that if the boats were damaged or sunk, the codes would simply wash away. They had not allowed for the possibility that the sea cocks of the damaged submarine would

U110 *and HMS* Bulldog.

not be opened in time to scuttle the boat – and it was this extra time which those brave sailors managed to take advantage of.

It might seem that the Germans had thought of almost everything to ensure their Enigma secret was safe. But they had no idea that a substantial, skilled team and network of determined people and machines in England, aided by the listening Y-stations, would be probing their messages at an almost microscopic level throughout the war. There would be tough times, with intense frustration and few positive and constructive results, and U-boat successes at alarmingly high levels. There would also be occasional surges of deciphering large quantities of decoded Nazi intelligence, giving the senior officers of the Allied armed forces a clear advantage in planning future actions and diverting shipping away from the Nazi menace.

At the same time, the Allies could not let on to the Germans through their actions that they had broken Enigma. Some German generals and senior officers already had their suspicions on this point, but fortunately Hitler was not convinced by them. This did not, however, prevent specialists at the German factories developing even more advanced and secure machines over the course of the war.

The Allies were walking on eggshells. Great efforts were made to find all sorts of methods to convince the Germans that Enigma was still intact. Allied spotter planes were flown over panzer divisions, or within sight of isolated U-boats in the north Atlantic; double agents dropped hints to the enemy that intelligence had come from other sources.

There was coincidence, and then there was too much coincidence, raising concern among the Nazis. Managing the decoded Enigma intelligence would be a full-time job for the Allies.

4

CODEBREAKING FOR AND AGAINST THE RUSSIANS

It is useful to understand the reasoning behind the UK and the US restricting certain intelligence sources when dealing some Allies, particularly Russia, while simultaneously giving them crucial information to help destroy the Nazi war machine in the East. What might be seen as completely unacceptable behaviour in peacetime might well be tolerated in war.

In June 1941, Operation *Barbarossa* commenced and brought to an end the German-Soviet Non-aggression Pact signed on 23 August 1939. Sources of British intelligence during this period were not always conveyed to the Russians, but they provided key intelligence to enable the Soviets to win important battles. The Battle of Kursk was one which helped to turn the tide against the Nazis, and British intelligence made a huge difference by warning the Russians of German intentions well in advance.[16] If the Russians had lost that battle the Germans may have had access to Russian oilfields, providing virtually unlimited fuel supplies and helping them to overrun Russia.

The British trusted the Russians as allies up to a point, but not completely. Their assistance was necessary to help destroy the

Nazis, but Britain was selective with intelligence, with enough credibility for them to take information seriously when it was proffered. As it turned out, this was a wise strategy. To avoid German suspicions that Enigma had been cracked, the British had to be creative in covering their tracks when feeding intel to the Soviets. So once again, an Allied plane might conveniently fly over a fringe perimeter area of mobilized panzers, or information would be passed so that it appeared an Allied agent had betrayed the Germans in the area – but now this was practised in the East.

Throughout the war, the Allies had to be creative in deceiving the Nazis as to why they often seemed to be in the right place at the right time. There was such a thing as too much coincidence, which would arouse suspicion. The fact that there was actually a Russian spy within Bletchley Park gave the Russians a degree of comfort that what they were being told regarding enemy intentions and planning by the British was in fact credible. The Russian spy was soon identified, and monitored, but he was largely confirming what Churchill was telling Stalin at meetings anyway; the British were much less concerned than if a German agent had infiltrated the base.

The author's parents were not from the UK. They came from Estonia, a Baltic country, which was overrun by the Russians, Nazis, and then the Russians again during the war. Back in 1931, a Royal Engineers radio operator, William Green Swanborough, went to Estonia, and taught the Estonians the principles of signals intelligence against military targets (i.e. the Russians) and the need to identify networks. He also taught them the importance of understanding enemy routines and patterns. Swanborough was a self-trained radio operator. He was authorised to provide Estonia with UK intelligence that would benefit the Baltics. In return he needed access to Russian intentions, and being close to the border, this was seen as a constructive exchange of information. The British needed to know about how their units were organised, their make-up and structure, their capabilities in times of war. Good intelligence, if targeted properly, at the correct time, can prove to be invaluable, even if you are not actually at war. The information quickly started to flow and would prove to be useful later on. When Swanborough returned to the UK, he arranged that the Estonians would continue to feed the UK with Russian intelligence.

This process continued up to the start of the Second World War. But of course Russia was later to become Britain's ally, at least for a period. There is a long history of Britain providing support, technical information and training to other countries when they are fighting against oppression and threat; but there would be times when the nations of the Baltic region, and not just Estonia, would be very much on their own.

The Molotov–Ribbentrop Pact, signed in August 1939, demonstrated that smaller countries could effectively be passed illegally from one major state to another. The German-Soviet Frontier Treaty that year was a secret addendum that supplemented the original treaty once Poland was invaded by Germany. Germany soon invaded their Russian 'allies' in Operation *Barbarossa* and tore up such agreements. The Baltics therefore had to suffer Russian, then German, then Russian aggression, and eventually fell under communist rule for almost fifty years from 1944, finally gaining independence in 1991.

Russia was an enemy of the Baltic States, and they fought against her purely for their survival, with high loss of life, mass deportations and extreme hardships. Ironically, when the Germans occupied Estonia, pushing out the Russians in 1941, many Estonians welcomed them. The reason was that inhabitants of the Baltic states – provided they weren't part of a persecuted group such as the Jews – were treated far better than under the Russians, and given considerably more freedom.[17] Germany considered the Baltics and particularly Estonia to be much closer to the spurious Aryan bloodline than many other occupied countries, and this was reflected in the freedoms permitted. The Estonian flag was retained for example, and the people had access to Estonian culture, religion, and churches of their choosing.[18] This was not to say the

Nazis could not be extremely ruthless, if they chose to be. But the Germans generally punished only those who had taken part in the underground movements. It was of course a different story for the Jews and Roma. Many Estonians spoke the German language, which would be to their advantage.

Russia had deported thousands of Baltic-born residents, broken up numerous families, many never to be reunited, and many were to suffer terribly in Siberia. In 1949, 20,000 Estonians were deported to Siberia and eastern Russia and overall, reports indicate that 61,000–62,000 Estonians were either deported to Russia or executed.[19] It is recorded that 60% of the deported Estonians died. Apart from the mass deportations, the population shrunk by around 7% during the Russian invasion.[20] The Russian oppressors burnt books and re-wrote Baltic history to purge Estonian influence.

Those refugees that fled from Estonia from the Russians were pursued relentlessly, and many of the population died fleeing Soviet oppression en route to the west. To the man in the street, the German victory over the Soviets could mean freedom from fear of arrest by the NKVD.[21] The Russian approach was one of mass terror, and generally far worse than that of the German military, unless you were one of their targeted groups.[22] At the outbreak of the war Estonia had approximately 4000 Jews, but by the time the Germans entered the country, only 1000 remained after deportation and flight. The bulk of the remainder would either be killed or deported under the Nazis.

Unsurprising then, that one oppressor was 'preferred' over another. The Allies did nothing to challenge the Russian's action in the Baltics, as in the early years of the war they had enough to worry about themselves, with the fall of France, and then the Battle of the Atlantic, and the relentless sinking of shipping by U-Boats.[22a]

By mid-1945, the Allies were recovering from the loss of enormous quantities of men, and mass casualties in defeating the Nazis. Then after the end of the war, there was the huge

The old town of Tallin bombed by the Soviets in March 1944.

task of co-ordinating the mass of refugees across Europe, with the assistance of the International Red Cross and other support groups. Roads, bridges, railways and infrastructure were ruined across Europe, particularly in Germany, France, Belgium, and the Netherlands. There was just too much going on, and too little resources. Even if you had the resources, it was going to be a challenge to get your men and women from 'A' to 'B' due to destroyed bridges, craters in the roads and heaps of rubble.

Places like Hamburg and Dresden were completely ruined, flattened in May 1945. The author's older brother can recall being in Hamburg on a train immediately after the war, with enormous devastation and nothing left standing in the city. Britain was virtually bankrupt after the war. The Allies were reeling from the loss of servicemen and women, material shortages at home, and needed to regroup. They were not prepared to challenge the Russians so soon after the end of the war, even if they came across extreme atrocities, or identified incidents and actions which, in peacetime, would have been high profile and completely unacceptable to the West. The Americans, French and British were trying to predict how the Soviets were expecting to carve up Germany and other states, to mould a much larger, and stronger communist Soviet/Eastern Bloc.

So how did all this affect military intelligence? After 1939 and the signing of the Nazi-Russian pact, it transpired that GC & CS had penetrated the Russian meteorological cipher codes. They had also read various army and naval intelligence. But when Russia was attacked in 1941 by the Nazis, the British stopped that intelligence work. By 1943, the British were once again gathering Soviet intelligence, with the agreement of America. In London, a Russian intelligence section was established at Berkeley Street. The staff increased at this location as Soviet intelligence traffic grew from late 1943. None of the gathered intelligence was shared with the Americans, particularly that of communist networks infiltrated. The British were keeping that information to themselves.

In the latter part of the war, around 1944, a small GC & CS Russian cipher section was set up in Park Lane, London, and later in Sloane Square. This implies that Russian intelligence was almost as important as German intelligence to the Allies at that time.

In 1946, GCHQ at Eastcote, which had evolved from Outstation Eastcote. and which took on the role of GCHQ after the war, was instrumental in breaking a Russian encoding system known as the 'Poets' cipher series. Encoded teleprinter ciphers were being broken by a combination of the British and Americans. Teleprinter-based advanced encoding machines would also be used by the Germans for the Lorenz series of encoding machines, and Bletchley Park and those that transferred to GCHQ Eastcote would have had some knowledge of the processes to break this type of cipher. This was based on an earlier British success called 'Coleridge', in the earlier part of 1946, used by the Russians for its armies and support services. *Coleridge* was probably one of two main Russian teleprinter systems, and was used in Europe for Russian army, navy, and airforce operations. *Coleridge* provided information on the Order of Battle, as well as training and other military information. This had to be filtered out from much administrative traffic to find the important intelligence the West needed.

Regarding the cracking of the 'Poets' series of cipher systems, one needs to appreciate that as the Russians penetrated Germany, Poland and other occupied countries in the latter stages of the war, they would have come across and captured numerous encoding machines used by the Germans; machines like the Lorenz S42, and others.[23] These were highly advanced encoding machines, far more secure than Enigma would ever be, part of the 'Secret Writer' suite of German advanced machines. But many would be abandoned or hidden by the Germans during the retreat back to Berlin. Some of these would have formed the basis of Russian encoding ciphers and systems in the post-war period. It was a relatively inexpensive way of having encoding systems without the cost of developing them. It would save time both in technical development and cost. But there would also be risks in taking this line, if others had access to the machines and were breaking your cyphers and codes.

On 29 October 1948, the Russians completely changed their cipher system, and there was a blackout of intelligence for the West, which meant they were effectively blind. This was nicknamed 'Black Friday' by the American NSA. It was reported that a Russian agent in America tipped them off. This was a game of 'cat and mouse' but with high stakes. It would be some time before the West could penetrate Russian and Eastern Bloc codes and ciphers again.

Even today, NATO forces are supporting the Baltic States with troops from the UK and elsewhere near the borders. A NATO Very High Readiness Joint Task Force (VJTF) of around 5,000 men has been created within the High Response Force (HRF). This is to identify and respond quickly to the 'trigger' of an impending attack and invasion from Russia over the Russian/ Baltic borders.

Other support means have been established to boost the defence of the Baltic States, including significant air cover, and additional monitoring in the Baltic Sea. This clearly unsettles President Putin and his Generals. The background and complexity of the Crimean and Ukrainian encroachments by Russian rebels is still in everyone's mind, and a repeat elsewhere is always possible. But the Baltics are NATO countries, so the area is even more sensitive than Ukraine. The Baltic countries have had more than their fair share of conflict and oppression. The large Russian population within the Baltic States, and particularly Estonia, might stimulate Russia to 'regain' its territory.

Clearly, there will be a range of listening stations to monitor Russian traffic in the area and elsewhere, to be forewarned of any impending Russian troop movements or planned attack. Satellites too, will be the eyes of the Allies and of the Russians, scanning for changes on the ground and near the coasts. Of course, much of the intelligence traffic will be encoded, and it is still the challenge to the West to decode it promptly. The Russians will also be monitoring Western communications on a large scale. A whole industry has grown up around the electronic equipment, systems, training, logistics and codebreaking. It isn't going away anytime soon. No one would really benefit from a major military action in the Baltics. It might be the trigger for World War Three, or at least a significant loss of life affecting not just military forces but civilians too.

The number of ethnic Russians in Estonia rose from 10% of the population in 1940 to approximately 26% today, the remainder being ethnic Estonians. More than 300,000 Russians now live in Estonia, many having come in after the end of the war, as life there was much better compared than in the mother country, for most.[24] Fifty years or so of communist rule allowed them to settle before independence occurred in the Baltics in the 1990s.

Once independence was declared, the Baltic States started changing the rules in their favour over the 'occupiers', who now had grown-up families. The imposition of certain stiff rules and restrictions on Russian residents in those countries has not helped the situation. Where did the EU concept of 'free movement of people' go? But of course, Russia is not in the EU, so the Baltic States can control immigration of Russians quite lawfully. If you are Russian, you will probably not obtain the same benefits as ethnic Estonians, and there will be some discrimination, as seen by outsiders. Russians can freely return to their mother country, but the number of Russians willing to do this and voting with their feet is tiny, just 37 ethnic Russians in the last two years. Clearly, they enjoy living in Estonia, and have a far better life there compared with Russia.

In a recent poll in 2019, Estonia came out near the top of countries that were anti-immigration. Others looking on from outside might believe this to be surprising, and indeed shocking, particularly for an EU country. But one needs to look back in history at the reasons for this. Across Europe and indeed the world, there are pockets of populations, some relatively small in size, who consider themselves to be free people and independent, and who are willing to defend their independence. Putin and any future Russian leader will always have one eye on the Baltics, and consider whether the Russian resident people are being heavily discriminated against in Estonia, Latvia, and Lithuania.

There may be many in Russia who would welcome a strong leader going in militarily, to 'protect' their residents in those adjacent countries, once ruled with an iron fist by the communists. There may be a 'red line', which the Baltic States and particularly Estonia must not cross to prevent Russian aggression. Estonia and others have had cyber-attacks in the past on a large scale, allegedly launched by the Russians. Cyber-attacks are a relatively new weapon, which could eventually trigger a war if they bring down the infrastructure purposefully in a modern country relying on the internet and computer systems.

The western Allies are conscious of the sensitivity of the region, geographically and politically. Just because NATO has armed forces in those Baltic States does not mean they condone all the actions and rules imposed on Russian residents by Estonians. If there is clear anti-Russian discrimination practised in any or all of the Baltic States, then sooner or later, Putin and his successors may take action. The cyber-attack, if it was indeed originated by the Russians some years ago, may have been intended as a warning for the Baltic States not to step too far over that red line.

In the Second World War, trusting the Russians with Western detailed sources of intelligence was playing with fire. But while Hitler was keeping the Russians occupied, it diluted to a significant degree the Nazi military force in the West, giving additional breathing space. Hitler had allocated some of his best troops to the East to fight the Russians. It suited the Allies to work with Russia, as the bigger threat by far was Hitler at the time. Had those German armies and panzer divisions been in France instead of in the East, the impact on D-Day would surely have been enormous. Over three and three-quarter million Nazi German and Axis soldiers would attack Russia. If even a fraction of these had been in France and Belgium, looking to the West, the Allies would have had a much tougher time, and D-Day may not have happened when it did. Or, it may well have failed, with disastrous consequences for the Allies, perhaps leaving Hitler time to develop weapons of mass destruction. The relatively reduced strength of German panzers on the French coast and further inland would prove to be of considerable value to the Allies later.

The Russian success at Kursk made a huge difference to the outcome of the war. That was partly down to the Allies providing them with crucial intelligence at the right time via British 'Tunny' decoding of advanced Lorenz Nazi encoding machines. The Russians were waiting for the German attack, and surprised them. The delay by the Germans in waiting for Tiger and Panther tanks prior to their assault would prove to be costly, and give the Russians much more time to build their defences. Managing the decoded intelligence so as not to give the enemy a clue that it was largely the decoding of German messages by the British that gave the Russians the military advantage was a high priority.

But to share our secrets on codebreaking methods with the Russians, and our sensitive *sources* of intelligence? That would have been a bridge too far. Churchill was certainly no fool, and could weigh up Stalin and his senior communist advisers and supporters. For now, they were our important Allies.

5

LETCHWORTH AND THE BOMBES

Before Alan Turing's great breakthrough in understanding how incorporating new machines would help process the Enigma encoded messages, he had already spent a great deal of time together with his colleagues on manual methods using logic, and an advanced form of trial and error. They looked for the settings of the machines, the sequences of rotors, the actual rotors selected, and their positioning by the German operators in the encoding machine before they started transmission. They searched for the Cipher 'Key'. To make progress they would not only need those clues but also 'depth' in the Cipher messages to give a good probability of breaking the key. Use of squared paper with lettering was one method, looking for patterns in the lettering. To mechanize the data processing, to create a 'menu', they needed a 'crib' or clue.

'Depth' to progress the decoding would be assisted greatly if the German operators of Enigma (or other encoding machines), failed to change the rotor or plugboard settings when they sent another message. The more messages they sent without changing the settings, the better the chance was of penetrating the cipher code. Enigma messages were kept relatively short, but sometimes there were exceptions. The longer the individual message, the more exposed the message might become. *Zygalski* sheets was a tried and tested Polish idea, invented by one of the three pioneering Polish mathematicians used originally. They overlaid sheets of squared paper onto a lightbox to find repeat letters, *Zygalski* sheets and 'Jeffreys' sheets were actually quite different systems, and each had its advantages and disadvantages.

'Jeffreys' sheets were a sort of catalogue of the effect of two of the rotor wheels, and the reflector wheel within Enigma. The process aimed to eliminate as many of the permutations of the encoded letters settings as possible, so that the remaining permutations were likely to be the pre-encoded text, the original secret message.

The 'Bombe' machine was a monstrosity of moving parts, and weighed around one ton. It was built on a substantial framework on a bronze-metal structure, in a rectangular large box. It had a mass of red-sheathed electrical cables and connectors at the rear, which needed to be plugged in various sockets before any processing could start. When people say that Alan Turing designed the 'Bombe', we must recognise that his diagrams and drawings and calculations needed to be converted into a practical, working machine. Turing required the considerable engineering expertise of others, and ideas from other mathematicians such as Gordon Welchman. Engineering expertise was necessary to provide a finished working machine. Turing could not have done this on his own, any more than an architect can construct a substantial building on his own.

There were no guidance manuals or instructions, other than Turing's brief sketch drawings, and mathematical calculations. Proper drawings needed to be prepared, few were actually detailed. A lot of hard work and time had to be put in to ensure the first Bombe could be practically constructed, and would operate as Turing intended.

Somewhere was needed to build the Bombe. Fortunately, a factory in Letchworth had been previously awarded a contract before the war to process Census results for the UK, and was called

BTM, or The British Tabulating Machine Company. BTM had commercial involvement with the Americans in their distribution of specialist punched card processing machines. Hollerith machines were an American invention, and would prove to be both useful and essential to help penetrate the Nazi war machine in the years that followed.

In 1908 the American firm gave a licence to BTM for marketing those special machines for early data processing. Over thirty years' experience of use and knowledge of the design,

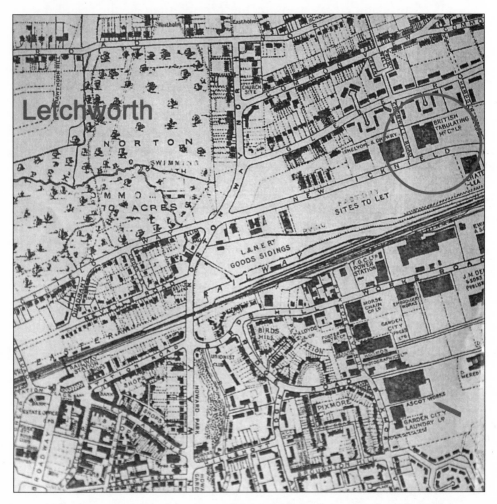

Map of part of Letchworth c. 1936 with BTM marked. (Photo courtesy of the Garden City Collection, Letchworth)

mechanisms and application of Hollerith machines would prove to be invaluable. This was going to be an excellent match for Bletchley Park. Discussions were held with their management, and a part of the factory was set aside for the build. The Official Secrets Act had to be signed by those working on the project and it was given a code name – Project *Cantab*. BTM referred to Bombes as the 'Cantab Contract', but it also had a code reference at the factory, being 6/6502. There was even a logo or symbol designed for *Cantab* by BTM.

In London, at their head office, BTM would sometimes refer to Bletchley Park as 'Bureau "B"' for security reasons. Letchworth, famous as the first Garden City, was roughly 33 miles from Bletchley Park. The BTM factory would be in Icknield Way. This was parallel with the railway line, and close to it. Tabbs Close, a cul-de sac, now stands where one part of BTM existed all those years ago, a rectangular-shaped building on plan.

One old map dating back to 1936 clearly shows BTM identified and marked, and the buildings nearby have text indicating 'Works'.[25] BTM was sometimes locally and affectionately referred to as 'British Tab', and was a vast building with smaller isolated blocks positioned opposite. Even today, the Garden City Collection Heritage site talks of 'British Tab'.

The key player at BTM was Harold' Doc' Keen, who innovated constantly and led a team to build the Bombes, making several high-speed versions to improve efficiency for Bletchley Park and the codebreaking outstations. Gordon Welchman, a close colleague of Turing and mathematician, worked with Harold 'Doc' Keen to form the practical design of the Bombe.

Keen built two prototype Bombes initially. Drawings and technical details would need to be prepared from Alan Turing's sketches under the greatest secrecy. The wheel drums would need to rotate and make electrical contact to run through many thousands of settings to find the letter sequences, and BTM already had some specialist brush-sensing technology. This was going to be extremely useful and pertinent to the new design. Switches would be based upon electromagnetic relays, and would later be further modified to make them more efficient, using, of all things, German design and technology.

Two engineers were allocated for testing, monitoring and maintenance, and feedback on issues was passed to Keen and his design team to make further modifications and improvements of the Bombe. Following testing of the prototypes, there was an initial production run of twelve additional Bombes with scramblers, to reflect the Enigma. The wheel rotors would run in synchronous pattern, so all the top drums would be driven together, the middle drums synchronized, and the bottom drums also synchronized. Keen's design was technically brilliant, and complex: a mass of carefully angled wire brushes in each of the rotor drums, fine and delicate electrical contacts to the rear, reams of electrical wiring and electromagnetic relays. A door at the rear gave access to electrical circuitry and test equipment, and the drive mechanism could also be accessed from the rear of the machine.

BTM would also house the 'super-bomb', or 'GIANT', a combination of four Bombe machines, so large and heavy it would remain at Letchworth until it was separated into four machines later and sent to the outstations as individual machines (Bombe numbers 266, 267, 271, and 278).[26] One of the four ended up being relocated to Outstation Eastcote (Bombe Number 278), and had an original name of 'MARATHON', being renamed 'LILLE' in June 1944, and 'ESSEK' in October 1944, eventually moved into the Yugoslavian Bay on the site. The remainder were sent to Bletchley Park.

'GIANT' was renamed 'SAVAGE' on 8 October 1944, being listed as Number 266 in the Bombe Register, Volume 2. 'GIANT' would be monitored via Bletchley Park personnel under utmost secrecy, until the machine was dismantled. 'GIANT' was not very successful, but demonstrates that innovation and experimentation was encouraged, at a time when both time and resources were limited.

'GIANT' was not operated by WRNS but by a special team of BTM operators, engineers, and visitors from Bletchley Park, in a secret part of the factory away from prying eyes. Keen was involved in the work, with close contact with Bletchley Park. Commander Travis, the Director at Bletchley, would make several visits to BTM to review manufacturing progress. The nature of the specialist work meant that there would have had to be constant progress reports and review to troubleshoot the problems in manufacturing and delivery times that would result from designing and making something which had not been created before.

Turing visited BTM along with Gordon Welchman, who designed the diagonal board improvement circuit for the Bombe and improved its operating efficiency. Here, they could check modifications out, look at production output figures and see the assembly of new Bombes, many being built as High-Speed versions. It must have been going through Turing's and Welchman's minds that more and more of these machines would be required to process the increasing German intelligence being intercepted every day. Assembly of the Bombes would be carried out in different buildings, but modular parts came together to be assembled in the main factory building in Icknield Way. The special, multiple-wired wheel rotors, with many hundreds of stiff, angled wires, would be assembled by rows of factory women, and quality control would have been a high priority, to ensure there were no short circuits once the Bombe wheels were assembled. Discussions would have been ongoing as to how to deal with the additional Enigma rotor which then formed a 'four-wheel' Enigma, bearing in mind the Bombes were essentially three-wheel machines.

The drums and other components were made in the basement of the Government Training Centre in Pixmore Way, about a quarter of a mile away from the main factory. The Bombe metallic frames, with a bronze-coloured finish, were made in other Letchworth factories and assembled in the main BTM factory building. Some components were made in a clothing factory down the road, to the west of Letchworth.[27] The weight of the machines would require heavy lifting hoists. Miles of electrical cabling were required, with thicker red sleeved cables for the rear, and special robust plugs and sockets which would be set carefully by the Wrens, who would operate the majority of the Bombes across the codebreaking outstations. This was modern modular assembly of manufactured and part-built components and whole sections, coming together to be assembled into the finished article and tested prior to dispatch to Bletchley Park and the outstations.

The first Bombe made at BTM Letchworth was transported to Bletchley Park on 18 March 1940.[28] The second machine was installed in August. Bombes initially took around six weeks to assemble, but as experience, speed, and confidence grew, one Bombe was coming off the production line at BTM each week. 211 were produced in total and each Bombe represented thirty-six Enigma three-wheeled encoding machines. 23,421 wheel-drum-rotors were made for the total number of Bombes, with some additional ones for spares. Bombes were eventually made in batches of six, and all the parts and modules from the other factory buildings were put together in the large main building in Icknield Way.

Each Bombe had nine rows of twelve wheels, plus three additional ones at the end, making 111 wheels per machine. Each wheel-drum had many hundreds of angled wires clamped accurately in place to make electrical contact at the back of the machine as they revolved around, helping to eliminate the enormous quantity of encoded settings, based on the Bletchley Park 'menus' written. Apart from 'GIANT' mentioned earlier, other special versions of Bombes were produced including 'Jumbo', with an electrical typewriter, and designed for weak menus; 'Ogre' was a combination of two Bombe machines, and there were a series of four-wheel Bombe machines, some designed by Wynn-Williams of TRE in Malvern.

In the official Bombe Registers at the National Archives, there is clear mention of 'Wynn-Williams' Bombes and H.S.K., standing for 'High Speed Keen' model. These were running much faster than the standard Bombes. Wynn-Williams designed the 'Cobra' attachment which had a multi-strand cable to enable four-wheel operation.

Bombe machine. (Photo courtesy of GCHQ)

One three-wheel Bombe version (Basic 39 point), used Siemens relays, and the reader is directed to the Chapter on Siemens to understand the relevance of this.

Letchworth would also be the base where the *Spirella* corset factory was used for crucial war work, including manufacture and assembly of wiring for the Bombes.

Spirella was an American-based company, and brought new technology into the area of undergarment manufacture. It prided itself on introducing sprung-steel – and later sprung-aluminium – corset stays for comfort, instead of the more common, but much stiffer whalebone stays. This technological innovation may have helped to convince the authorities that Spirella convinced the authorities that *Spirella* workers could become involved in the most top secret war work, involving precision assembly of components for the Bombe machines. *Spirella* was certainly used to innovative technology and production techniques. In 1942 the production of *Spirella* corsets was relocated to London, whilst the factory at Letchworth concentrated on manufacture of Bombe components, parachute making, and 'war work'. From autumn 1942, the BTM factory ladies worked day and night at Letchworth. Over two hundred workers were on the day shift, and roughly half as much on the night-shift. Their speciality would be to wire up the complex wheel-drums of the Bombes, a process which must have appeared rather strange and confusing, if you did not know what purpose those components would have in the final product.

None of the labour force would have had a clue what they were really making, and what use it might have. Much of the wiring for the Bombes was assembled here by teams of female workers, probably enjoying the challenge and change from making women's corsets. A photograph in the Letchworth Garden City collection, termed 'Wizards with wires', shows BTM workers at the Spirella factory, busy making Bombe parts with wires and components. Other photographs show workers making parachutes on a large scale. Thank heavens then, for ladies' corsets, and the skilled female labour force, some of whom clearly had unique, transferable skills.

The *Spirella* building, built between 1912 and 1920 in three phases, was designed by Cecil Hignett, a well-respected local architect. Thankfully it still exists today, but has since been refurbished, at a cost of over ten million pounds, after many years of disuse and deterioration, and now houses around twenty modern Letchworth businesses, only a stone's throw from the railway station. The building has beautiful landscaped surroundings opposite Letchworth's unassuming, single-storey police station. In the 1990s the *Spirella* building was reopened by H. R. H. the Prince of Wales, after major refurbishment and upgrading, but maintaining the style and character of both the building and site. The large ceiling heights and substantial windows makes for a pleasant working environment with lots of natural daylight and excellent ventilation. This would have been welcomed for the factory workers all those years ago, as many other factories would have been quite basic by comparison.

Spirella was seen by many as a caring employer, almost philanthropic in their methodology and approach. It looked after its staff and workers. Even before the war, there were regular worker training sessions, and an involvement of staff in the changes made to the designs and production. If you got

Spirella *building today. (Photo: Ronald Koorm)*

Workers in the Spirella *factory making Bombe components. (Courtesy the Garden City Collection, Letchworth)*

married as a worker, you were given high quality best *Spirella* underwear as a gift. Indeed, *Spirella* goods would have been expensive for most people. An impressive arched ballroom lies behind the main building, which was used for training purposes before and during the war.

Down the road was Irvin's, or 'Irvin Airchutes' a factory making parachutes, set up originally by an American Hollywood stuntman, Leslie 'Sky High' Irvin. It was reported that in excess of 20,000 persons were saved by an 'Irvin Airchute' parachute, by the time of VE day, becoming grateful members of the 'Caterpillar' club. *Spirella* helped with parachute-making too, and worked closely with Irvin's.

Over time, many of the surrounding villages to Letchworth made modular parts to modify, improve or expand the many Bombe machines. If you were instructed to make a cable with many wires and strange connectors at either end, you just didn't ask questions. It was 'war work'. Even after the war, the men and women making these parts were under strict instructions not to breathe a word to anyone of what they did. Imagine working day after day on long shifts and even at night, making the parts and not being allowed to tell anyone in your family what you were doing. Not your partner, your mother or father, brothers or sisters, gran, friends, or your neighbours.

'The Tabulating Machine Company' later became International Business Machines (IBM), which was to dominate computer technology and computer production in the late 1950s and 1960s. The Hollerith machines, used for processing the large quantity of punched cards which harvested intelligence data, now moved from Bletchley Park to the farm in Drayton Parslow.

There were some disagreements as to who should manage the punched card Hollerith processing section, and a difference of opinion on how the data should be best used. Freeborn was told in no uncertain terms how to manage his processing of data by people at Bletchley who were relatively unfamiliar with processing this type of data on a large scale using the machines.

Freeborn knew what he was doing. Freeborn remained loyal to BTM, and realised that this was a sensitive situation. He could not afford to upset Bletchley Park, as BTM had considerable orders from the Government and Bletchley Park for a range of specialist equipment. The Hollerith machines were considered as an added bonus.

There are some reports of specially modified Hollerith punched card machines sent to Bletchley Park. They indicate some of these modified machines were attached to some Bombes, whilst others were free-standing. It is not entirely clear to the author how the interaction between the Hollerith machine and the Bombe could have worked, as they were for completely different purposes. Further research on these aspects of integration of Hollerith machines with BTM Bombes is still required.

A high level of security also applied to the Outstations like Stanmore and Eastcote, and those near Bletchley. Walls have ears, as the posters declared at the time. As we have seen, there was infiltration of Bletchley Park by at least one agent, but thankfully not by the Germans, but the Russians. After considering all the options, they only monitored the spy, and even fed him some information which they wanted the Russians to swallow.

The first Bombe, called 'Victory', was delivered to Bletchley Park in 1941.[29] It was later improved by mathematician Gordon Welchman, with his famous 'diagonal board', a small electrical additional circuit, which improved the data processing and efficiency of the Bombe dramatically. First-year efficiency was 98.8%. Turing was delighted that the Bombe could be made even more efficient than before, but most likely annoyed that he himself had not thought of that improvement. 'Victory' had its name changed twice, first to 'Leo' and finishing up as 'London', having been moved to Outstation Eastcote on 6 September 1943, when the outstation had only just been established. It was partially dismantled when it arrived and not used except for training purposes. The Official Bombe Register, Volume 1, has a note towards the latter part of its time, indicating 'Used solely for Instruction'.

If you were a factory worker in a specialized section making parts, whether at BTM, *Spirella*, or elsewhere, there was a 'need to know' approach, and many elsewhere in other parts of the factory would not be aware what 'X' or 'Y' Block or section, was doing. You might have met in the works canteen for a chat and a smoke and something to eat between shifts, but you kept quiet. Best not to ask too many questions.

The initial BTM Bombes at Bletchley Park would be operated by servicemen, but shortages of manpower forced Bletchley to rethink and consider WRNS operators, which then snowballed after an initial trial period. Wrens would operate the vast bulk of the Bombes, and they would understand the idiosyncrasies of the Bombe machines better than almost anyone, as it was they who spent the most time setting them up, plugging them in, and monitoring them. There would have had to have been close liaison between the outstations and BTM on technical issues, so the engineers on site could resolve problems with the Bombes. BTM might send a technical person to an outstation on occasions, where an issue was challenging the RAF and GPO engineers, but this was unlikely to happen very frequently or for an extended time, as they would be needed back at Letchworth on the manufacture and production of the machines. Only a few Bombes, part of the 'GIANT' installation at BTM, would not be operated by Wrens, and be nurtured by Bletchley Park personnel and BTM senior staff in a corner of the factory. One estimate indicates that around one third of BTM's factory production would be involved in production of Bombe codebreaking machines, a substantial proportion of the factory's output.

Letchworth became a key operational part of codebreaking during the Second World War. BTM was fortunate to have brilliant engineering minds like Harold Keen to manage the Bombe production, and make improvements. It was a stroke of luck to have the rights to marketing and selling Hollerith punched-card machines, as they came in handy for filtering intelligence data. Having the labour resources in both skillful engineering and

BTM in Letchworth, main building. (Courtesy the Garden City Collection, Letchworth)

assembly of components at BTM, *Spirella*, and even Irvin's took a load off the minds of Turing, Welchman, Travis and possibly even Churchill. There were very strong American links with the city of Letchworth, through Hollerith, Irvin's, *Spirella*, and the origins of the American IBM company dealing with BTM. The US began playing its part in helping to defeat Hitler long before D-Day.

Today, Letchworth does retain some of the history of BTM in the Garden City collection, with numerous photographs and information. The pre-war and post-war period at BTM is particularly well-covered in this respect. But because of the secrecy surrounding the Bombes, and the making of them, relatively little information is available; a few photographs internally and externally of the factory, and of some of the individuals who worked there either side of the war. Whilst the local history society and a few relatives of the people that worked there during the war may know of the key part that BTM played, and that of *Spirella* too, few outside Letchworth are probably aware. Those enthusiasts who are into codebreaking will most likely have some knowledge, probably centred around the important figure of Harold 'Doc' Keen, and maybe also the construction of the 'Giant' Bombe. But few others. It is fortunate that the *Spirella* building has been retained and in modern use for commercial business. It is a key section of the large jigsaw puzzle of British and Allied World War Two military intelligence.

'Doc' Keen, who always carried a bag around with him, hence the nickname 'Doc', was high up in the top ten individuals who made Turing's Bombe a practical reality, the unique data-processing machine to break German intelligence. Keen produced a lot of the development work for the Bombe machine, and later improvements too. Keen's team of engineers worked relentlessly to make the Bombe production line work efficiently, carrying out modifications, liaising with Bletchley, TRE, *Spirella*, and Dollis Hill to keep the momentum going.[30] Coordinating all those modular components from the different buildings, arranging the material supplies and knowing that delivery dates had to be achieved no matter what, would put intense pressure of both staff and management. It was a complex juggling act, with quality control of the Bombes an important stage during construction. Organisation was clearly one of BTM's greatest strengths. At a time when there would have been materials and skills shortages, heavy demands on local power supplies, and a balance to be struck with other, important non-Bombe work in the factory, it was a remarkable feat of engineering on a production line to keep the codebreaking outstations operational.

The fact that the factory also ran the 'GIANT' Bombe for a time, with assistance from Bletchley, puts it into the category of a codebreaking outstation, at least for part of the war. So, one could almost say there were six codebreaking outstations in total, and not just five. Either way, without Letchworth, the whole process of codebreaking during the Second World War would have been very different.

6

INCREASING THE WHEELS

The development of Enigma was ongoing throughout the war. What started off as a three-wheel machine soon became a four-wheel machine, with many more permutations and increased security. Not only that, but operators could select from a range of wheels, from five rotors, and later, seven or eight rotors, and then could put them into different orders even before setting the starting point for the codes. The *Kriegsmarine* were far more disciplined in their approach to security than most of the other armed forces (apart from the *Abwehr*) and introduced additional codebooks and strict protocols to keep their information and messages under wraps. The *Abwehr*, or secret service, directed by Admiral Wilhelm Canaris, had their own Enigma version.

In contrast to the Navy, some of the Army operators of Enigma were slapdash, giving opportunities for the Allies to penetrate their messages in part or completely, at least for a time. Some would use the name of their German girlfriend, or the first few letters of her name, to start the setting up procedure, or as part of a message. 'E' is the most frequent letter that occurs in the German language. Analysis at Bletchley Park discovered patterns in certain phrases, letters, and common abbreviations, which all came in useful in providing tools to help penetrate Enigma.

The German Navy's Enigma at the start of the war, the Model M3, had several additional wheel rotors compared to the other armed services, rotors numbered VI, VII, VIII. This increased the permutations of letters significantly. The naval cipher for Enigma was known as 'Dolphin', but there would be many more ciphers, based upon the wheel settings, wheel orders, plugboard, etc.[31] But the introduction of four-wheel Enigmas caused Bletchley Park and its outstations a real problem. The Bombes were designed for three-wheel Enigmas as can be seen in the pairings and layout of machines in photographs.

The problem for the Allies was how to keep on using the Bombes, which were designed for three-wheel machines, but still try to crack the codes of the newer Enigmas. There was roughly a three-pronged approach to this problem.

Firstly, you could still use the three-wheel Bombes. Whereas a Bombe was set up for 36 three-wheel Enigmas, with a bit of ingenuity, one could possibly reconfigure the Bombes to do less processing than before, but to incorporate the row of wheels below the third row as the fourth wheel. So no longer could it represent 36 Enigmas. It would become effectively become less efficient than before. This was a simplistic approach, and would have its own problems and challenges.

Another approach was to add a sort of super-extension lead with an added piece of machinery, and electrically connect it to the three-wheel Bombes. That was a system called 'Cobra', and it used around 2000 wires to make up the connecting cable. Some extension lead! This enabled the Bombe machine to still tackle 36 Enigmas as before, but with a four-wheel capacity.

Twelve Cobras were built, and these were designed by Wynn-Williams, who was based at Telecommunications Research Establishment (TRE) in Malvern. TRE was a radar research base, but had a name to throw off curious people. Wynn-Williams contributed greatly to developments in the

Bombe machines, and the 'Robinson' machine, which came later on. Cobra was built at the Post Office Engineering Establishment with Tommy Flower's input. Flowers was later to design and build the world's first semi-programmable computer. That would be a massive task, and he would require numerous competent engineers to assist him. Cobra had an electronic sensing unit built-in, which was quite an advance for the time. The Cobra attachment was not particularly successful, and there were various problems with it. Essentially, it was found to be unreliable. Cobra attachments were sent onto Outstation Stanmore and to Outstation Eastcote.[32] They were mainly targeting the German North Atlantic Naval intelligence.

The other system was designed by Harold 'Doc' Keen of BTM at Letchworth, and called 'Mammoth'. 'Cobra' was eventually set aside, and 'Mammoth' was put into production on a larger scale. This decision did not particularly reflect well on Flowers, although he was a brilliant engineer who had worked his way through night school. Flowers had to overcome various prejudices as regards his ability, particularly when he came up with the idea of the 'Colossus' computer some time later, and wanted to put that design into practice. Colossus would have to incorporate much innovation and techniques which were then seen as highly dubious by others, and it was a big risk in terms of materials, resources, and cost.

Fortunately, for the Allies, initial mistakes made by the Germans in setting up the four-wheel Enigma allowed them access into the workings of the upgraded Enigma machine and its codes. Access to naval codebooks in the daring raid on the sinking U-boat, and a German trawler, also helped to intercept the U-boat messages.

It was the introduction of the four-wheel Enigmas that made Bletchley management and others realise the need for escalating the quantity of codebreaking base outstations. More Bombes and operators were required. The outstations extended beyond Gayhurst, Adstock and Wavendon to Outstation Stanmore in 1942, and Outstation Eastcote in late 1943. This would also spread the risk of attacks on the bases, and damage to the machines and personnel. It was a wise decision.

The race to produce high-speed Bombe machines was under the direction of Harold 'Doc Keen at BTM. But the first high-speed experimental machine would not be available until March 1943. These would have an extra row of wheels and slashed the time to produce a typical Bombe run. BTM would produce a high-speed wheel-drum, which had a rotation speed of 1000 rpm. A copied Siemens, German-designed, relay facilitated the read-out of the output, and was part of the Allied race against time to keep up with the changes the Nazis were making to Enigma. These modifications, plus the developments at TRE Malvern under Wynn-Williams, moved the technology and designs forward at a time when speed of intelligence processing was a critical factor in informing the senior military officers and commanders of the intentions and advance planning of the Germans.

American Bombe. Most were manufactured at NCR in Dayton, Ohio, USA.

The US Navy would specialise in making their own four-wheel Bombe machines and use them to good effect. They were produced by the NCR company. There is an original machine at the National Security Agency Museum in Washington DC. The secrecy of Allied codebreaking was kept intact, and the Germans never did realise what Bletchley Park and its outstations were doing, or how successful they were in breaking German codes. One slip of the tongue, one careless message, and the Germans would have attacked the outstation bases and Bletchley to destroy them, and would have also changed their settings and procedures to make their messages impenetrable.

Four-wheeled Enigmas indicated the Germans were becoming cautious, and other advanced encoding systems such as '*Lorenz*' teleprinter attachments were being introduced, which would make Enigma seem like a simple child's puzzle in comparison.

Enigma intelligence was still being sent daily in large quantities across Germany, France, Italy, Greece, Belgium, North Africa, and elsewhere. The Swiss, neutral at the time, also had their own version of Enigma, the Model 'K', with six different wheel orders. They had shown interest in the machine well before the war. This model had no plugboard, so was far less secure than later models. The Swiss acquired over 250 of them for their armed forces. The Germans intercepted these, and read intelligence links from the foreign office in Bern to Washington, London, and Berlin. They had acquired two Enigma machines and rewired them to the Swiss specification. Providing the setting of the machine remained the same for a long time, the Germans could read the Swiss messages. Eventually, it appears that the Germans discovered the wiring of the wheel rotors and recovered new settings, which gave them a way in.

Whilst the Germans did not see the Swiss as a direct threat, they would have been curious to establish what dialogue had been exchanged between Switzerland and Britain, perhaps transferring funds across those countries, which frequently occurred, or making new alliances in secret. Finance was a key service industry in

Switzerland, and there would be opportunities for countries and individuals with political leanings to take advantage of the secret movement of funds across Europe.

Being neutral as a country, did not mean you were immune from being spied upon by others. There was much to be gained by the Nazis in fishing for key information in the financial dealings of the Swiss.

Intelligence was particularly of interest when the Nazis suspected some of their own senior officers were liaising with Russian agents in Switzerland, perhaps even plotting against the Fatherland. The Swiss were of great interest to both sides of the war. The British also needed to know what they were planning.[33]

7

ADSTOCK, WAVENDON, AND GAYHURST

These were the initial three codebreaking outstations. These would be the buffer for Bletchley Park, so badly needed, to make space at Bletchley and to spread the risk of a Luftwaffe attack. With the three satellite stations, came logistics problems: how do you provide the listening station coded messages to them quickly? How do you prioritise the encoded messages that come into Bletchley Park, and which outstation gets which message? Additionally, how do you receive back the decoded message or part-decoded message securely from the outstations? All this had to be thought through and managed efficiently. Later, with other outstations even farther away, that process became critically important, to avoid delays, mistakes and security breaches.

Wavendon opened as the first codebreaking outstation in March of 1941. It was at Wavendon Manor (sometimes called Wavendon House), close to Bletchley Park. Automatic typewriters were added on some of the machines to print 'stops' of the bombe rotors or drums. Wavendon and the other two local outstations to Bletchley Park had low-profile security to avoid attracting attention. There were still military personnel at the three outstations, and all the discipline and rules that were expected of naval establishments.

Wrens operated the machines. The designation for Wavendon was O.S.W. The very first Bombe which had been delivered by BTM to Bletchley Park, 'VICTORY', was relocated to Wavendon in 1941. It was sent to Outstation Eastcote on 6 September 1943, partly dismantled, and as we have seen eventually used for training purposes.[34] Wavendon had single-storey huts and structures to house the Bombes, away from the main building, Wavendon Manor, an impressive country house, had a small lake in the grounds. Daphne Child, one of the Wrens at Wavendon, skated on the lake in winter, a welcome break from the gruelling hours attending to the Bombes.

Adstock, also geographically close, designated as O.S.A. in Bombe registers, had Bombes in outbuildings and stables. The smelly and damp stables were commented on by Wrens who operated the machines. These were early days, and Wrens had to get used to the new machinery quickly, the operational quirks, and the protocols. Adstock would be requisitioned, including the house and stables, based on instructions and reports in October 1942.[35]

By the end of 1941 there were six machines at Bletchley, five at Adstock and another five at Wavendon. This number would increase at Wavendon and Gayhurst Manor significantly, as BTM ramped up production. Historic England confirms that five Bombes were at Adstock.

Diana Payne, a Wren, started off at Bletchley Park, and was then posted to Wavendon. The high, substantial windows in the room where the Bombes were kept minimised the noise of the machines to a degree. Security seemed to be minimal, but it was rather out of the way, and few would know about the location. Some time later, Diana was again transferred, posted to Stanmore in 1943, where she received promotion. This illustrates how personnel moved around codebreaking outstations, as the need for resources at various bases grew over time.

In January 1944, Wavendon closed and their machines (14 Bombes), were relocated to the remaining outstations. Tracking the relocation of Bombes is generally straightforward in the two volumes of the Bombe registers, temporarily on loan to the National Archives at Kew. Many of those Bombes ended up at O.S.S. (Stanmore), and O.S.E. (Eastcote).

Wavendon and Adstock had some advanced Bombes, called 'Jumbos', as the war developed. Modified and advanced Bombe machines were being made, modified and adapted at BTM and with help of Wynn-Williams at TRE in Malvern. 'Jumbo' was two Bombe machines connected together and had an electrical typewriter. It had no indicator drums, so the typewriter was an addition. The noise created by this machine was apparently like a machine gun owing to the connecting components and design, so it must have been quite a trial for the Wren operators, and would not have done their hearing much good.

There are several reports which have cameos and short descriptions of the experiences of operational Wrens at the three smaller outstations. 'Divisions' or parade, was held on the bases, and in the case of Gayhurst Manor, this was in front of the manor house. Twelve Wrens slept in a bedroom where Sir Francis Drake apparently slept, and they were in bunk beds. The Bombes were in a hut, a good walk away from the Manor itself, and the ground was rather wet in the hut. There were some concerns about the risk of an electric shock. The manor roof was used by Wrens for sunbathing in good weather. Overflying pilots sometimes had a good view of the sunbathing women, causing mild havoc at the time. There were around two hundred Wrens at Gayhurst during the war, some operating the Bombe machines, some in a support role.

'HAVOC' was in fact the name of one of the codebreaking Bombes. There was downtime for relaxation at dances, as the US 8th Army was in the area. In the locality, there was much surrounding woodland, and the Wrens had to traverse through the woods to pass from the Manor House to the Bombe hut and back. Probably not so much fun in the dark after a nightshift in winter. The limited number of Bombes and operational personnel would have affected the way the outstation was managed; still a military base, but nowhere the scale and size of somewhere like Outstation Eastcote. There were far fewer staff compared with Stanmore or Eastcote. However, it still was operated as a shore-based naval base, and uniforms, saluting, shift-work, and 'Divisions' were all part of the setup and formalities.

When Wavendon closed in 1944, the larger outstations continued to perform their codebreaking functions, with many hundreds of Wrens, engineers, RAF staff, and a few civilian and general post office engineers.

These smaller bases were all geographically still quite close to Bletchley Park, but sufficiently far away to survive intact in case Bletchley did get a visit from the Luftwaffe. As these three bases became operational, yet more space was needed elsewhere as the quantity of intelligence messages intercepted was growing at an alarming rate.

Wrens who worked at Bletchley Park were sometimes billeted at Woburn Abbey. Some who did commented on a three-week training course at Mill Hill before being posted to Bletchley, instead of the normal two weeks, which most others endured. Working on Bombes or Colossus machines, they had to travel into Bletchley Park each day, and Woburn became home for a while as the War office had requisitioned the house. The sitting room on an upper floor was classed as the naval foc'sle. Church parade was compulsory on Sundays, unless you were on shift, marching into the village.

There were around 200 Wrens at Woburn, considerably stretching the resources of the plumbing and sanitary facilities. Heating and hot water were spasmodic and in short supply. However, this was largely compensated for by the beautifully landscaped, vast surroundings, with extensive land, trees, several lakes, and wildlife. Drills and kit inspections were ongoing, and not particularly welcome after long days at Bletchley or the outstations, standing on your feet all day long, but were a necessary part of naval life. Irrespective of where a Wren was stationed, there would be the formal uniformed parades, both in daytime and in the evenings

after night shifts. There were billeting officers at Bletchley
elsewhere, to help coordinate the billeting and accommoda
of Wrens and other personnel and the spread of them across
town and villages. Those who operated at Adstock, Gayhurst
Wavendon would most likely have some basic accommodation
those bases.

Some of the country houses used as bases across England ha
history of ghosts and unexplained happenings, and the Wrens w
soon made aware of this, if it was a location for their posting a
duties. Going about the buildings and surroundings in pairs w
probably wise, especially if you wanted to wander around at nigl
Gayhurst Manor House still has reports of strange occurrenc
if you study the reports from people who have stayed there. Tl
house was completed by Sir Everard Digby, one of the conspirato
in the Gunpowder Plot. It had several 'priest-holes', conceale
hideaways for Catholic priests.

But for the Wrens in wartime, such stories didn't worry then
too much, as they were far too exhausted from the setting up o
the Bombe machines, changing the wheel-drums, plugging anc
unplugging the cables at the back of machines and recording
the output. Then there would be the constant walks across to
the outbuildings, stables or wherever the Bombes were situated.
A good night's sleep was essential, to be refreshed for next day's
parade, and another day operating the codebreaking equipment.

On 4 June 1942, H. D. Fletcher from Hut 6 wrote a report
outlining the Bombe machines available at the time and their
location.[36] He suggested they should be looking for 'a really large
place' to provide for expansion, and suggested Stowe School as an
option. The status of Bombes is set out below, being the quantity
and spread of the Bombe machines in mid-1942:

Hut 11A (B. Park)	8 Bombes
Wavendon	16 Bombes
Adstock	5 Bombes
Gayhurst	16 Bombes

At Wavendon there were 100 Wren 'watchkeepers' listed, and Gayhurst had 150. The basic number of Wrens to operate a machine was eight, based on four watches of two. However, there had also to be allowance for sickness, training, and for those who were allocated to operating special machines at some of the outlying sites. The intake was planned at 20 Wrens per week, but it was recognised by Fletcher that there would be a delay in getting new Wrens fully operational on Bombes on arrival, about a fortnight. Fletcher goes on to make the case for more machines and more Bombes, as well as the personnel to support and operate them. Seventy Bombes were being manufactured by BTM to be delivered in the next few months, of which 25 would be delivered by the middle of September 1942. Roughly half would be high-speed versions. That meant there was a need for housing for about 45 other Bombes from BTM after September, An estimate was provided of a need for a further 400–450 Wrens. The exact number of Wrens could not be fully ascertained at the time, as this depended upon how many of the Bombes would be of the High-speed Wynn-Williams design, or indeed the 'Mammoth' type modification. But Fletcher thought that was a good estimate, based on eight per machine, if one allowed for the four watches for rotation of Wren personnel, two Wrens per machine per shift. The country houses, like Gayhurst, would have on average 16 machines each, and possibly fewer for smaller sites like Adstock. Clearly, they had to move quickly to identify the larger site or sites out there.

Fletcher gave Bletchley Park the two clear options: either find other country houses to repeat the Gayhurst and Wavendon requisition process, and assume that one may have to compromise with smaller sites and limit Bombes to four per site, or find a much larger site. Time was of the essence. The disadvantage of having many small sites with a few Bombes would mean that logistically, the management of those sites would prove difficult, large-scale processing of intelligence would have to be split across many different sites, communication might not be as effective. So, a large site, or sites ... but where?

Adstock, Wavendon and Gayhurst were doing their bit, and doing it well, The expansion of intercepts as war progressed was proving to be more difficult to manage logistically by the day. Churchill could not afford the Allies to fall behind in gathering and processing German, Italian and Russian intelligence. Someone's eye eventually fell on a site in Stanmore, Middlesex.[37]

Stanmore was going on the list for scrutiny and consideration, along with others, but not before evaluating a much larger area hidden away in the Buckinghamshire countryside; a well-known public school with acres and acres of land, not a million miles away from Bletchley Park. Making a wrong decision here could be disastrous. Get the location wrong, and German agents could provide the Luftwaffe with bombing coordinates to remove Allied cryptography and codebreaking capabilities.

Large amounts of technical equipment and machines, of men and women, trucks, lorries, supplies, cabling, signage had to be concealed. The risk of exposing an outstation, even just one, couldn't be permitted. Communications aerials of any size would not be allowed, as the risk would have been too great. If a Y-station aerial was taken out by the Luftwaffe, one just had to reconstruct it. If bombing had occurred on Bletchley Park or the outstations, the damage to the Bombes, the Typex machines, the telephonic landlines, the personnel, could well have been catastrophic. The choices would be summarised in detailed reports for the senior managers to consider. A decision was needed soon. The pressure was on.

8

WRENS AND BOMBES

The history of each Bombe machine can be tracked in some depth via both the Bombe Registers, including date of manufacture, and delivery, where it was located and sent, any modifications made, date of modifications, etc.[38] Also, whether it was a special High-speed version, and if so, which type, the date it was relocated in some cases and where it ended up, if it might have been used for training purposes, and even if it was found to be reliable or not. Some Bombes were renamed, and that can cause a degree of confusion when trying to follow their history and location. 211 Bombes were made in total. Most were destroyed and dismantled after the war, with few surviving post May-1945. Eastcote had some of the remaining surviving Bombes and other codebreaking equipment after the war finished.

It must be remembered that the Bombe was only one important stage in the decoding of the German messages. It still required intellect, logic, manpower, and a lot of woman-power to bring together all the elements to process the Morse code received from a 'Y'-station. Bombes were originally positioned in Hut 1, and later moved to Hut 11 at Bletchley. Bombes were usually named after a city or large town.

The history of each individual Bombe and key modification can be found in the two brown-covered Bombe registers, Volume 1 and Volume 2, currently at the National Archives in Kew. There was a liaison officer at Bletchley Park coordinating closely with the BTM factory in Letchworth.

WRNS personnel had been tried out on Bombe machines at Bletchley in the early years of the war, and this seemed to be the key to expansion across the new codebreaking outstations. They had to overcome the prejudice of male officers and managers in the early years at Bletchley Park, as there was some doubt as to their ability to do the Bombe setting and monitoring work competently. One officer's report was something along the lines of 'Wren X is clearly not suited to this type of work. Wrens Y and Z seem to apply themselves well to the task, and have proved themselves capable.' There would be far more positive reports on their performance than negative ones.

WRNS Director Mrs Vera Laughton was responsible for WRNS personnel. When she first applied to work at the Admiralty, she was initially rebuffed with a 'No women allowed' comment. She persevered, and eventually became a Dame after the war, after giving many year's loyal service, retiring in 1947.

The downside or consequence of the influx of Wrens was the additional management and coordination needed to control the new outstations. There was the need for additional training, instructors, and accommodation sites, management of supplies (from Bombe parts to toilet rolls), establishing and maintaining communications links, provision of maintenance staff, site security, morale and health monitoring, management of shifts and leave/travel passes, coordination with naval and RAF officers, and much more.

Whereas Wrens were categorized into 'Specialised' branch and 'General duties' branch, there would now be an extra category of Special Duties 'X' personnel for Bletchley Park and codebreaking-outstation work. Yet no special flash insignia on the uniforms was permitted, owing to the secrecy of the work, which upset some as they did not receive formal recognition for their war contribution, at least not until very recently, decades after the war had ended. Many did not realise they were training for such a role, even after having signed The Official Secrets Act.

Outstations Eastcote and Stanmore did at least have more permanent accommodation, and were adapted for the codebreaking equipment with the necessary power supplies and stores, etc. These were shore-based naval stations, and ran as such. They had 'berths' to sleep in. The huts for sleeping accommodation were named after warships and aircraft carriers. HMS *Formidable* was one name which rang a bell with a retired Wren. The sites had a quarterdeck, ensign flag, and a foc'sle. Ratings had to salute the officers, and attend 'Divisions', the formal parades. One should not be seen to walk across the quarterdeck. You marched quickly, and saluted the Ensign. When the first Wrens arrived in 1943 at Eastcote, they were shocked to find that they were still building part of it.

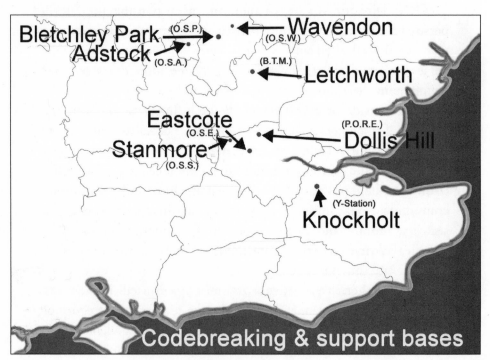

Map indicating key sites including Stanmore and Eastcote.

No good complaining, you just had to get on and make the best of the situation. Things would improve as blocks and sections were completed.

Signing the Official Secrets Act was the first duty when arriving on the base for the first time. Early Wren intakes at Outstation Eastcote would even have to construct their own bunks if they wanted to sleep that first night. Outstation Eastcote alone had 800 Wrens. Promotions in the ranks were limited, and it took a good time to be eligible for the rank of leading Wren or even Petty officer.

They all needed naval uniforms, feeding, training, retraining of new methods of operation, an understanding of the need for absolute security, the ability to swap from setting up and operating a Bombe machine to operating a checking machine, and acceptance of naval discipline. Additionally, they would need to understand the complex instruction menus received from Bletchley, have the ability to recognise defects in the machinery and liaise with RAF and Post Office Engineers – and know not to ask too many awkward questions.

Wrens and personnel used to move around from site to site at times. It may be after training that you were allocated to Stanmore, then after several months transferred a few miles south-west to Eastcote. You might later be transferred to Bletchley Park. Some welcomed the changes, others did not. Of course, Bletchley benefitted from the transfers, as by then the Wrens would have gained much experience. It is likely that those who progressed well in their tasks would be considered for transfer, based on officer's reports and scrutiny. With five satellite stations and the hub of Bletchley Park, there was a good spread of the risk against bombing and a good pool of talent. The spread of external outstations allowed the senior staff and Churchill to sleep at night. It also meant the workload on some of the Bletchley staff could be transferred elsewhere, to a degree.

Wrens were put on a sort of trial at Bletchley in the early 1940s. This would establish their skill level and ability to learn instructions.

Although one or two found the work was not for them, on the whole, they proved themselves as able as men to do the job. With men away fighting, WRNS, ATS and WAAFs filled the gap. Whilst there would be the need for discipline, as with all the armed and support services, there would have to be a great degree of goodwill and trust to act as a sort of 'glue', to ensure the organization was robust and flexible.

It was not the case that Wrens were only used on Bombe-setting and Bombe-monitoring operations. At Bletchley Park, there were several Wrens and ATS personnel in the codebreaking huts, and supporting the 'Newmanry', a specialist section, and elsewhere across the Park. In 1943 there were sixteen Wrens in the 'Newmanry', and this number increased as time went on. But the operation of the Bombe machines was principally down to the Wrens, who had the discipline to maintain accuracy and fine attention to detail, as one slight mistake could have serious consequences.

Some Wrens later also worked on the 'Robinson' and 'Colossus', more advanced machines, but these were for Bletchley alone, and not operational at any of the codebreaking outstations, at least, not until after the war.[39] Reports of Wrens working with the advanced Colossus computer in the latter stages of the war commented that it took time to adjust to this complex machine. There were times they were left alone with it, churning away. Fortunately, there were engineers available to sort any technical problems out. They would be trusted with a high level of responsibility, as it would have taken many months to design and build those machines.

Wrens were vetted as to character and ability beforehand by senior officers, and filtered down to those who would be suitable for the work. A Bombe-operator would have little or no clue as to what effect the decoded messages would have on the enemy, as she usually did not see the final text, unless she was in a privileged role at Bletchley Park. It must have been similar to being trained in writing a computer program, then running the programs daily, but never being told what effect the program had, or what the purpose was; a strange task to carry out day after day.

Mathematical brilliance was certainly not essential, but absolute accuracy in following instructions was imperative. Attention to detail would be everything in their role. The core information provided to the Wrens for setting up was the 'menu', a diagram of letters and links with various drawn lines, which looked like a cryptic puzzle. If one set up the Bombe even slightly incorrectly, it would never come close to the answer looked for. The plugging up of the cables at the rear of the Bombes, based on the menus allocated, was always done in pairs. The sockets were attached to the long, red-sheathed drooping cables, and had to be aligned very carefully to prevent the pins of the sockets being damaged. It was fiddly work. They had to avoid misaligning the plugs to the delicate sockets as damage would have resulted and delays caused.

Once the rear cables had been aligned and plugged in, after a few more checks the machines were ready to start a run, assuming the menu had been followed for setting up the Bombes. Menus were a combination of letters and numbers with linking vertical and horizontal lines provided by the mathematicians at Bletchley. There are some examples out there of menus which were actually used at Outstation Eastcote. Gobbledygook nonsense to an outsider, they were the key interface to communication with the Bombe machine to arrive at the decode, if set correctly by the operator.

Pairs of Wrens would look after a machine in a bay of 8–12 machines, and each Bombe had the processing power of 36 three-wheel Enigmas. To avoid making errors in connecting the cables and fiddly plugs, the work was checked and then cross-checked. The bays, divided into names of countries, and then into cities and towns, were managed by a senior Wren officer, who would have had a record of which Bombes were being worked on, and who was allocated to operate them. New instructions came in frequently. It was a juggling act to ensure there were enough resources available to operate the Bombes on all the shifts, both day and night.

Outstation Eastcote – A Bombe room with Wrens in attendance. (Courtesy of GCHQ)

Wren at a checker machine station within a Bombe room. (Courtesy of GCHQ)

The Bombe would become the equivalent of the Wren's 'Baby'. 'Baby' would need devoted attention from her Wren, routine oiling and maintenance, care in alignment of wheel-drums and contact wires, using tweezers from time to time to prevent electrical shorts and false 'stops' of the drums. The reward to 'mother' would occasionally be an output which went a long way towards deciphering the coded message, after checking on a checking machine, and later on a Typex machine, to simulate Enigma and produce German text. But it was a monster of a baby, with multiple wheels which had to be changed, set up and aligned on a frequent basis. Unfortunately, positive output was not always forthcoming.

A Bombe 'tantrum' might involve an electro-mechanical breakdown, needing the services of the RAF and GPO engineers to sort it out. The many internal wires, angled to make close contact with the rear of the machine, often became distorted, and needed constant attention to avoid false stops. Tweezers to align the wires and prevent short circuits were essential, as were small fingers that could tighten and align the sharp wires correctly. GPO and RAF engineers would have to carry out the routine maintenance, often coming in between shifts late at night. Oil would seep onto your fingers from the lubrication of the spindles, and there would be the constant smell of warm oil in the bombe bay rooms. The Wrens would become used to the aroma of the Bombe machines, boosted by the heat given out by the friction of the mechanical rotating movement around the spindles of the wheel-drums, the metal wire brushes, and the relay switches behind the drums. It was most fortunate that BTM in Letchworth, had experience of metal wire-brush technology, as without that expertise, the machines would have probably broken down more frequently than they did.

The Wrens had to know what they were doing, at all times, to avoid making the problems worse. Delays in processing new intelligence could not be tolerated. Men's lives could be at stake. When they sorted the problem themselves, they must have experienced elation and breathed a sigh of relief. Small feminine hands in aligning the fine wires in the wheel-drums may have been a distinct advantage, in the relatively small space of the internals. Callouses and abrasions on hands and fingers would have been common. Gloves might have been worn by some, but they probably would have been too restrictive in the small spaces, where precision alignment of components was essential.

This was a 24-hour, seven days a week operation. Routine maintenance was factored in, and some machines reallocated for training, as some of the materials might have been found to be poorer quality than expected and the odd machine unreliable, with many breakdowns. The Bombe Registers, or logs of Bombes, had several entries indicating problems with certain machines. A few Bombe entries in the register comment on poor quality of materials.

On one site, a Wren decided to tidy up her make-up and hair by positioning a small metal compact mirror on the codebreaking machine. A bright electrical flash occurred, and left her compact slightly worse for wear, partially melted and destroyed, as the electrics shorted. She was advised to do her make-up elsewhere than the machine room to avoid possible electrocution. A new cosmetics-compact would have to be acquired, although suitably insulated compacts to prevent electrical mishaps would not be available. Incidents like this were relatively rare, but reminded the operational personnel that the equipment was live electrically, and you had to be extremely careful with the voltages and current that were present.

Wrens needed to be 5′ 8″ tall to work in the Bombe codebreaking bays, as the uppermost wheel-drums were positioned near the top of the tall machine.[40] Colossus, a later development, would be even taller than the Bombes. Being tall and strong and with high stamina was a great plus because of the very long hours. Windows would be covered over to a degree to avoid viewing inside the rooms. The minimal daylight would be quite debilitating. On some sites, additional security walls were built outside the huts to further limit window access. It is not known if that was carried out at Eastcote, but plans studied of the site indicate that it probably was not, except high blast walls and barbed wire did exist around Block 'B'.

Checking machines were smaller table-mounted machines, with four wheel drums, often positioned in adjacent rooms with a Wren operator. They would have periods of inactivity and then be forced into action to test the output of part of the Bombe run. This would be a sort of quality control check, testing the plug-in cabling permutations at the front of Enigma, the plugboard. The checking would help decide if the menu was giving the sort of results intended, and Bletchley Park would then have to be informed, so they could do a Typex check at their end.

The checking machines were, in some cases, later moved into the Bombe rooms, and this did not please many of the checker Wrens.[41] This was because the Bombe rooms were very noisy, a bit like multiple knitting-needles clicking away continuously. Thirty-six wheels on a typical bombe, although not all necessarily turning at the same time, were extremely noisy. Now multiply that by, say, eight to ten Bombes in a finger of the block and then others in adjacent areas, and the noise would be quite intolerable at times. You would have had to certainly raise your voice quite loudly to converse in the Bombe rooms.

While Bombe wheel-drums could only rotate in a clockwise direction owing to the angled internal wiring, the checking wheels could rotate in both directions. This saved the operator valuable time. Semi-soundproof screens were later devised and positioned around some of the checking machines, and these can be seen in one of the photographs, with a checker-girl looking quite bored, probably thinking about her boyfriend somewhere in France. If you were operating the Bombe, it may be your next shift allocated you to checking duties. This meant at least you could sit down for the shift.

The checking duties were relatively popular with Wrens, although some preferred setting and monitoring the Bombes to the process of checking Bombe output. If you were in an adjacent room with your checking machine, it would be a lot quieter, and you could maybe read a book for some of the time, awaiting Bombe output to check, or even daydream. But all eyes would be on you when the output from the Bombe urgently needed the checking process. When a positive Bombe output which had been checked was sent onto Bletchley via a scrambled telephone line, if the call came back down the line after a short pause of 'Job Up', that meant success. 'Job's Up, Strip!'⁴² That meant the machine needed to be stripped of wheel-drums and reloaded/reset using a completely different 'menu' setting supplied by the Park.

The checking system was an important stage in the decoding process, a form of a quality control check relevant to the Enigma plugboard settings. Checking reports would be communicated back to Bletchley Park's Hut 6 machine room by a Wren on a scrambler telephone, when they had a 'good stop'. 'Norway' Bombe-bay might have a good stop on the 'OSLO' Bombe. Or 'France' bay may have a good stop on the 'PARIS' Bombe. It was up to Bletchley Park to then give the outstation permission to move onto another menu and message by scrambler telephone.

The Wren Bombe-operator would have to pass across to the checker the initial basic information in order for her to start the checking process. This would include the Stop number, wheel order, Ringstellung setting, and stecker position of the input letter. Checking sheets would be filled out, and letters circled and entered on the sheets as the checking machine gave an output. It would take time to get used to the process. Less experienced Wrens might work alongside a more experienced individual to get to grips with the checking process and completion of the checking sheets. Then there would be 'Check Stops' to monitor the performance of both the operator and the Bombe machine. This would be a highly technical process, albeit adapted so that it could be communicated to non-technical people. Each Wren involved in the process would have to pull her weight and be efficient, to work as part of a team. Without their input, Bletchley mathematicians and cryptographers would have been totally unable to decipher such a large scale of enemy intelligence. With experience, a Wren would become extremely proficient at setting up the machines, transferring the key data to checking sheets, having an intuition when there was likely to be a positive outcome on the check. She was surely elated when HQ confirmed the success of the job.

Bombe runs took on average 15–16 minutes, but sometimes much longer, even hours. If it were not for Gordon Welchman's 'diagonal board' circuit, the Bombe runs would have been far longer, and fewer messages would have been processed in the same time. However, just because there was a 'stop' of the wheel drums did not mean you automatically had broken that message code. There would be many false stops and much resetting of the machines, checking of readings at the end of the machines, checking against the menus, reporting to the Wren officer in charge of the block. Some stops might be due to short circuits of the Bombe-wheel internal wires, which would need to be located, corrected by the Wrens, the drum reloaded and the machine restarted.

Visits may be needed from the maintenance crew on call at the time, to rectify faults in the mechanism or the cabling connections. Mistakes made in plugging into the sockets to the rear of the Bombes could cause short circuits. Much time would be spent checking and rechecking the plugs.

The monotonous nature of the work, and the fact that most of the time you had no idea what the message actually stated, its level of importance, or its impact on the war, meant it could be a rather lonely and possibly a depressing workplace. Some found the work across the outstations to be incredibly boring, but others saw it as exciting and a new venture, which was quite unique compared to other roles in the Navy or services. There were always pubs to visit at least, and American dances to attend, and theatres to visit with free or reduced tickets for military personnel.

At Outstation Eastcote, visiting the pub could be a challenge as there may have been an eight-mile, even a twelve-mile exclusion zone from the centre of the base, according to some reports. This was intended to further reduce the possibility of loose talk by Bombe operators, Wrens, and Engineers.

Those who breached the rule could be expected to be confined to barracks for an extended period. Local publicans might have wondered why there were fewer Wrens coming for a beer. At least one Eastcote Wren did take a chance but was found out, and had to suffer the consequences, of being confined to barracks.[43] Post-war at Eastcote this restriction on local pub access would be lifted.

From time to time, there would be a morale-boosting exercise to bring together the Wren operators and others involved with the codebreaking machines and give them a talk. This talk might convey that work they did some weeks ago on the Bombes resulted in an Allied success somewhere in Europe or the Atlantic. It could be a particular series of messages that enabled the sinking of an Italian cruiser, or bombing of an armaments supply train in France.

This would then 'join the dots' for the Wrens and RAF engineers. This provided some meaning to the repetitive and monotonous shift work. It gave the personnel purpose for their long hours at the base. They were saving Allied lives, but it was difficult to make that connection stuck in a large machine room in North-West London or elsewhere, day after day.

At Eastcote, these information talks probably took place in the Assembly Block near the Lime Grove entrance, known as Block 'A'. The Assembly block was constructed as the base developed. Or the talk might have been confined to part of Block 'B' which was the most secure part of the Outstation Eastcote site, on the north side of the footpath. Knowing that your efforts may have helped move the battle against the Nazis forward, even in a small way, would improve morale.

Of course, the Wrens could not tell others outside the base any of this confidential information. Most would not give away anything even decades after the war.[44] They would become expert at understanding the menus issued to them, in respect of setting up of the machines quickly, as time was imperative. They would also become expert at training others who had recently joined the section, including, later at Eastcote, American Signals soldiers from the US Army.[45]

The Wrens would become expert at aligning the long, dangling cables at the rear of the Bombes, and cross-checking with a Wren colleague that a particular connecting plug at the end of the cable had been inserted in a particular socket carefully, so as not to damage the pins and connectors. They checked, double-checked, even triple-checked just to make sure no errors had been made in connecting the sockets.[46] Then, setting the letters corresponding to the menu on the Bombe, they would they be ready to turn the start switch and stand back while it went through its processing cycle. They could do no more until the machine stopped. Then it would be for the Wren operators to determine whether this was a viable stop to go to the checking machines, or if it was a malfunction, and if so, whether they could fix it themselves, or needed further assistance from the RAF or GPO engineers. The more shifts you did, the more experienced you were in working out whether a Bombe 'stop' was due to a malfunction or not.

During odd moments of contemplation, they would have probably thought about their boyfriends or brothers over in France, Italy or North Africa. They would dream of the next few days off-shift, when they would go and visit friends and family, or go up to London to see a show or attend a dance. Long shift working patterns could eventually allow a four-day pass. Food would have been a daydreaming occupation too, as the food at the outstations, particularly Eastcote and Stanmore, was not the best. Those American servicemen's dances were a good excuse for a decent meal. And sleep, sleep, sleep. Tiredness, both physical tiredness and emotional stress, would take its toll.

There would be a medical room in most facilities and outstations, probably at Bletchley as well. There, an overstressed Wren could be put to bed by a senior officer, given some headache pills, and allowed to rest, sometimes for days. There were reports of near nervous breakdowns in some cases. The mental breakdowns happened at more than one outstation, and Bletchley Park may even have had its share too.[47] A release of weeks, and perhaps even months of stress, which had been bottled-up by the Bombe operators and message checkers.

One young Wren, 'Ruth', was put to bed in the sick bay room, and spent several days sleeping, eating almost next to nothing.[48] Eventually she was allocated a special pass for two weeks leave. She went home, but returned back fit and refreshed for work. Ruth had only been eighteen when she first arrived at Outstation Eastcote.

Constant shift pattern changes caused a form of jet-lag. Not all found they could sleep well during daytime, upsetting their circadian rhythm. Particularly when there were reports of your loved ones elsewhere being bombed night after night, the death or serious injury of a relative or partner, the impending approach of D-Day, with uncertainty around each corner. But Wrens were resilient, and most affected by stress and tiredness quickly came back to work after a few day's rest having de-stressed in sick bay. Outstation Stanmore's Admiralty allocation figures show that there were two sick bay support Wrens allocated to the base, probably rotating on a shift basis. A similar arrangement would have been likely at Eastcote.

Many Wrens and others were confined to barracks for several days or even weeks near D-Day, to avoid the possibility of leaks to the outside. This would limit external contact, so the Canteen/Galley, plus a bit of open space outside the huts and barracks, would be the only escape you could experience away from the Bombes and sleeping accommodation. Smoking was a release, and plenty of cigarettes were available. Smoking would not have been allowed in the Bombe rooms as the equipment was quite delicate and the risk of fire would have been too great. The extinguishers on hand must have been of the type that could be used on electrical fires. There would be fire sand-buckets too, in the long corridors.

Eastcote had a fire practice drill of sorts for 'D' watch fire team, with Wrens moving portable hose fire-equipment on a trailer through a gate on the public footpath.[49] When they had to transport it through the gate to bring it inside, the Wrens discovered it could not fit through the opening, so the practice was reluctantly abandoned. In the event of a real fire, the local fire brigade might even have had to sign The Official Secrets Act before they would be allowed to leave the site. (That assumes the secrecy forms wouldn't have also gone up in smoke!)

The constant relocation of personnel, including Wrens, meant that you had to go where you were allocated at a moment's notice. When they had shortages of personnel, you just had to pack and go to your new base. It might be from the initial training camp at Mill Hill, Wimbledon (or elsewhere), to Stanmore, to Eastcote, to

Bletchley and back to Stanmore. It would be a challenge at times. But you would make new friends or possibly bump into old friends and colleagues from other bases.

It would not be like working as fighter or bomber crew, where you quickly learnt how to cope and to lose close friends in battle. But you were just as important to the overall objective. If it was tactical intelligence, all well and good. If it happened to even hint at a *strategic* move on the part of the Germans, that was like gold dust, and of particular importance. You were doing your bit for the war, even if most of the time you had no idea exactly what impact it was that you were making. Most would have to tell white lies to relatives and friends, about what they were doing 'I'm just typing boring reports,' or 'It's a training camp, really, that's all I can say.'

Joining the Wrens, particularly at a young age, might meet considerable opposition from parents naturally fearful for their daughter's safety. 'Why don't you just do typing at Clarke's down the road?' or more often 'Why not marry your sweetheart Jim, and just settle down like other girls?' But many would be proud of seeing their daughter in uniform, and doing something to help the war effort. Some would have been debutantes who wanted to 'do their bit' for the war and join the Wrens or WAAFs. This is where the social mix of classes came in, and it would prove to be quite a shock for some, initially.

Everyone would have to get on, once you were enrolled and on the training programme, usually a two-week camp. You wouldn't normally have a choice where you would be posted to after training at Mill Hill, but one or two managed to get a posting of their choice.[50] Many were shocked to find it would be a rather basic shore-based camp, and not a ship. Where were those handsome sailors that we were told about at training camp? In the Navy, one usually expected to be with sailors, ships, the sea, and certainly not tarmac and rows of huts. Most of the codebreaking outstations had relatively few men, maybe a few maintenance engineers, technicians, Royal Marine security guards, or some RAF personnel. After initial training, having arrived at Eastcote or Stanmore, the newer Wrens may have been trained how to teleprint.

Bletchley expected the senior officers at the codebreaking outstations to ensure everyone was doing their job, and doing it efficiently. In most cases, it was the combined effect of the mass of decoded intelligence filtered through back to Bletchley Park that made the greatest impact, not a single key breakthough. Eastcote, Stanmore, Wavendon, Gayhurst, Adstock, BTM, Dollis Hill, Drayton Parslow, and others were but cogs in the big wheel of intelligence decoding. And this machine was largely driven by thousands of skilled and semi-skilled female personnel. The Wrens' training at Mill Hill, Wimbledon, Scotland and elsewhere, would provide basic skills, but the Bombe activities would require supplementary training at the codebreaking bases.

They would have to learn on the job quickly. The statistics of errors and efficiency would be recorded and monitored by senior personnel. Thankfully, Wrens had a very high level of efficiency, and apart from 6812th US Signals division, who were quite exceptional in intelligence operations at Eastcote, they were at the top of their game in operating the Bombe machines.

The quantities of WRNS and other personnel on Special 'X' Duties are shown here on some charts and graphs, but the reader needs to be aware that there was a build-up of personnel, transfers of staff, new arrivals, resulting in a final peak number of personnel at each individual base. There were also ATS and WAAF personnel at some of the bases, and particularly at Bletchley Park. These should not be overlooked, as they also had challenging roles to play.

Apart from relocation of Bombes between stations, sometimes they were renamed and moved from bay to bay on the same outstation site, even up to half a dozen times.[51] It is a bit of a mystery why some machines were renamed quite so many times, particularly when they were broadly the same machine. It is the case that modifications were sometimes made, improvements, diagonal boards added, some converted into high speed versions later, etc. That must be why some were renamed.

Those which were for the American (6812th Signals) Bombe section at Eastcote were generally named after American locations and (USA bay) was then written in the Bombe register in brackets. American names included 'HOUSTON', 'MINNEAPOLIS', 'ATLANTA', 'PHILADELPHIA', 'ROCHESTER'. The registers indicate the date of delivery from BTM Letchworth, together with the date the Bombe was operational, shown as 'In action'. Information as to whether it was a High Speed Keen (H.S.K.) machine or a Wynn-Williams high-speed modified machine was recorded.[52] The fact that a particular machine had diagonal boards, and how many, was recorded. Clear notes were made by hand as to whether a machine was performing poorly, had to be sent for modification, or was reallocated for 'instructional use', training.

Bombe number 20 was initially named 'ZULU', changed to 'DUNEDIN', then a transfer to O.S.E. as 'ZEEBRUGGE', 'YANNINA', 'LILLE', 'LARISSA', and finally 'GHENT' (O.S.S.), when it was relocated from Eastcote to Stanmore. The name 'LARISSA' on a Bombe at Eastcote can be seen in one of the black and white photographs published at Bletchley Park. All the names would be controlled on the Control Board by a senior rating or officer, recording bay location and who was allocated to operate them on a shift by shift basis.

The Bombe registers make for a fascinating, if quite difficult read, as the ink is sometimes difficult to decipher, and there are a few amendments and crossings-out in places. They are a historical record of one of the most significant times in Britain's history. The two roughly A5-sized books have old brown paper covers and a basic contents near the front, with the names of the machines listed. Blank sheets of lined paper sometimes appear with various lengthy gaps before entries of Bombe names recommence, and the reason for this is unclear. When looking at the various names, many of the cities and places chosen at the time would have been Nazi-occupied, and the writer did not know if they would ever be freed from Nazi oppression.

The one entry that stands out in the Bombe registers is written in red ink at the bottom of each Bombe entry, 'Out of Action 23/5/45 for dismantling'. Victory! It would be highlighted clearly in red ink on each page. This would close one chapter of history, and open another.

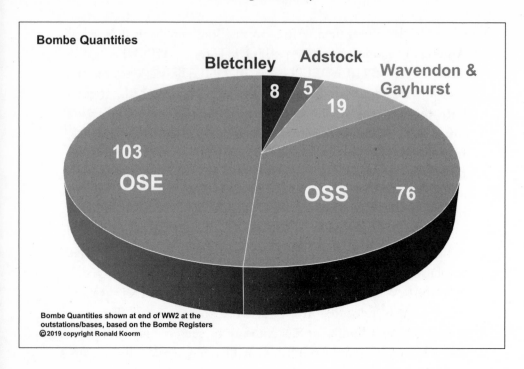

Bombe Quantities

Bletchley — 8
Adstock — 5
Wavendon & Gayhurst — 19
OSE — 103
OSS — 76

Bombe Quantities shown at end of WW2 at the
outstations/bases, based on the Bombe Registers
©2019 copyright Ronald Koorm

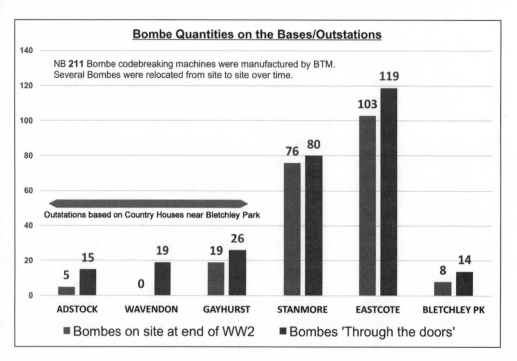

Bombe Quantities on the Bases/Outstations

NB **211** Bombe codebreaking machines were manufactured by BTM.
Several Bombes were relocated from site to site over time.

Outstations based on Country Houses near Bletchley Park

Site	Bombes on site at end of WW2	Bombes 'Through the doors'
ADSTOCK	5	15
WAVENDON	0	19
GAYHURST	19	26
STANMORE	76	80
EASTCOTE	103	119
BLETCHLEY PK	8	14

■ Bombes on site at end of WW2   ■ Bombes 'Through the doors'

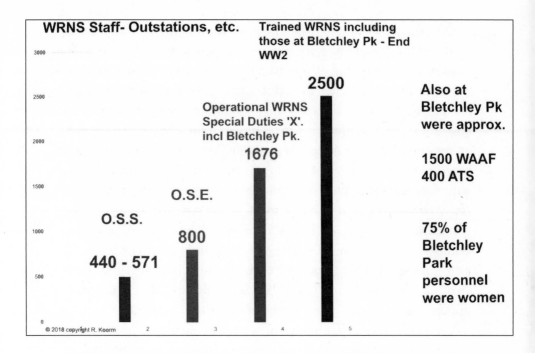

The table below is based on the author's research of the registers of the Bombes at Eastcote.

Bombe Register Entries of BOMBES AT O.S.E. (Eastcote) which were there mainly for the duration of WW2	103	Including those (ten) Bombes allocated to USA 6812th Signals on the base
Bombe Register Entries of BOMBES at O.S.E. which were eventually transferred later, mainly to O.S.S.	16	
TOTAL of Bombes Permanently or temporarily at O.S.E. based on entries added up	119	Including those (ten) Bombes allocated to USA 6812th Signals on the base

(Observations abstracted from Bombe Registers Volumes 1 and 2 based on entries inspected, but please see further information below.)

Initially, there appears to be a divergence from the 'official' figures as shown on the commemorative plaque at the site (110 Bombes). However, the changing of Bombe names for a considerable number of machines, the transfer to and from bases, and moving machines around the various bays on site, renaming them yet again, all added to the complexity and confusion for the record-keepers at the time. Some Bombes were assembled collectively, and built together as one, and then split, ie the 'GIANT', although this counts as four individual Bombes. Tracking the Bombes was never going to be straightforward. A lot depends how one interprets the entries in the register, and cross-references them. Double-counting Bombes is easily done. 'LARISSA' is in Volume 1 as entry 153. It also appears as entry 300 in Volume 2, and indicates the name changes to 'LILLE' and 'LYONS'. So 'LARISSA' may have been double counted, purely due to the entry in both volumes.

One can change the name of a Bombe machine a thousand times, but it is still essentially the same basic machine, even if it had been modified. Entries 118, 142 and 144 are likely to have been the same machine, 'ZEEBRUGGE', 'THEBES', and later 'GHENT' when it was transferred to O.S.S. Entry 275 states it was renamed 'DOORN' on 18/5/44. 'ZEEBRUGGE' was also later changed to

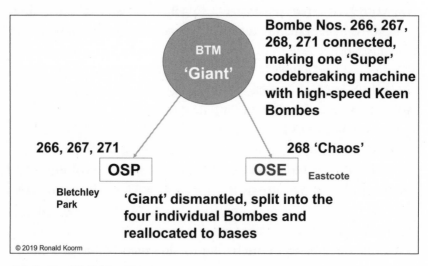

Splitting the GIANT Bombe.

'LILLE'. 'DOORN' is also mentioned under Bombe 269 at O.S.E. Clearly, double-counting of Bombes will affect the totals, and can give a false impression of the quantities that existed.

The author now believes that 103 Bombes at Outstation Eastcote is much nearer the mark as the final quantity, allowing for the renaming of Bombes, and transfers. This quantity may be slightly increased, when one considers some Bombes went to O.S.E. and were transferred to Stanmore or elsewhere. It all depends how you count the entries in the registers. One hundred and three Bombes represents almost forty-nine percent of all the Bombe machines made at BTM, Letchworth. This total figure includes the ten Bombes allocated for the 6812th U.S. Army Signals Division. Bletchley Park appears to have had up to eight Bombes, based on papers inspected at the National Archives, but several other sources indicate it had only six. Eight bombes accords with the Bombe Registers. Eight was enough to use some for training purposes, and some for fully operational activities.

One must appreciate that Bletchley was the director, HQ and hub of intelligence, but it was principally the codebreaking outstations that did the Bombe processing, with over 200 machines.[53] As no original Bombes now remain, it is purely the Bombe registers and other supporting information at the National Archives and Bletchley Park that we rely upon to establish the quantities and types that were made.[54, 55] Sadly, there do not appear to be any other Bombe machine records remaining in Letchworth, where the Bombes were manufactured.[56] This was probably largely because of the secrecy during wartime. Further details of the relationship between BTM and GC & CS and the arrangements can be found in the depths of The National Archives.[57]

Considering the relative importance and input that Letchworth as a city had, the city does not metaphorically shout about what it achieved. Perhaps it's because both older and younger generations wish to put that all behind them? Information is available to a degree, if you look hard enough, but when I first went to Letchworth, many years ago, I was completely unaware of the role it played in the war. Since revisiting the city a couple of times, I am of the opinion that a commemorative monument or something similar is warranted, to be positioned near the station or city centre. Maybe it's there already, but I have not found it.

The Garden City Collection has some interesting historic records, and can even be searched online. However, you can be sure that if the same events and activities that occurred at Letchworth had happened at Bletchley Park, or in London, those in charge would be making a very big thing of it. Letchworth and the surrounding villages housed an astonishingly talented collection of determined individuals, across different locations of the city, each of them concentrating on their roles and responsibilities. Letchworth Garden City can be proud of all of them.

9

OUTSTATION EASTCOTE TO GCHQ

The selection of Eastcote as an outstation was possibly a strange one. It was initially considered as a base for a casualty station following the new second front in France, but that idea was quickly scotched as being impractical. It did have the advantage of a degree of relative seclusion in the suburbs, away from important buildings, bridges or structures, and around nineteen acres of land to house buildings and personnel. It may have been because of the relatively close proximity to the 'Post Office Engineering Establishment' in Dollis Hill that Eastcote and Stanmore were selected.[58] So engineering and technical advice could be quickly obtained, and specialist engineers would be available to attend on-site to sort out problems which the resident RAF and Post Office engineers were unable to deal with, or perhaps just wanted a second opinion. At the time of establishing these bases, no one would have known that Eastcote would become GCHQ after the war.

From the 1920s land at the north of the top of Lime Grove was owned by Telling Bros. Prior to this, there had been several owners, including a rubber planter and his wife. South of the public footpath, the previous owners included a gentleman of Swakeleys House in Ickenham, and a development company, the British Freehold Corporation. The Government acquired the land under requisition powers. There used to be tall poplar trees near where what is now Kent Gardens (previously recorded as allotments) and the old Assembly Block on the site.

The 1935 map provided illustrates the considerable area of open fields around Highgrove House and beyond. Cattle grazed on the open meadow. It would have been a tranquil scene, soon to be changed. The work commenced on buildings at Eastcote in September 1943. It has been reported elsewhere that Outstation Eastcote was established following abandonment of a decision to provide a hospital base there for future D-Day casualties.[59] It was deemed unsuitable for the casualty base, probably for being so remote from the coast and the transport links.

Until it came into being, the largest codebreaking outstation running Bombes was Outstation Stanmore. This was north of Eastcote, but not very far distant. Outstation Stanmore was established in 1942, also known for a time as HMS Pembroke III and later Pembroke V. (Further information on Pembroke can be found later on). At Eastcote, alongside the 800 Wrens, occupied on four shifts, support staff included around 100 RAF and Post office engineers, there to maintain and repair the Bombes.

The site was divided in two by an old public footpath, running east-west, dating back to *c.* 1565, and is still there today, although the site was developed in the early 2000s as a housing estate. Highgrove House is still adjacent, but the house was rebuilt many years ago after a fire, was used for social services accommodation, and later turned into luxury flats. The footpath is around a quarter of a mile long, and walking along it one has a good idea of the scale and size of the outstation. In 1935 the lake at Highgrove almost reached the public footpath at the north end of the site.

Highgrove itself was had 23 acres of land, dominated by the house, the large lake, and outbuildings. Large meadows or fields were to the north and east, around 19 acres, which were

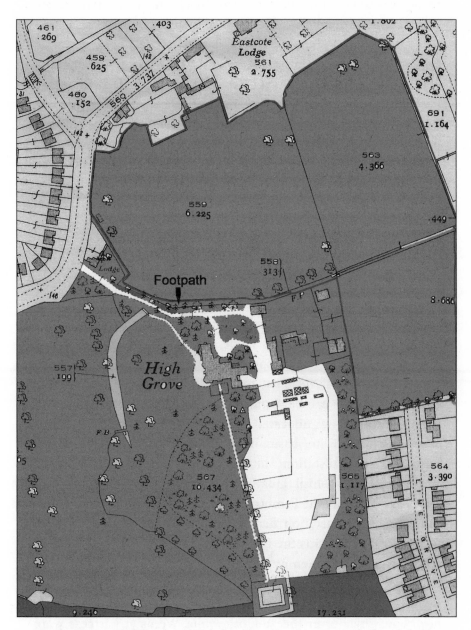

Map by Eastcote High Road c. 1935 before Outstation Eastcote was built and showing Highgrove House, footpath and fields. Fields outlined would become the site for Outstation Eastcote and, later, GCHQ.

to become Outstation Eastcote in 1943. The relevant fields for the outstation are marked 559, 563 to the north of the public footpath, and 313 and 689 to the south. The public footpath separates Highgrove from the north fields. Field number 558 was a smaller plot of a third of an acre to the east of Highgrove House, with several individual buildings. It would later become the north part of Kent Gardens, with residential housing linking back to Lime Grove. Lime Grove is one of the oldest roads in the area, and extends south to north, terminating at the bottom of the south-east field, marked 689. Kent Gardens, further to the left, did not exist at the time, being built on areas shown as greenhouses, based on the 1936 map, which were almost certainly part of the Highgrove estate.

The housing estate development on the old site, Pembroke Park Estate, was constructed after 2007 when the site was sold, and spreads across both sides of the footpath.[60] The site was roughly bounded by Kent Gardens, Deane Way, Lime Grove, and Eastcote High Road. Post-war, it was to be called RAF Lime Grove. The name of the housing development 'Pembroke Park Estate' comes from the WRNS naval term for the site 'Pembroke V' or HMS Pembroke V. This can be confusing, as Pembroke V was the name for those personnel allocated to Special duties 'X', carried out across a wide range of bases, including Bletchley Park, Outstation Eastcote, and Outstation Stanmore. If you had done your two weeks training at Mill Hill, or in Scotland, or elsewhere, and saw your posting was Pembroke V, it could have been at any of those bases.[61] Outstation Eastcote was abbreviated as O.S.E. in documentation such as the Bletchley Park Bombe Registers. But if you were a naval officer, Wren or similar, then you would probably have used the term HMS Pembroke V.

Bunks for personnel were two high, and separated from neighbours by clinker breeze-block walls. Wrens at Eastcote were billeted at around 70 persons per hut. Heavy snorers were a hazard if you were a light sleeper. The records for the Women's Royal Naval Service Officers (WRNS) 1939–1945, indicate that some personnel allocated to Pembroke V (London) were on accounting duties. It is not clear if that was just a cover for the secret bases, or if they really were carrying out accounting work. Other entries in the database show 'HMS Pembroke V (base for WRNS units in London)' and 'HMS Pembroke V (secret base, WRNS, Bletchley Park, London).[62]

There was one isolated report of an attack on a Wren, on the footpath, and patrols were increased by the police and military accordingly. The culprit was never found, and there did not seem to be a repeat attack. Apparently, the Wren was shaken up, but thankfully no real injuries occurred. Some Wrens admitted to being petrified at night after a nightshift in Block 'A', and ran across the footpath lane as fast as they could, to get back to their sleeping quarters in Block 'B' or to have a meal before bedtime.

Attending 'Divisions' was compulsory; standing on parade in the freezing cold and rain after a nightshift in the early hours, was not exactly a Wren's favourite pastime, when all you really wanted after your shift was your bunk bed. Some Wrens did get promotion, but there were no guarantees, so you just had to hope your efforts had been noticed by a senior officer.

Wrens had to tackle anything and everything that came their way, and that meant doing a spot of work in the galley kitchens, unless you were an officer. The accommodation was better than Bletchley Park (unless you were based in the mansion), the huts at Eastcote being of a more permanent nature and better built than at Bletchley. However, the food was insufficient in quantity and lacking in quality. Wrens looked forward to going to American servicemen's dances, where the food was in a different league. It wasn't all about meeting handsome American servicemen. Finishing a long shift on Bombe room operations, a meal might be as basic as cheese on toast. Some reported seeing 'oven beetles' in amongst their food, and even food poisoning occurred. In the galley the floor open-gully drainage left a lot to be desired. Only half an hour was allowed for a break during the shift, and in that time one had to rush across the lane to the dining hall on the other side of the lane, gobble your food down and rush back to the Bombes or the checking machines.

Some Wrens didn't bother making the trip across the footpath, and made do with something they had brought over for a snack. There would not have been enough time to rush down the road to Eastcote, Local cafes in the parade of shops were visited frequently during the daytime by off-duty staff. At least it wasn't in the middle of nowhere, and one had fairly good transport links into London. It would be around a brisk ten-minute walk from the Lime Grove entrance to the shops, longer to get to the station, which was farther south along the high street.

The locals would have known of the existence of the base, as they would have seen the personnel and vehicles and supplies going in and out. They would not have known what went on inside, but many would have been curious, and no doubt there would have been some local gossip about the base. What was quite curious was

Outstation Eastcote – control board for the Bombes. (Courtesy of GCHQ)

that public footpath adjacent to Block 'B', with the codebreaking machines, remained open to the general public. Churchill could easily have given the instruction to seal it off at both ends, for reasons of national security. We know it was kept open during the war, as reports and diary accounts of Wren personnel mention the need to cross the lane to go to the galley for a meal, and being quite scared of meeting undesirables late at night.

Of course, they may have played the security aspect down to avoid alerting locals, and if the footpath had been closed, that might have started tongues wagging and be of interest to an enemy agent, perhaps. This way, there was better integration with the locals. The high walls and barbed wire and armed guards were just accepted as a security measure, which could have been guarding military toilet rolls, for all the locals knew. It is not entirely clear if some of the windows at Eastcote or Stanmore had screens.

Statistics on errors in using the Bombes across most sites indicated that accuracy by Wren operators was exceptionally high, generally. Wrens were sometimes told that they had to be extra careful when doing their job, as Mr Churchill himself might be reading the output of one of their messages. This in fact, was quite possible, as Churchill had a lockable, buff folder of recent intelligence on his desk every day, to examine a summary of the decoded information.

Aligning the plugs and sockets to the rear of the machine was a time-consuming task, especially as the cables were rather long, drooping vertically down the back of the machine. Standing on tiptoes may have been necessary for the upper sockets, if one was the minimum required height of 5′ 8″ After a Bombe 'Stop', sometimes the Wrens were told they had the wrong number, and that meant starting again and checking everything. The Wrens would need to take down the result readings accurately at the end of the machine run.

As the German Enigma operators were instructed to change the settings of the machine every 24 hours, this meant everyone had to be on their toes, and alert for those changes. That was Bletchley

Park's problem. They were the ones preparing the menus based upon the encoded messages coming in.

Some reports state that menus were telephoned down to the outstations from Bletchley Park. If this were so, then it would have been a curious process, as the menus were a sort of diagram, and would have been perfect for a facsimile machine to transmit them, but they had not been invented at the time. So there would have had to be some detailed description of the menu. With practice, however, it would be possible for someone at the receiving end to insert the menu letters from Bletchley Park in the correct places with the horizontal, vertical and diagonal linking lines between the letters in the correct places. That would be a skill to be learnt by experience, and one which the mathematicians at Bletchley would have to be proficient at. One mistake, and the Bombe would never locate the correct settings on the Bombe run. It would all then be wasted time and resources.

Many of the Bombes had to have modifications to turn them into high-speed versions, or have relays upgraded to the newer, modified relays, based on a well-respected Siemens design.[63] Most Bombes had the 'diagonal board' electrical circuit, which was Gordon Welchman's brainchild for improving efficiency and reducing the processing necessary. Entries in the official bombe registers indicate the actual number of diagonal boards for any particular Bombe machine. Some machines had more than one.

It wasn't all work for the Wrens. Plays were arranged on the base in the Assembly Hall, with the Wrens and others taking part in amateur dramatics, and there were various societies and social events. Hockey games with RAF personnel on nearby open land and parks were sometimes organised to break the monotony. If you went up to London via the tube train, you hopped on at Eastcote station and went on the Piccadilly line. It would have been quite exciting for the girls that lived outside London, as the types of trains were specific to the capital, and rather fun. Your pass limited your time away from the base, but you would make the most of it.

Severe winters at Eastcote could freeze the water pipes for several weeks and stop the heating working. Multiple layers of clothing was the only solution. At least during these exceptionally cold spells Wrens were allowed flexibility in clothing, otherwise they could have frozen to death. The lack of heating and hot water in mid-winter must have hit morale quite hard.

The shift work played havoc with metabolism. 'A' watch shift patterns were 8–4, 4–12, 12–8 on Bombe operations and monitoring the machines, with alternate nights in the checking room and checking the 'Stops'. Good 'Stops' were phoned through to Bletchley. Some referred to the Bletchley communications link as 'The Hot Line'.

Apart from routine maintenance, the Bombes rarely stopped unless they were being relocated. Bombes did not stop for Christmas Day unless they were being overhauled. Even operating the Hollerith punched card machines at Drayton Parslow, staff had to work on Christmas Day until around 4 p.m.

Based upon the 800 peak WRNS personnel, around 200 were on each shift, this correlates with the 103 or so Bombes allocated to them (including 10 machines used by the Americans). Some equipment was brought over from the US, including some specialist machines, but there was a reluctance by the British to give away all the details of the Bombes to the Americans. Eventually they manufactured their own Bombe versions back home, and they concentrated on four-wheel Bombes. Many were for the benefit of the American Navy, who had their fair share of U-boat attacks, and also required intelligence on areas such as Sicily.

The ratio of two Wrens to an individual Bombe was the basis of management calculations for assessing personnel required at the bases, plus the other support and administrative staff.[64]

Noise levels were so high at times that some Wrens after the war stated that they had suffered hearing loss. Some Y-station radio listeners also complained of hearing problems after the war, being on long shifts, day after day, with headphones raising the levels of fading signals. If the same set-up would be used today, the

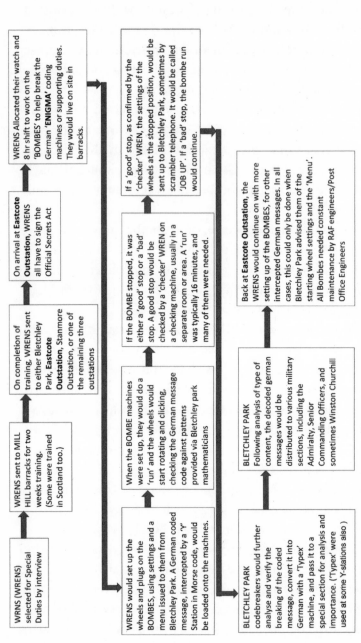

WRNS (WRENS) selected for Special Duties by interview

WRENS sent to MILL HILL barracks for two weeks training. (Some were trained in Scotland too.)

On completion of training, WRENS sent to either Bletchley Park, **Eastcote Outstation**, Stanmore Outstation, or one of the remaining three outstations

On arrival at **Eastcote Outstation**, WRENS all have to sign the Official Secrets Act

WRENS Allocated their watch and 8 hr shift to work on the 'BOMBES' to help break the German **'ENIGMA'** coding machines or supporting duties. They would live on site in barracks.

WRENS would set up the wheels and plugs on the BOMBES, using settings and a menu issued to them from Bletchley Park. A German coded message, intercepted by a 'Y' Station in Morse code, would be loaded onto the machines.

When the BOMBE machines were set up, they would do a 'run' and the wheels would start rotating and clicking, checking the German message code against patterns provided via Bletchley park mathematicians

If the BOMBE stopped, it was either a 'good' stop or a 'bad' stop. A good stop would be checked by a 'checker' WREN on a checking machine, usually in a separate room or area. A 'run' was typically 16 minutes, and many of them were needed.

If a 'good' stop, as confirmed by the 'checker' WREN, the settings of the wheels at the stopped position, would be sent up to Bletchley Park, sometimes by scrambler telephone. It would be called 'JOB UP'. If a 'bad' stop, the bombe run would continue.

BLETCHLEY PARK codebreakers would further analyse and verify the breaking of the coded message, convert it into German with a 'Typex' machine, and pass it to a special section for analysis and importance. ('Typex' were used at some Y-stations also)

BLETCHLEY PARK Following analysis of type of content, the decoded german messages would be distributed to various military sections, including the Admiralty, Senior Commanding Officers, and sometimes Winston Churchill

Back at **Eastcote Outstation**, the WRENS would continue on with more setting up of the BOMBES, for other intercepted German messages. In all cases, this could only be done when Bletchley Park advised them of the starting wheel settings and the 'Menu'. All Bombes needed constant maintenance by RAF engineers/Post Office Engineers

A simplified diagram of the contribution of 'WRENS' (WRNS) at Outstation Eastcote and elsewhere.

Copyright © 2018 Ronald Koorm FRICS - v8

Codebreaking process operated by WRNS personnel at outstations. Note that while most Wrens were based on site at the outstations, some were billeted in the surrounding locality, and travelled in.

employer would have had to carry out detailed risk assessments of the health and safety of their employees, and probably would have had to provide hearing-protection under the Noise at Work Regulations. Health and Safety was not a priority during wartime.

Talks in the Assembly Block at Eastcote didn't just revolve around successes. A potential security breach in a café in Eastcote, where personnel would have a coffee and a smoke when they were not on duty, involved an officer from the base finding a scrap of paper on the floor of the café. But this was no ordinary piece of paper. It contained information which was clearly from one of the huts at the outstation, of coded information, or possibly even a Bombe menu. A member of the public would see it as some sort of puzzle. But the person who picked it up knew that this was potentially a major security breach, and there were two, possibly three, options. Either a Wren, engineer or RAF engineer had been careless, and somehow carried the paper in their pocket or bag, and it ended up on the floor. Or there was a German agent at the outstation. Or there was a German agent in Eastcote liaising with a staff member.

One can only speculate as to what went through the officer's mind at the time, who to notify, when and how to communicate the security breach. If there really was a German agent involved, surely they would soon know of it as the Luftwaffe would be finding their way to Outstation Eastcote before too long. We have no evidence that there was a German spy at Eastcote, or that a member of the Eastcote team was somehow compromised. This incident was almost certainly option one, carelessness. A series of security talks were held on the base in the Assembly Hall. Held by a senior officer, the importance of not carrying papers or items outside the base without authorisation was stressed. Such lectures were carried out in a sensitive but firm way. Officers relied on the Wrens and RAF engineers, and morale was important. They never did find out how that piece of paper ended up on the floor of that café.

The reader should by now appreciate that the Bombe, whilst a useful tool, was just that, an electro-mechanical tool. It wasn't a computer, even though certain media presenters and some others seem to be misinformed on this point. Before the Bombe could be used, the brains at Bletchley Park had to do their bit. Although mostly a male-dominated cryptographic team, there were also very able women too. Margaret Rock and Mavis Lever, amongst others, were known as 'Dilly's girls'. Lever, with support from a Bletchley mathematician, Keith Batey, decoded an important piece of Italian military naval intelligence, and a number of Italian warships were sunk as a result by the British. The British Navy had been forewarned of the intentions of the Italian fleet at the battle of Matapan.

Meanwhile Wynn-Williams from TRE in Malvern (the radar research base) continued to make various modifications and improvements to the Bombes over time, they were adapted with high speed drums, either High Speed 'Keen' machines or Wynn-Williams designs. All this happened whist Tommy Flowers was developing a more sophisticated machine, to crack the much more complex 'Lorenz' or 'Tunny' encoding machines. His Colossus, the world's first semi-programmable computer, did not go to the codebreaking outstations but was reserved for Bletchley Park; but two Colossi did arrive at Eastcote just after the war, when it was the new GCHQ.[65] They were assembled as Mark 2 versions.

Wrens who had cared daily for the well-being and setting up of the Bombe machines would be dismantling them at the end of the war in May and June 1945. Some de-soldered wires and relays/contacts, putting the connectors onto boxes, which would later be sent to be sold off as army surplus. One Wren recalls, after the war had ended, rolling some coloured Bombe wheel-drums across the floor, as if playing skittles. Around 50 Bombes were retained at Eastcote post-war, with 16 remaining operational, and active. The rest were mothballed. None remain, as eventually they were all dismantled.

From records, 106 bombs fell on the Eastcote area between September 1940 and May 1941, which was well before Outstation

Eastcote was established. Bombing came close at times when the base was in existence. Indeed, from bombing maps seen, a slight adjustment by one German bomb-aimer could have easily flattened and destroyed Eastcote without too much trouble. The detailed information for actual bomb patterns for the Eastcote area when the outstation was working have not been found. However, bombing maps for Harrow are available, the borough which housed Outstation Stanmore. One bomb did apparently fall on Block 'A' at Eastcote, being the barracks portion where the Wrens slept. It was an unexploded incendiary bomb. It was not targeted specifically at Eastcote.

If Outstation Eastcote had been heavily damaged by bombing, there would have been the remaining outstations, but it would have severely affected the processing of encoded German military intelligence, as there were large quantities of Bombes and operational personnel on the base. Although still a threat, this was not concentrated bombing as compared to the central London docks or other strategic targets.

Four GPO technicians worked at Eastcote on 12-hour shifts. They would help to maintain and repair the Bombes along with other RAF staff. The Bombes used some components which may have been from GPO-type equipment, relays, etc. The GPO engineers would have been familiar with many of these modules or components.

Although intended to be mothballed from Bletchley Park, Colossus 'RED' and 'BLUE' were used for a combination of training and other uses, such as helping to calculate GPO parcel processing logistics, and also for Cold War processing, some of which may still be classified even today. The Russians were thought to have acquired various 'Tunny' or Lorenz machines, during their invasion of Germany and surrounding states, the first time anyone had seen what Lorenz looked like. The British assumptions about the processing and rotor/wheel design had been correct. Colossus could therefore be useful in trying to break Russian intelligence messages, if Lorenz or similar were being used.

At Eastcote, the machines worked more efficiently than before, due to the improvements and modifications made on site by the team. Much more useful than the Bombes, Colossi could be programmed up to a point, so could be used for computation of different problems. There was still an important human element involved. A reconstruction of Colossus is now in the National Computing Museum at Bletchley Park, following years of dedicated work and effort by the late Tony Sale and his team.

Both Colossi from Eastcote were eventually transferred to GCHQ Cheltenham in the 1950s, but ultimately were destroyed/dismantled. Colossus 'BLUE' was dismantled in 1959, 'RED' in 1960.

When Eastcote became GCHQ on 1 April 1946, staff turning up in Pinner for lodgings could call their employer GCHQ but were absolutely prohibited from mentioning intelligence operations. The process of transfer from Bletchley Park was handled exactly like a military operation (which of course it was), in four separate phases. The National Archives contains the paperwork on the relocation to GCHQ Eastcote. The directions were signed and dated 23 February 1946, some weeks prior to the actual move, giving time for managers and personnel to get organised.

Director's Order Number 75, dated 14 September 1945, concerned the transfer of GC & CS from Bletchley to Eastcote, where all sections of SIGINT (Signals Intelligence), would be concentrated.[66] The direction refers to the transfer to Civil Service status of certain personnel, and to uncertainty about terms and conditions pending advice from the Treasury, and the new status of military service personnel who would be going to Eastcote.

The establishment of GCHQ at Eastcote was designated 'X' Day. March 28 was the very start of the transfer, inasmuch as the first tranche of people and equipment would cease work at Bletchley on that date at the end of the day. The batches were called 'Waves' of personnel and equipment, four in total. Some would not be finally in place at Eastcote until 6 April.

The paperwork shows a different date for 'X' for each individual Wave, being the actual transfer date for that section. So, one had

X-1, X, X+1 and X+2 written in sequence for each wave, with corresponding dates adjacent, and a clear description of what would be happening on each date. 'Wave 1':

X-1 March 28th Cease work after completion of normal day's duties.

X March 29th Party 'A' moves to Eastcote and is billeted during the day. Party 'B' assisted by Party 'C' packs and loads the vans to transfer to Bletchley Park.

X+1 March 30th Vans move to Eastcote. Parties 'B' and 'C' move to Eastcote by van and coach and are billeted during the day. Vans unloaded by party 'A' and preliminary arrangement of furniture effected. Empty cartons, etc loaded on vans which will return to Bletchley Park so as to be ready for Wave 2 on the following morning.

X+2 March 31st Entire staff returns to work, completes arrangement of furniture and settles in.

Each Wave was further divided in three parties: Party 'A', Eastcote advance party; Party 'B', B/P Loading Party; Party 'C,' Remainder. 'Certain members of Party 'B' will have to travel in the removal vans as security guards, the remainder in coaches.' Staff in Berkeley Street, London, would start to move on 8 April. GC & CS was to be no more, but instead 'GCHQ' at its new Middlesex base.

GCHQ was sometimes used as a cover name at Bletchley Park, but was generally known as GC&CS. A new account was opened at Barclays Bank by the crossroads in Eastcote for the new operational base. The date of the opening of that account was 1 April 1946. Settling in to GCHQ at Eastcote was expected to take a minimal amount of time. Staff were expected to hit the ground running, and ensure there was no letup in the operational side of gathering intelligence and processing it. The lack of bomb damage at Eastcote meant that GCHQ could be established after the war without having to do mass reconstruction before it was operational.

The Swiss were provided with several Enigma machines after the war by the British, but this was only so the British could crack their secret messages when they used Enigma. The Swiss purchased them from the British, probably at a substantial discount to facilitate the sale. The days of trust in Russian allies were over, if they had ever existed. German-occupied territory was being carved up.

Many thousands of refugees were escaping from the occupied Russian countries, the Baltics and elsewhere, and fleeing to refugee camps in Germany. Russia was trying to stop the haemorrhaging of civilians from those war-torn areas, resorting at times to quite horrendous methods.[67] It would need that additional labour force to help beef up the Soviet Army, as well as producing food and material for its revival post-war. Things were moving quickly. Berlin would be later be blockaded, and pressure put on the West to give up Berlin in its entirety. Eisenhower would later be criticised for not driving towards Berlin in the latter stages of the war, preferring to go after pockets of SS in the mountains. That would have significant repercussions later on, and allow the Russians valuable time to acquire much territory, unopposed.

The origins of GCHQ had been formed back in Room 40 at the Admiralty, and then via Watergate House in London, Queen's Gate Kensington, and again via GC & CS at Bletchley. All these were stages of learning, application, and development of more advanced cryptographical methods. Now the British were in new intelligence territory. The stakes were becoming higher every day. Yet, most of our Bombes and Colossi had been disposed of. Churchill had been worried that if the Russians had access to Colossus, that could be very damaging for the West. But was it less damaging than destroying most of the machines and burning the drawings?[68] We were now dependent on the US to come to our rescue if the worst happened.

It was not long before Eastcote GCHQ became aware of the 'Venona' project. An interception of Russian intelligence by the West in Canberra, Australia, started to expose a ring of eastern Bloc and Soviet agents across Europe and the west. Based upon further analysis of past intelligence via Bombes, Colossus, and other devices, it transpired that there was a complex puzzle to be solved, and one which could expose many spies and threats to the West. Initially, GCHQ at Eastcote had only casual, informal dealings with this project, but eventually funding was made available to pursue the intelligence as part of the team on a formal basis. 'Venona' became high profile in 1947 and the National Security Agency (NSA) in the US was involved to a significant degree. One could argue this period led to the rise of 'McCarthyism', rooting out communists in America and elsewhere.

Tracking spies became a full-time occupation, and Eastcote helped in this regard by analysing historic messages in depth. The discovery of a major spy ring infiltrating the West shocked the US and European leaders. Eastcote played its part in the analysis of past Russian intelligence data, maybe using even the Colossus machines, or perhaps, at least some of the 16 Bombes that were operational and remained on the site. This was almost James Bond material. As there was suspicion that the Russians had acquired several Lorenz machines in the closing stages of the war, Colossus would have been perfect to help decode the Russian and eastern Bloc intelligence until they changed their systems.

'Venona' exposed agents such as Guy Burgess, Donald Maclean, John Cairncross, Rosenberg and others. The authorities had to tread very carefully, in case exposing some agents would result in others running for cover. Proof of passing secrets was not always easy to find, and Eastcote assisted in this intelligence process.

In the 1960s children in American schools practised anti-nuclear drills. crawling under their school desks. A scary time, and the safety of those children would revolve around Kennedy and Kruschev and their military and political advisers. If America had been attacked by Russia, Britain would certainly have been attacked too, as there were American bases there.

Eastcote's role in 'Venona' was to go back over old messages, decode and process them to find links and connections which could then be put together by others to find the bigger picture of infiltration. It was a bit like tracking your internet history, looking for clues and words and phrases, codenames, references, and other relevant information. This was a time-consuming process, and whilst staff were allocated specifically to the project on the base, eventually it would wind down for others to progress elsewhere. The Soviets learned of the exposure of 'Venona' by the West in the late 1940s, and the entire project was closed in late 1980, several years after GCHQ had relocated to Cheltenham.

The Russians clearly wanted information on the development of the West's nuclear weapons, rocket and jet engine technology, which the Americans had a head-start on, having acquired several important scientists such as Wernher Von Braun and others. The Russians had also captured several German scientists. Information would be sent to Eastcote at the London Signals Intelligence Centre to be evaluated. The spread of Soviet agents and penetration of both American and British senior posts rang warning bells across the West. Sure, several spies and Russian agents were captured, but many more would return under cover back to Russia and the Eastern Bloc before there was time to intercept them. Arguably, 'Venona' was Eastcote's high point after the war, playing its small part within a broad, worldwide team of analysts and cryptographers. It knocked the confidence of the Western powers for six, and would take some time to recover from.

An Eastcote female resident who lived locally to the base after the war told the author that one day she bumped into a relative whom she had not seen for some considerable time coming down Lime Grove, one of the entrances of the GCHQ base. She was surprised to see him, and he appeared equally shaken. After exchanging pleasantries, he said he had to rush, and yes, he told her, that he was working on the base, but was not permitted to say what he was doing there. She was none the wiser many years later. It remained ingrained in her memory for years.

At several of the author's talks, on more than one occasion people have talked of a certain woman and neighbour who worked at the Eastcote base after the war, but never told them what they did there. It is highly likely most of what they knew will go with them to their graves. Locals at Eastcote recall American Marines jogging around the base, and surrounding area after the war. Some of the wooded areas around the Ruislip Lido and footpaths nearby would have made good training grounds.

Personnel at GCHQ of course, needed accommodation, and this was provided in various lodgings around Pinner, Eastcote, Rayner's Lane and elsewhere. Some were billeted at a local golf club. Pinner was very popular for staff accommodation, and not far away from the base. It had good transport links to central London.

A football team was established at GCHQ, and cricket matches and tennis in the summer months. Bearing in mind the prohibition on mentioning that their work involved 'intelligence', contact with the locals in the area would have to be guarded. Visits to the nearby pubs no doubt boosted the publican's takings at The Black Horse and The Case is Altered significantly for a good few years, until the base was closed.

There were links to Ickenham, a few miles away, for relaxation and other sports. The Foreign office had access to several places in and around London. Swakeleys House, a seventeenth-century Grade 1 listed mansion and estate in Ickenham, situated between Ruislip and Uxbridge, had been requisitioned during the war. It was later acquired by the Foreign office. This site was used by GCHQ Eastcote personnel to wind down and relax, Or there were trips to Central London, much as the codebreaking Bombe Wrens did during the war, but without the air raids.

The Old Eastcote Association was established in 1946 for keeping in touch after the war, but of course The Official Secrets Act still applied. If at an association meeting one reminisced about setting the Bombe wheels or checker machines and was overheard by a member of the public, in theory the long arm of the law could reach out, via The 'Act'.

The failure of Hitler's agents to identify and expose Bletchley and the outstations enabled the British to continue on quickly after the war with intelligence gathering, albeit on a reduced scale. The enemy had changed overnight. In one way the stakes were even higher than before, with the atomic bomb threat.

Soviet use of Lorenz and other advanced German encoding machines to transmit their messages meant Allies were listening for as long as they could. That was until the Russians changed their approach to cryptography, and caused an intelligence blackout, The West was effectively 'blind' to Eastern Bloc intelligence. Times were already changing, and there was a pressure to catch up with our enemies in intelligence-gathering skills.

10

THE AMERICANS ARRIVE

American servicemen operated Bombes at Eastcote, from 6812th US Signals Corps detachment (part of ETOUSA cooperation), and there were 10 machines allocated for them in a special part of the site. Training of the Americans fell to the Wrens, and it must have been amusing to the newcomers at Eastcote to be instructed how to set up a Bombe and operate it by an eighteen-year-old Wren, who had barely had enough time to learn herself. The Americans did not live on site. Those who worked at Eastcote were initially in a tented camp in Ruislip Woods, later to be billeted near Harrow on the Hill, and were bussed in each day. One of their billets was named 'Hollywood'.

The attachment of American personnel to Bletchley Park and outstation duties was as a direct result of a visit made to Bletchley in 1942 by senior American officers. A Captain Johnson, on a second visit to England, obtained Foreign office approval to have some Signals US Army personnel attached to both Bletchley Park and Outstation Eastcote.

Some 290 Americans made up 6811, 6812, 6813th Signals Detachments. The 6811th Signals went to Bexley, Kent, at an intercept station. The 6813th Signals were allocated to Bletchley Park, in Hut 6 and Hut 3 in 'D' Block. They integrated quickly with the British in codebreaking and intelligence analysis. The Americans had some considerable success in operating their allocated Bombes at Eastcote.

The 6812th Signal security detachment APO 413 US Army came over to England along with other Signals Engineers, and they would be trained to use the Bombes at Outstation Eastcote by the Wrens. They operated their machines from 1 February 1944. It was thought they had access to eight Bombe machines, increasing to ten. Their efficiency was anywhere between one quarter to one third above the British in terms of output runs per day. Twenty minutes per Bombe run, including setting up and connections, was fast. This indicated that the training phase managed by the Wrens had gone extremely well, and that the Americans were very fast learners. By VE day, the section, from commencement of operations, had broken some 425 Enigma keys. Their valuable contribution had ceased by 7 May 1945. Here is the 'diary' of one US Army Eastcote Bombe called 'MING'.

25 January 1941: Bombe delivered to Bletchley Park.
7 March 1944: Transferred to Outstation Eastcote, and put into one of the bays for the United States Army (Signals Division), operational bays.
26 May 1944: Identified for instructional training duties.
10 May 1945: Out of action and dismantled, along with most of the other Bombes, based on Churchill's instructions.

Those Bombe names identified as being included within the American US 6812th Signals bay are HOUSTON, ATLANTA, PHILADELPHIA, MINNEAPOLIS, MING, ROCHESTER, OMAHA, MING, NEW YORK and SAN FRANCISCO. This makes ten allocated Bombes. Bombe 'NEW YORK' was operational 1 May 1944, 'HOUSTON' in May, CHICAGO in June. 'HOUSTON' would suffer technical problems on 29 November, but those were rectified by 6 December.

In July 1944 'MINNEAPOLIS' and 'ATLANTA' were operational, and in that same month a large quantity of solutions for menus were identified.[69] In August three more US Bombes were added, 'PHILADELPHIA', 'SAN FRANCISCO', and 'OMAHA' delivered 30 August and in action by 5 September. December achieved the highest production per Bombe machine. The last, or tenth Bombe for the Americans was 'ROCHESTER' (Bombe number 313), put into action 12 September 1944. There was a direct teleprinter link to the US section for the menus from Bletchley Park. The success and efficiency of processing Bletchley Park menus to decode the messages by the Americans was beyond all expectations. The 6812th Signal Security Detachment provided a report dated 15 June 1945 outlining the workings of the Bombe machines, the menus, the checking process for stops, in the greatest detail. They clearly had an excellent understanding of the complex processes.

As regards the Bombe 'Checking machine' process, they provided a listing in the report of around six status levels, including 'Good Stop', 'Bad Stop', Confirmation, Contradiction, Hut 6 Stop, and one other, together with the description of 'Check Stops'. The latter were stops on the Bombes to maintain a continuous check on the Bombe and the operator, a sort of quality control test. The wheels of the checking machine would be rotated to check the links on the menus. All this would be useful for their own Bombes built in Ohio.

After the war ended, there were many Americans on the Eastcote base, including US Marines and US Army, even a serviceman's children's school. The Americans had the Signals Intelligence Service (SIS), the Armed Forces Security Agency (AFSA) and the Special Cryptographic Advisory Group (SCAG). The US Navy had a substantial presence and were in Block 4 and Block 1 on the base. The US Marines moved into Block 1 as barracks in 1974, and numbered between 60–100 men. The American School settled into Blocks 1 and 2.

The Americans integrated well both during and after the war. Some would settle here permanently. Their own Ohio-built Bombes were used to help their navy to penetrate German, Italian, and perhaps even Japanese encoded messages. The Americans built 121 four-wheel Bombe machines in total to penetrate U-boat intelligence traffic. This amplified the ongoing attack against the Nazi *Kriegsmarine* resources, and helped to push the U-Boats away from the Allied convoys eventually. Figures indicate that NCR (National Cash Register Company) in Dayton, Ohio, had manufactured 155 Bombs by May 1945.

The sharing of Bombe technology between the British and Americans was a sensitive matter. It was probably because of the fear of a leak. The British had worked long and hard for the Bombe, and perhaps the Americans would not have been so careful with this precious asset. But common sense prevailed, and even Bletchley Park acknowledged that sometimes risks had to be taken to make progress.

To ensure a degree of compatibility between the British and the Americans, the Combined Cipher Machine was developed. This was a combination of a modified Typex machine and an equivalent USA machine. These modifications and developments were ongoing, and extended post-war, later using teleprinters. Typex was very successful as an enciphering and decoding machine. It had reduced many of the stages that troubled Enigma, and any errors produced were but a fraction of the Enigma equivalent processes. One could type, encipher and transmit messages as a single operation. It was an elegant solution and proved to be useful in a different form, after the war. The Americans gained something useful out of the British Typex technology, but it would be only one of the routes chosen by them in order to develop better security systems for the future.

The innovation and ability of the Americans would not stop there. One of the sub-basements of Selfridges, a famous department store in London, contained a Bell Laboratories American 'SIGSALY' encryption encoder for voice transmissions of messages during the war. Developed in 1943, it was highly complex in design and construction and very advanced. It was used by Churchill to communicate by telephone with President Roosevelt from 1943 via Churchill's Cabinet War Rooms some distance away, near Whitehall. This was operated by a team of

US army technicians. It was a highly complex series of machines, wired-up and connected together underground. It took up a great deal of space, giving out large amounts of heat due to the quantity of valves it used, and would require a substantial power supply. The damp-proofing and asphalt tanking in the basement would need to be constantly maintained and monitored, to keep any seeping groundwater away from the electrics. The machines in total weighed 55 tons. A team of thirteen American technicians would operate it. SIGSALY was the first encoding system to be used with Pulse-Code Modulation technology applied to speech and telephones. Setting up a telephone call would take around fifteen minutes. A part of the machine is on display at The National Cryptologic Museum at Fort Meade, Maryland.

SIGABA at the National Cryptological Museum.

The US Army's SIGABA encoding machine was extremely complex, and reports indicate this system was never broken during the war. SIGABA was known about by the Germans, but the design, although similar to Enigma, had many advances which outshone the German machine, and made the encoding more random-like. The Germans could not decode it, and the Japanese failed also. It seems the Allies had learnt from the weaknesses of the German encoding machines. It could have easily been the other way around, but the Allies were much better organised in decoding processes and innovative techniques.

The Americans post-war would leapfrog the British in terms of computer technology, mainly because the British had much of its technology and systems cloaked under The Official Secrets Act, which stifled British computer development and innovation. In contrast, the Americans just got on with it. The experience of their personnel in operating and modifying Bombes would have certainly helped in creating the appropriate environment for innovation and enterprise.

11

SIEMENS AND NON-MORSE MESSAGES

A relay is principally just an electro-mechanical switch, and the Bombe would need many of these to operate. British relay designs were functioning satisfactorily up to a point, but it was noted that a German Siemens relay was a much better design and far more efficient than ours. The German company Siemens had distribution across Europe and elsewhere. Siemens' British offices were closed down at the start of the war by an Act of Parliament that targeted enemy manufacturers, factories and companies.

The company had been in the UK since 1843 and in London since 1850. At BTM Letchworth, and possibly at Dollis Hill too, closer examination was made of the German relay design. Some modifications of British relay design were made, and effectively they now had a copy of the Siemens relay. It was quickly introduced to the newer Bombes being constructed at BTM, Letchworth in late 1943. A noticeable increase in Bombe efficiency resulted. So the Germans helped improve British codebreaking machines with their design of relays, due to their superb engineering.

The first Siemens BTM relays were eventually installed at Outstation Eastcote in early 1944. Bombe number 250 is an example of one machine delivered to Eastcote that had the Siemens relays installed.[70] The Bombes would work more efficiently and reliably than before. Copying of equipment by the British was probably also done on the Typex Enigma-emulator machine to a degree. Siemens, under the name Siemens and Halske, also manufactured an encoding machine, called T52, *Geheimschrieber*, or Secret Writer. It was far more advanced than Enigma would ever be, even more advanced than Lorenz. The first patent was granted for this model in July 1930. T-52 was used by the Luftwaffe and *Kriegsmarine*. The British called the intelligence links *Sturgeon*. Both *Sturgeon* and 'Tunny' (Tunny being based on the Lorenz SZ40 and 42 models), would give them plenty of headaches, and no amount of Turing's Bombes would be able to help.

The T-52 and *Sturgeon* link would be military intelligence via landline mainly, and not readily accessible to the Allies, although the Swedes did manage to intercept certain Sturgeon landlines. From time to time Bletchley Park did break the T-52, but infrequently compared to Lorenz. The Model T52d machine was one of the most secure *Geheimschreiber* models, and seemed initially virtually impossible to crack, due to its twelve rotary wheels. It would be connected to a Siemens T-36 teleprinter to operate and decode messages effectively. There was a keyboard for direct text entry and no need for assistant operators, as with Enigma. Lorenz was based on teleprinter messages transmitted mainly via radio, so the British were in with a chance of intercepting those encoded messages.

'Tunny' really had two meanings, Firstly, it sometimes referred to the general German non-Morse intelligence generated by those German specialist machines, teleprinter intelligence traffic *Fish*. Secondly, it was to become the British-built version of the Lorenz machine, which was reverse-engineered by a man called Bill Tutte, with some help. No one in the UK had even seen a Lorenz machine. Imagine trying to reverse-engineer a micro-computer design from a different country and designer, without ever having seen it, from snippets of computer code generated by it. It did not mean the British could forget about the Enigma intelligence. The quantity of Morse code from Enigma machines would be many hundreds of time the quantity of Lorenz, or similar non-Morse encoding machines. This was simply because the Enigma was the main encoding machine across the armed forces and built in very large quantities.

The Lorenz S40/S42 and T52 Secret writers were built in much fewer numbers, intended for the German High Command on strategic communications. They were complex, expensive to build, and required even greater attention to detail. The Siemens T-52 model was extremely heavy, and not designed to be portable. The T-52 cipher was eventually cracked by Bletchley

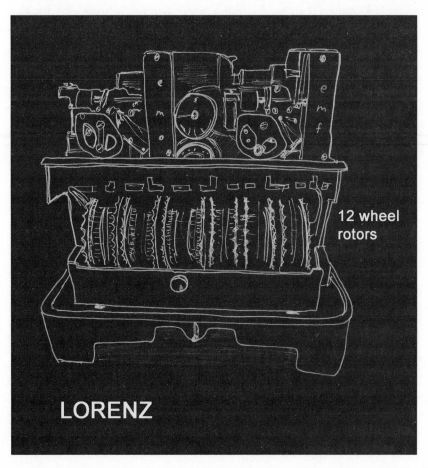

Park experts, which was a major achievement, considering no one had ever seen the machine.

Carl Freidrich von Siemens was the Director in charge of the company until 1941. He was not in sympathy with the Nazi regime, but had to tread carefully, as factories would be required to produce much equipment for the military, and of high quality. Siemens would be allowed to make electrical goods and components, and steered away from heavy armaments, which were better suited to other factories and producers. It did make some weapons and ammunition, but on a relatively small scale compared to others. It would concentrate from the end of 1943 on manufacturing a wide range of electrical equipment for the German armed forces. Siemens used forced labour during the war, worker slaves, in its factories. Siemens management argued they had no choice due to shortages of local labour, as the men were fighting for Germany and the women often in heavy armaments factories.

It has been estimated that around 80,000 forced labourers worked at Siemens during the war. This was a huge operation, requiring intense organisation and strict management control. Photographs exist of Siemens vans and lorries being used to broadcast Nazi instructions to the public with mounted loudspeakers. The 'Siemens' name is on the front of the vehicle in bold lettering. Commencing in 1940, Siemens relied more and more on forced labour. Towards the end of the war Siemens acquired forced labour from concentration camps. But the Allies were successful in bombing many of Siemens' factories in the Berlin area, and this significantly affected production, along with shortages of raw materials and equipment. They spread the factories farther afield, and put several in occupied territory to spread the risk of Allied bombing attacks.

It must have been a management nightmare to keep production going, satisfying ever-increasing demand for parts and equipment, particularly in the latter stages of the war as the Allies got nearer to Berlin. Transport of materials and equipment was becoming haphazard, as railways and roads were constantly bombed and attacked. Senior officers crying out for replacement equipment and parts from Siemens would have to wait much longer than before, and that would affect the efficiency in communications, particularly with their radio and electrical equipment, constantly on the move. The design and construction of radio receivers and transmitters had to be robust, to cope with vibration from vehicles, tanks and armoured personnel carriers. The equipment was not always treated with great care, when one had to move at a moment's short notice, and throw the equipment into the back of a truck and drive over bomb craters. Yet it was expected to work on the battlefield.

The Germans were excellent engineers and designers. Their gunsights, binoculars, rangefinders, and cameras were precision instruments. It was as much about keeping the flow of raw materials coming into factories as other factors affecting production. The constant bombing and harassment by American and British bombers, aided by the P47-Thunderbolt and the American P-51 Mustang armed with cannon and rockets, impacted severely on the supply chain of German materials, fuel and equipment. As the occupied countries were gradually clawed back by the Allies in late 1944 and early 1945, the Nazis and their production factories had fewer options.

As the war ended, the factories closed. Equipment and machinery was quickly and ruthlessly acquired by force by the Soviet army, now in control of large areas of Germany and the capital. Almost ninety per cent of the remaining factory equipment and stock was acquired.

Siemens did, of course, resurrect itself post-war, and became one of the most successful German precision engineering companies, but has formally acknowledged the darker side of its war history.[71] In 2018, the assets of Siemens amounted to some €28,281,000,000, and the revenue for the same year was €83,044,000,000.[72] They recovered from the trauma of the war to become a major worldwide blue-chip company, in engineering and technology. In the late 1990s Fujitsu Siemens, a business joint-venture acquired the modern development of BTM, ICL, before it went back to being Fujitsu-owned in 2009. Few would have seen the irony of this acquisition at the time.

Considerable funds have been set aside for compensation to recompense those with relatives who suffered forced labour at Siemens, and many other German factories. Following acknowledgment of regret in Siemens' history in respect of forced labour and related issues, in 2017 Joe Kaiser of Siemens made an official apology to Jewish people at a presentation for an Award for Tolerance and Understanding: 'It is important to me that we do all we can to prevent injustice from repeating itself, both in Germany and around the globe. That is our obligation and our unequivocal position.'

12

OUTSTATION STANMORE

Few people appreciate that Outstation Stanmore was not on the RAF control site at Bentley Priory but was positioned further to the east a few miles distant to be relatively unobtrusive, and for very good reason. The site was at the junction of Brockley Hill, an old Roman road (Watling Street) and the A410. The base was redeveloped for housing some years ago. In mid-1942 it was the largest codebreaking outstation, with in excess of 440 Wrens operating the Bombes and equipment. By 1943 there were 22 Bombes in Block 'B' at Stanmore, and by July 1943, 45 Bombes. By October of that year, there were 29,660 square feet of net floor space for the Bombe machines available. At its peak, Outstation Stanmore had 571 Wrens operating Bombes over three watches.

There were also 49 RAF and three naval personnel, and a few civilians. Around 630 overall. Some sources report 49 Bombes[73] in total at Stanmore at its peak. Others record 50, even 60 Bombes, but the definitive assessment is contained in the Bombe registers, which track the manufacturing and delivery dates, as well as the relocation dates and locations of each Bombe machine.[74]

It transpires that 81 Bombe machines passed through the doors of Outstation Stanmore during the war. That represents around 38% of all Bombe machines made, and is considerably higher than the 49 mentioned elsewhere. Some were there for relatively short periods, and many were relocated later to Outstation Eastcote as it became established. Those 81 machines would not have been at Stanmore simultaneously, but the importance of Stanmore cannot be overlooked. This is reflected in the large numbers of operational personnel at the base.

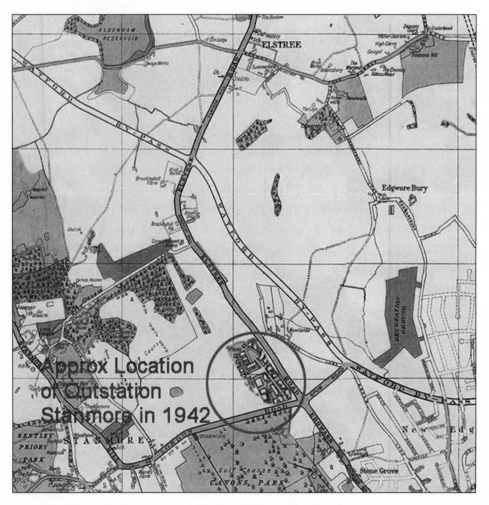

Site of Outstation Stanmore overlaid onto a 1932 map of the Stanmore area.

One machine went from Stanmore to Eastcote and back again to Outstation Stanmore, the reason for this being a mystery. The machines which ended up at Stanmore, based on the Bombe Registers, amounted to 76. The discrepancy between the 81 mentioned above and the 76 is that the missing five were relocated elsewhere, most likely Eastcote, at various times. When one combines the totals for both Stanmore and Eastcote, it transpires that around 85 per cent of all Bombe machines were at those bases, indicating the importance of both of those sites.

Stanmore became operational in November 1942, as Bletchley Park realised there was a need for a great many more Bombe machines than at Adstock, Wavendon, Gayhurst, and Bletchley. A report from Hut 6 in June 1942 indicated Bletchley Park and its initial three close support outstations were running out of space and suffering a shortage of Wrens to operate the machines. Stanmore had to have the Bombes quickly, together with a significant number of trained Wrens, and supplementary engineers to repair and maintain them. However, Stanmore was certainly not the first choice to supplement Wavendon, Gayhurst and Adstock.

Stowe School in Buckinghamshire was first choice as an expansion base for Bombe processing operations. Geographically, it was not too far from Bletchley. Stowe was considered in 1942. It was a relatively large site, away from factories and potential bombing targets. It did not go down too well with the school, however. So eventually, Stowe was ruled out and Stanmore was developed, becoming the largest outstation serving Bletchley Park in November 1942 prior to Eastcote coming on board. If Stowe had been prepared for housing Bombes, then it is quite possible that neither Stanmore nor Eastcote would have existed as outstations. It had great potential capacity for additional hutting and outbuildings, although they would have detracted from the aesthetics of the beautiful landscaped surroundings of the site. But it was to be Stanmore that was selected. A 'cover story' was needed to explain what Stanmore existed for, bearing in mind the substantial amount of Wrens and support staff needed to operate the Bombes.[75] The cover story chosen, and suggested in writing on 21 October 1942, was to say the Wrens at Stanmore were needed for confidential naval clerical work.[76] Travis did not object to this 'clerical work' cover, so that was the cover story arranged, and the site became operational.

In the early years Outstation Stanmore was referred to by the Wrens as Pembroke III. Later on, it had to fall in line with other onshore naval bases under Special Duties 'X' and become Pembroke V. It was a military base, and had all the formalities of a naval ship. On 26 October 1942, a letter was produced confirming their 'Lordship's Approval' of administrative and related staff for Stanmore, the new codebreaking outstation.[77] There were to be several officers and general administrative personnel, mostly Wrens, including cooks, switchboard operators, teleprinter operators, a motor transport driver, civilian boiler maintenance staff, a civilian gardener/ handyman, plus several security staff from the Royal Marines police to guard the base, with one Sergeant in charge of eight men. Sixteen Wren cooks plus an officer's cook would prepare the meals for the base, with the assistance of twenty-five general stewards for dining and support duties. One additional steward would be for the Wren officers. Two Wrens would be allocated sick-bay duties, who would later be supporting the individuals hit by the continuing stress and fatigue of operating the Bombe machines and support equipment. There would be two first officers, two second officers, two third officers, split between administration and 'quarters'.

A Chief Wren at Stanmore would take responsibility under the direction of the Chief Officer (WRNS), at Station 'X', Bletchley Park, who was then promoted from Senior WRNS officer. Eighty-one key staff for Stanmore were therefore approved, including four civilians. This did not include the operational Bombe Wrens. The core organizational team of mainly Wrens, plus a few others, would keep the wheels of Outstation Stanmore oiled with food, clothing, showers, toilets, barracks and beds. All that was needed now were the Bombe machines from BTM at Letchworth and the Wrens to operate them. It was agreed that once the numbers at Outstation Stanmore exceeded 300 personnel, a supply officer would also be required.

The high number of personnel at Stanmore reflects the importance and relevance of the outstation. Bearing in mind the 81 Bombes that passed through the loading bay doors at the site, and the constant changes, allocations and reassignment of many of the Bombe machines to Eastcote in 1944, the coordination and management of this process must have been organised as a military operation.

'Divisions' like other bases, were compulsory as parade inspections, and there would be some similarities to the later Eastcote base. Stanmore was not the size of Eastcote, but still had a considerable floor area for the Bombe machines, together with various barracks and staff accommodation.

The official designation in the Bombe registers for Stanmore was O.S.S. A picture exists of the Wrens at Outstation Stanmore in full uniform, standing to attention outside one of the larger huts, and looking very professional. Area for area, the allocation of Bombe space varied tremendously across the bases. Reallocating and moving Bombe machines around, this had to be taken into consideration.

Bletchley Park	6,800 square feet Bombe space
Stanmore	29,600 square feet Bombe space
Eastcote	33,120 square feet Bombe space

If one applies the Stanmore quantity of bombes to these figures (ie the Bombe Register record of 76 Bombes), we arrive at the following square footage per Bombe:

Bletchley Park	1,133 square feet per Bombe
Stanmore	389 square feet per Bombe
Eastcote	321 square feet per Bombe

It may be that the figure of 49 Bombes mentioned elsewhere was too low in quantity, but it may have been based on a figure at a particular time when the site, but it may have been based on a figure at a particular time when the site was still being expanded, so may have been accurate for a particular date and time.

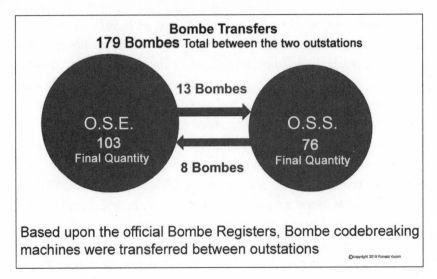

Bombe Transfers
179 Bombes Total between the two outstations

13 Bombes

O.S.E.
103
Final Quantity

O.S.S.
76
Final Quantity

8 Bombes

Based upon the official Bombe Registers, Bombe codebreaking machines were transferred between outstations

©copyright 2019 Ronald Koorn

Transfer of Bombes between outstations.

Bletchley Park obviously had much more space for Bombes than either of the larger outstations, and Eastcote was relatively cramped compared to the others. But of course, Bletchley had to fit in thousands of people across the site, from mathematicians, to typists, military officers, cryptographers, linguists, and others.

The training centres, such as the one at Mill Hill in North London only a few miles away, worked overtime to increase the output of trained Wrens. Some land lines were linked to Bletchley Park, which helped transfer of data and intelligence output. The role of the GPO in assisting with telecommunication links was significant; this was many decades before British Telecom or 'BT' separated the telecommunications arm of the post office from the postal delivery and processing service. Engineers would be needed to maintain and repair the equipment, and some may later on have moved across to Outstation Eastcote.

At the time of establishing Outstation Stanmore the area was fairly rural, but also part of a growing suburb of outer London, with reasonable access to central London when needed with a terminus close by. Positioned by Watling street, the old Roman Road (and named Elstree Road on older maps), it gave good access

Enigma showing key parts. (Photo by permission of The Bletchley Park Trust)

Above: *Bletchley Park Mansion.*

Left: *Wrens at Wavendon Manor. (GCHQ)*

Outstation Eastcote, 'A' Watch (one of the four 'watches' on shift work at Eastcote). (GCHQ)

Wrens on parade at O.S Stanmore. (GCHQ)

Labels visible on map: Celandine Rd, River Pinn, Esso, High Rd Eastcote, Black Horse, Azalea Walk, Azalea Walk, Azalea Walk, Azalea Walk, Celandine Rd, Flag Walk, Flag Walk, Spring Dr, Blagrove Cres, Blagrove Cres, Aitken Cl, Footpath, B466, Ellis Cl, Flowers Ave, Flowers Ave, Flowers Ave, Wren Ln, Lidgould Grove, Coleridge Dr, Eastcote Outstation [Approximate position relative to Pembroke Park Housing Estate- Prepared Ronald Koorm FRICS], Google, Kent Gardens

Overlay map of Outstation Eastcote. A housing estate, Pembroke Park, was constructed at Eastcote following demolition of the blocks circa 2007. The overlay produced by the author is an attempt to graphically superimpose the old offices and blocks onto the modern estate roads. The common datum for alignment of the blocks to the residential estate was the public footpath, (reported to be 16th century), which still remains. The scale is approximate, and the footpath seems to have been slightly amended for the development of the residential estate, at the western end, nearest to Eastcote High Road. From the overlay shown, it is possible to appreciate where the old office blocks/huts were, relative to the modern estate roads. The housing developer may even have had something similar for planning purposes, before the site was constructed, but this has not been confirmed.

Statue of Alan Turing in Sackville Gardens, Manchester. (Courtesy Catherine Cronin under Creative Commons)

Above: *Memorial plaque in Sackville Gardens. (Courtesy Catherine Cronin under Creative Commons)*

Below: *Manchester mural of Alan Turing. (Courtesy Dunk under Creative Commons)*

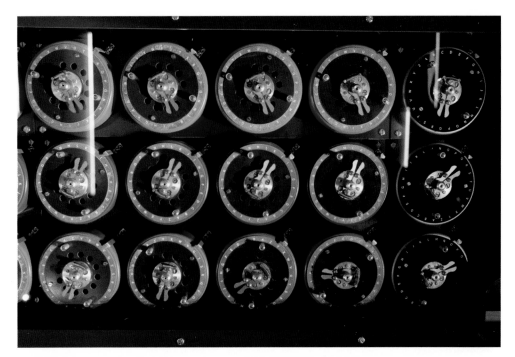

Bombe drums.

Rotors. Gordon Welch: 'The task of the Bombe was simply to reduce the assumptions of wheel order and scrambler positions that required "further analysis" to a manageable number.' (Courtesy Michele M F under Creative Commons)

Above: *The maze of wires that the Wrens had to deal with. (Courtesy Sagesolar under Creative Commons)*

Below: *Siemens & Halske T52 German cypher machine, the* Geheimschreiber, *or secret teleprinter, more difficult to crack than Lorenz. (Courtesy Tony Kent under Creative Commons)*

Above: *The rebuilt PHOENIX with relay gate open. (Courtesy Elliott Brown under Creative Commons)*

Below: *Colossus valves. (Courtesy Dave Addey under Creative Commons)*

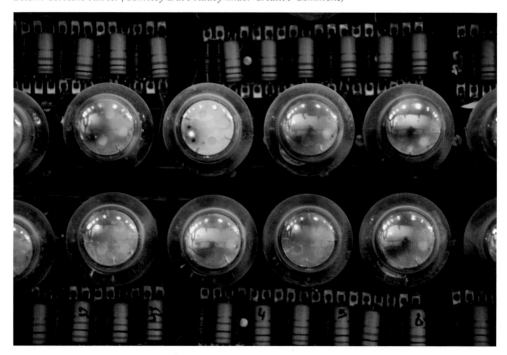

north, which would be a route towards the northern support outstations and to Bletchley Park. Inspecting maps prior to the establishment of Stanmore, there were open fields with a golf club and woods to the north, and several ponds.

The National Orthopaedic hospital at Stanmore was slightly to the north. It can be clearly seen on older maps of the 1930s.[78] The main road north went via Elstree, a few miles away. Bentley Priory was some distance to the west of the site, being the central RAF defence, control and filter room, which passed information out to 'Group' and sections.

There have been several accounts of Wrens based at Stanmore, some who had moved from Bletchley Park or one of the other bases, and several in later years moved across from Eastcote. One such Wren was Diana Payne, referred to earlier in the chapter on Wavendon. Following her gaining experience at both Bletchley and Wavendon, her transfer to Stanmore resulted in promotion to Petty Officer. She was then in charge of ten Bombes in a large room. Her work was feeding the Bombe team the menus, and setting up and monitoring the machines with the assistance of two more junior Wrens, who would do much of the setting up work.

The stress of the unique work, day in day out, would sometimes result in nervous breakdowns and extended sick-bay rest. Sometimes it would be so severe that the individual was invalided out of the service. Not everyone could cope with the long hours, the noise of the rotating wheels, the intensity of the work. But most took it in their stride.

There was constant upgrading and improvement of Bombe machines, and relocation from some of the smaller outstations to Stanmore and Eastcote. Inspection of the Bombe registers indicates that several machines also moved from Eastcote to Stanmore and vice versa. This would usually involve renaming the relocated machines, to avoid confusion. The importance of these two bases grew over time as the quantity of codebreaking machines increased and more personnel were brought in. Wrens lived on site in barracks with bunk berths, much as at Eastcote.

The food at Stanmore was not of a good standard. Cold cheese on toast was mentioned by several Wrens who worked and lived there during the war.

As expected, shift work was the norm, with standard eight-hour shifts and half an hour for lunch or dinner, and 'Divisions', or parades in all weathers. 4pm–12 midnight was considered to be the antisocial watch, as that severely limited your social life. However, one Wren elsewhere reported that this was her favourite shift at Gayhurst Manor, as she could then go horse-riding early in the morning. Kit inspections were relatively frequent, and you had to give attention to detail in presentation, if you were to satisfy the officers. 'Leading Wren' was a senior promotion which few achieved, but was something to aim for.

There may have been contact with Bentley Priory, not far distant, for social events and similar, the base that coordinated air movements for the RAF, and later monitored the D-Day assault. However, there is no specific evidence to confirm it.[79]

Being transferred to Bletchley Park from Stanmore would have come quite as a shock, as the Bletchley base was full of civilians as well as military personnel. At Bletchley, there were times when Wrens were permitted to wear their own clothes, and at least one visiting officer was shocked at what he saw, and asked why the Wrens were not uniformed. There were times when most military personnel were instructed to stay in uniform, but there were relaxations of the rules, which was something unique to Bletchley Park.

One Wren, Ann, went initially to Eastcote, then Stanmore, then a spell at Bletchley Park, and back to Stanmore. That would have been quite disruptive, with the constant travel arrangements, passes, training, varying shifts of hours, and Special 'X' duties. At least the food would vary a little. Another expressed sadness that the 'sub-stations' (outstations), are nowadays rarely mentioned. She felt they had been largely forgotten, and that only people like Alan Turing and Bletchley Park itself were known to the general public to any degree. A fair point to make.

High walls and barbed wire surrounded the many single-storey buildings at Stanmore, and were guarded by Royal Marine soldiers. Stanmore was close enough to central London to go for a night out, on the Bakerloo line. Dancing up town in the clubs in the West End and Covent Garden was a good outing. If your pass allowed the extra time, you could stay at the YWCA and have a bed for the night.

Several annoyances were part of the job at Stanmore and the outstations. The oil from the lubrication of the Bombe wheels would sometimes transfer across onto your cuffs of your shirt blouse, and make a horrible stain; a devil of a job to remove, when your uniform had to be pristine at all times. The noise could be quite overwhelming, with wheels and drums rotating and clicking away. But the sound of the tea trolley was always welcome.

At the end of the war, Stanmore was decommissioned, with dismantling of machines and destruction of files. Churchill had personally ordered the destruction of machines and drawings for fear of them falling into the wrong hands. Some of the Wrens would be sent to Ceylon or elsewhere to continue the fight against the Japanese in intelligence gathering. Stanmore was the second outstation to be decommissioned, after Eastcote.

Some mentioned after the war that it was so frustrating to be operating these Bombe machines for hours and hours on end and not be told what they had achieved in practical terms. But at Outstation Eastcote, they did give 'pep talks' to Wrens and engineers who worked on the codebreaking equipment, to boost morale, and to tell them about any recent successes, based upon their efforts.[80] Perhaps this was not done at Stanmore. Those talks were welcomed, as they gave a purpose to life and a bridge to the reality of war and winning battles.

As Outstation Stanmore was situated in a part of North London close to open fields and open land, one assumes that relaxation time in the better weather could have included local walks and accessing the 'fishpond' marked on maps to the north of the site. Elstree in Hertfordshire was not far away by bus or car, Edgware was to the south-west. There were far, far worse places than Stanmore to spend the war, and the extent of general enemy bombing would have been much less than in the docks or central London.

Stanmore Park nearby was used as an RAF base during the war, and in 1939 was used as the Balloon command centre. The Poles required a radio base in Stanmore, and sought support and funding for radio intelligence against the Russians from the British. They established a Radio Workshop in Stanmore, managed by a Pole called Heftman who had worked for AVA, the Polish radio company. AVA were involved in making replicas of Enigma for the Poles. Heftman had escaped to the UK and then built a range of spy radio sets for S.O.E. in Stanmore, under a specialist Military Wireless Unit. One source says this work was done at Outstation Stanmore, where the Bombes were situated, but this is not confirmed, and it's much more likely that it was at Stanmore Park.

The 2236 Air training Group is currently based in Elliot Road, Stanmore, on, or very near the site, in a separate modern building. A small plaque exists at Stanmore Park commemorating the old

King George VI and Queen Elizabeth, escorted by Air Chief Marshal Sir Hugh Dowding, visit the Headquarters of Fighter Command at Bentley Priory, near Stanmore, September 1941.

RAF base, and the fact it was the (Barrage) Balloon command centre during the war.

In the museum at Headstone Manor, in Harrow, Middlesex, there is a large bomb map pinned up.[81] It shows the pattern of mines, V1s, V2s and general bombing during the war in Harrow. To the right-hand corner of the map is a symbol and note of a V1 bomb hitting part of Stanmore, very near to the old codebreaking base. One V1 German flying bomb hit the outer perimeter wall at Outstation Stanmore during the war, but caused little damage, and none to the valuable codebreaking Bombes or operational personnel. The author cannot be sure that the VI indicated on the map was the actual V1 flying bomb that impacted the perimeter walls, but it is likely. The date of the impact was 18 March 1944. There is much conventional bombing shown close by, and one bomb fell to the inside of the junction between London Road and Brockley Hill, very close to the base.

So it appears that Outstation Stanmore was extremely fortunate not to have been flattened by a combination of general bombing and a V1 bomb in 1944. It must be emphasised that this was general bombing by the Nazis and not specifically targeted at the codebreaking outstation.

Of some interest are the bombing records near Bentley Priory the RAF HQ during the war. A V2 bomb came very close, perhaps a hundred yards or so to the south of the Bentley Priory building on 27 January 1945 at 03:55. There is a record of a crashed aircraft also very close on 16 October 1940, but it is not clear whether this was friend or foe. Conventional bombing was within a hundred yards of the building, so it was a close call at times. The control of aircraft movements was in the lower floor, below ground level. If a V2 had hit the RAF HQ, it would have been extremely serious, and an alternative base, perhaps RAF Uxbridge, would have had to take over. A lucky break then, and had Goering known of the near miss, and the implications of a direct hit on the RAF base and the nearby codebreaking station, he would have been more than a little upset.

The Headstone Manor Museum is worth a visit, aided by an enthusiastic army of volunteers and guides, and at time of writing has a small section on the war. They have a display case with a small rubber gas mask for children in the form of Mickey Mouse. The museum volunteer guide commented to the author that she thought it was quite disturbing and frightening. Which it is. One wonders if Walt Disney had his children try it out initially, before it was issued to the public?

13

EASTCOTE BEYOND GCHQ

The Crown Estate had purchased the Eastcote site in 1947. Once Eastcote was identified as being too small for the new intelligence base for the Government Communications Headquarters, the work was gradually transferred to Cheltenham, over roughly four years. This meant some sections would be retained at Eastcote for a period of time, whilst Cheltenham was established as the main intelligence centre for the UK. The move was largely completed by 1952. This was a period of uncertainty, as the Eastern Bloc was being established post-war, and learning about what your enemies were up to had to go up a gear, and one. Eastcote intercepted Eastern German and Russian coded messages at the start of the Cold War from approximately 1948-1952, and on a limited basis beyond.

The American Signals Intelligence Service and Armed Forces Security Agency played their part. The LCSA or London Communications Security Agency remained at Eastcote for a time, but was renamed in 1965 The Communications Electronics Security Department, or CESD. The LCSA was overseen by Major General William Penney as Director in 1953. In the same year the Joint Speech Research Unit was established at Eastcote by Dr John Swaffield.

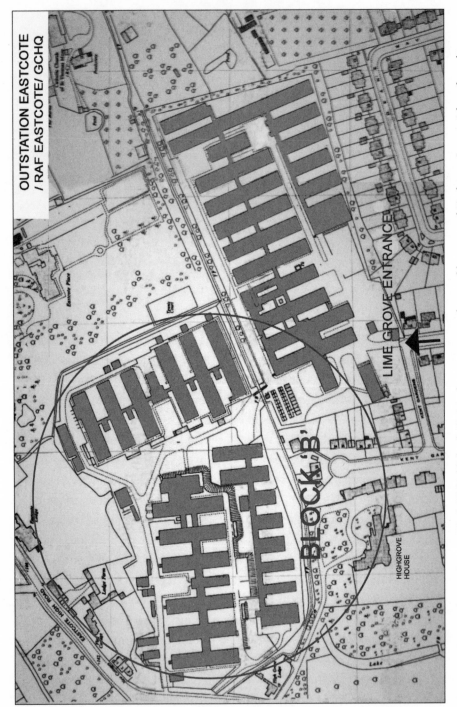

Outstation Eastcote layout showing Block 'B' highlighted. (Original map courtesy of www.old-maps.co.uk/Ordnance Survey. Adapted graphics - Ronald Koorm)

Aerial view of Eastcote showing site.

In March 1952 Eric Jones became director of GCHQ and took over from Commander Travis, This was the period where it was being relocated to Cheltenham. Once GCHQ had relocated to Cheltenham, the base at Eastcote became known as RAF Eastcote, or RAF Lime Grove. Multiple uses of the site included a psychiatric health clinic, a zoological veterinary surgery, a mortuary (in Block 3), an American servicemen's school, a GPO parcels logistics station and a rationing control base, amongst others. The GPO had a presence on the site from the early 1950s. Colossus was probably used as an experiment to calculate and determine GPO parcel logistics, but it is not known how successful this was in practice.

The Post office used Block 3 from 1950 or so, and GCHQ used Block 2. Mention is also made of the Census office, which was incorporated at Eastcote, and brought together from other locations. Early computers were used to process the Census data, using punched card machines. A worker on the base went to Eastcote in 1952 to work in 'X' Group, and help maintain the Colossus computers with engineers from the post office. This was in the days when it was quite usual for electrical and electronic engineers to be working for the post office.[82] The Official Secrets Act applied to all staff. There were mature Wrens on site working alongside him, and his specific role was to adjust the photo-electrical cells of the Colossus machinery that read the reels of punched tape, which flew past at alarming speed. A large number of punched-card female operators were employed at the Eastcote base. New computers were being introduced and they still had access to Hollerith machines for some tasks, these having been developed further compared to the ones used at Bletchley Park during the war. In the late 1950s an *Elliot 405* computer was the pride and joy of the base, until others came along. A printer had been adapted for Braille at Eastcote, and was used elsewhere to help train programmers. Some blind programmers would be able to operate the adapted machines.

One pupil of the American school on the base told how he travelled from Knightsbridge to Ruislip, and then by bus to Eastcote. Some American pupils refer to the school as USAF school Eastcote. Rumour has it that a famous *Dallas* TV star, Victoria Principal, attended the school after the war. It must have been strange growing up as a child somewhere like Eastcote, and then going to live in the US. But children had to learn to be resilient during the war, being displaced from their homes, moving from place to place, from one country to another.

There was an important US Air Force base not far away, in South Ruislip, where, in the Cold War era, spy plane film footage taken with sophisticated aerial cameras over Asia and Russia was brought in via Northolt Airport and analysed in detail by specialists.[83] The Gary Powers incident would soon shock America and the West, and make them reappraise their options for collecting intelligence. Satellites would largely replace spy planes in future years, although drones would also play their part, eliminating the risk of capture of a pilot.

Typing pools were set up at Eastcote post-war, and whilst many relocated in the late 60s, in 1973 there were still approaching 200 typists. An Eastcote local recalled that a rifle range was established for the American servicemen near Block 'B', adjacent to the Eastcote High Road on the west of the site. If that was true, one can only assume and hope that the Americans did their risk-assessments. The high masonry walls around the base and near the High Road would have provided adequate protection, on the assumption the wall was well maintained. The high masonry walls around Block 'B' were probably designed to withstand bombs and blast. The US Navy had personnel at Eastcote, and their numbers increased in 1984/1985.

The US Navy was one of the last occupiers of the Eastcote site, until 2006. US Marines were barracked on site in 1974. They moved into Block 1. Locals remember them marching and training in the area. MOD police guarded the entrances. A Joint Technical Language Service (JTLS), provided technical language interpretation/translation services. The US Embassy in London would bring in USMC Eastcote-based staff from time to time for guard and security duties. The Property Services Agency had a base on the site in later years, as there was a lot of property to manage, repair and maintain. They may also have used this as a property management base for the wider area.

From the processing of the British Census, to the administration of the Price Commission, to the support of American schools on military bases around the western world, the site was extensively used to the advantage of both the British and Americans, working closely together as friends and allies. This demonstrated the 'Special Relationship' was still alive and well.

Of course. 'Special Relationship' also referred to the financial support given to Britain by the Americans to survive during wartime and equip British forces. Much of the equipment was on a lend-lease basis, and Britain would be in their debt as a result of their borrowings, for armaments, equipment, food and supplies, all allocated to allied countries by the US. Enacted in March 1941, the official title was 'An Act to Promote the Defense of the United States'. It stopped abruptly when war ended with the defeat of Japan. Some equipment was contractually to be returned to American manufacturers and suppliers unless it was destroyed. It is not known how much of that actually occurred in practice, and it is suspected very little equipment and supplies was returned. At 2016 rates, it seems Britain and its Empire acquired around $340 billion of goods from the US for wartime activities. That is some 'Special Relationship'! Russia, China and others also benefitted from this process in in the war. It is quite amazing that the money was approved by Congress. Pearl Harbor may have had something to do with it.

There were probably in excess of 1,000 specialist people working on the base post-war, in the field of intelligence, cryptography, traffic analysis, cipher security, and communications. These were supplemented by other non-specialist personnel and security people. A substantial Government and semi-military base was operational here.

In August 1998, a visit was made to Eastcote by one ex-Wren, who had worked at the base, and an ex RAF engineer, who serviced many of the Bombe machines, just a few years before the base closed down completely and was abandoned. Walking down Lime Grove, those two people who had worked at the base were surprised at the appearance of the place. The old Bombe bays had been converted into offices for the Americans. Pictures of various deserted and dilapidated outstations prior to demolition and sale, seen in books, articles and online can be disturbing and sad, bearing in mind how much effort was put in to make those bases operational years ago.

The Eastcote site was sold in 2007, and a developer started demolishing the buildings commencing at the top end of Block 'B'. Apparently, the MOD had plans for the site in 2004 but abandoned them, and sold the site for housing. There were various planning objections at Hillingdon Council to try to block the development, but the developers, Taylor Wimpey, won through in the end. 385 houses were built on the site, spread north and south, with the original public footpath remaining to divide the site into roughly into two.

The developers caused a bit of problem for the surrounding gardens of the adjacent private housing. The author, at the time running a chartered surveying and design practice, was contacted by telephone one day by an irate lady householder next to the site. She said she had gallons of water in her garden appearing from nowhere, once the excavators were in action. 'It wasn't like that before they started work!' Alas, I declined to get involved with the householder and the builder, as I was too busy at the time. But if circumstances had been different, and if I had become involved, and then needed access to that building site following the demolition, perhaps I would have found the odd piece of evidence – an old newspaper, a cigarette packet, an old diary, or perhaps even a crumpled piece of paper with a Bombe menu written on it. Not that I would have realised at the time what that 'menu' was, as I had yet to discover the history of Eastcote and the codebreaking outstations. One wonders what interesting bits and pieces the demolition contractor put into the rubbish skips?

A plaque was unveiled in 2014 to commemorate the servicemen and women who worked at the base, and a ceremony was held with representatives of the RAF and the Mayor of Hillingdon present. The metal plaque with inscription is positioned on a raised, slightly angled brick plinth, behind a green painted steel railing, not far from a pedestrian crossing on Eastcote High Road. Ruislip, Northwood, & Eastcote local history society played its part in convincing the developers of Pembroke Park estate to name some of the estate roads after people who have a connection to the wartime base. Flowers Avenue and Wren Avenue are but two. Without their involvement, nothing would exist at the site to indicate anything of what went on there.

The short inscription does not really indicate the complexity and challenges of what went on all those years ago. It doesn't indicate that Outstation Eastcote was part of a large infrastructure which required a massive degree of cooperation, dedication and sacrifice by men and women, to defeat the Nazis and later provide the start of a modern intelligence service, which developed into GCHQ Cheltenham. Historic England have a website which lists monuments and sites, and one refers to RAF Eastcote. Whilst most of the facts are correct on this website, it does have an error, saying that 80 Bombes were at Eastcote, and not the plaque-inscribed number of 110. The plaque states the site had a military hospital and barracks in 1942 and was used for intelligence activities between 1943–45. It was, in fact, used for intelligence activities after 1945, as GCHQ, and Historic England do acknowledge the GCHQ connection.

As regards people that visited Eastcote after the war, one special lady was Mavis Batey. Mavis Lever (later Mavis Batey), and others, were afforded a work environment to flourish by 'Dilly' Knox at Bletchley Park, where his female workers were very much seen as assets, with the ability and flexibility under him to try new things out and experiment in codebreaking techniques. That eventually paid dividends, with major achievements for him and his team, saving countless British and Allied lives. After Mavis Lever's codebreaking breakthrough mentioned earlier contributed to the major success of the battle of Matapan for the Royal Navy, so pleased was the Commander of the fleet in the Mediterranean that he visited Bletchley Park and shook hands with the team, and thanked Mavis Lever for her efforts in codebreaking Italian intelligence.

Mavis had learnt very basic Italian to do her job. Using the Italian word 'PER', meaning 'for', helped her crack codes where others had overlooked the possible 'cribs'. She looked for an 'X' representing a space after the word 'PER', followed by a name or title. Her intuition was correct, and the Italian codes were penetrated bit by bit. She used a system devised by Knox called 'rodding', a series of lettered 'rods', and helped to break Enigma messages which did not have a plugboard at the front of the machine. The number of permutations of letter settings was far fewer than with the plugboard. Mavis later married Keith Batey, another codebreaker at Bletchley Park, who had helped her when she became stuck on a codebreaking problem. Post-war, she would play an important part within the new GCHQ at

Eastcote, working on intelligence. It is not known how long she remained at Eastcote, as she later worked in the Diplomatic service. She was recognised for her exceptional work and made an MBE in 1987, although there may have been restrictions about her wearing it, for reasons of national security.

Joan Clarke also visited Eastcote after the war. She was once Alan Turing's fiancée until Turing broke the engagement off. Clarke appeared to be aware of Turing's homosexuality so was it not a shock to her, and she was not apparently too concerned by it. Clarke was classified as a linguist at Bletchley Park, but had no foreign languages, so was rather unique. She had worked in Hut 8 at Bletchley, and worked her way up from a clerical support person to deputy of the Hut 8 cryptological section. Quite an achievement. She married in 1952 and became Joan Murray. She may have seen Turing at Eastcote after the war, when Turing became a consultant to GCHQ. They apparently remained good friends until Turing's death.

Many local people around Eastcote or Stanmore have no idea what went on at the bases, and are surprised when they attend a talk on the subject, or read articles and references to them. Hardly anyone knows that Outstation Eastcote transformed into GCHQ after the war. Bletchley Park wasn't all about Alan Turing.

Just because bombs were not dropped on the outstations and people did not die, or become injured, did not mean there was no sacrifice by those who worked there. Some probably suffered from various degrees of mental-cognitive-impairment later on, and hearing-loss over the years, due to being exposed to those unique environments. Most would not be able to speak of their experiences to family or friends, even after government declassification in the 1970s and later. The stress would have mounted up and taken its toll.

We are only now starting to recognize the impact of stress and mental effect on war veterans and take them seriously, to give them support. Such mental health support did not exist back then. We owe those people a great deal.

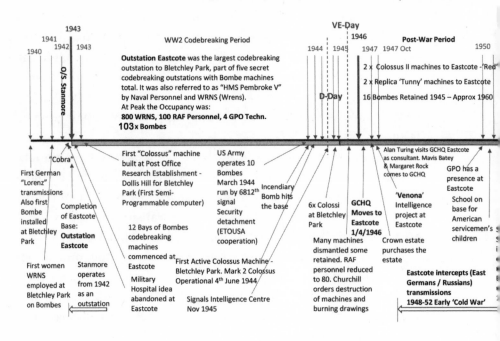

HISTORICAL TIMELINE OF 'OUTSTATION EASTCOTE' – (HMS PEMBROKE V / RAF

WW2 Codebreaking Period

VE-Day

Post-War Period

Outstation Eastcote was the largest codebreaking outstation to Bletchley Park, part of five secret codebreaking outstations with Bombe machines total. It was also referred to as "HMS Pembroke V" by Naval Personnel and WRNS (Wrens).
At Peak the Occupancy was:
800 WRNS, 100 RAF Personnel, 4 GPO Techn.
103 x Bombes

D-Day

2 x Colossus II machines to Eastcote - 'Red'
2 x Replica 'Tunny' machines to Eastcote
16 Bombes Retained 1945 – Approx 1960

O/S Stanmore

"Cobra"

First German "Lorenz" transmissions
Also first Bombe installed at Bletchley Park

First women WRNS employed at Bletchley Park on Bombes

Completion of Eastcote Base: **Outstation Eastcote**

Stanmore operates from 1942 as an outstation

First "Colossus" machine built at Post Office Research Establishment - Dollis Hill for Bletchley Park (First Semi-Programmable computer)

12 Bays of Bombes codebreaking machines commenced at Eastcote

Military Hospital idea abandoned at Eastcote

US Army operates 10 Bombes March 1944 run by 6812th signal Security detachment (ETOUSA cooperation)

First Active Colossus Machine - Bletchley Park. Mark 2 Colossus Operational 4th June 1944

Signals Intelligence Centre Nov 1945

Incendiary Bomb hits the base

6x Colossi at Bletchley Park

Many machines dismantled some retained. RAF personnel reduced to 80. Churchill orders destruction of machines and burning drawings

GCHQ Moves to Eastcote 1/4/1946

Alan Turing visits GCHQ Eastcote as consultant. Mavis Batey & Margaret Rock comes to GCHQ

'Venona' Intelligence project at Eastcote

Crown estate purchases the estate

GPO has a presence at Eastcote
School on base for American servicemen's

Eastcote intercepts (East Germans / Russians) transmissions
1948-52 Early 'Cold War'

Eastcote beyond GCHQ

COTE)   -   **Prepared by R.Koorm FRICS**   -   **NOT TO SCALE** © 2019 Ronald Koorm
History of HMS Pembroke V Eastcote -Version 7 -R Koorm.docx

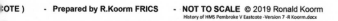

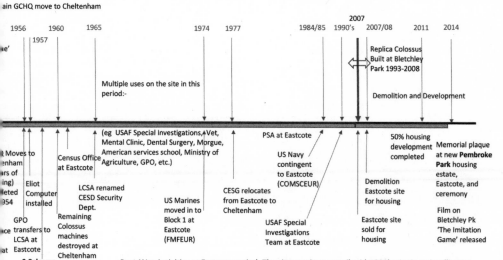

ain GCHQ move to Cheltenham

| 1956 | 1960 | 1965 | 1974 | 1977 | 1984/85 | 1990's | 2007/08 | 2011 | 2014 |

2007

1957

Replica Colossus
Built at Bletchley
Park 1993-2008

Multiple uses on the site in this
period:-

Demolition and Development

(eg USAF Special Investigations, Vet,
Mental Clinic, Dental Surgery, Morgue,
American services school, Ministry of
Agriculture, GPO, etc.)

PSA at Eastcote

50% housing
development
completed

Memorial plaque
at new **Pembroke
Park** housing
estate,
Eastcote, and
ceremony

US Navy
contingent
to Eastcote
(COMSCEUR)

Census Office
at Eastcote

Demolition
Eastcote site
for housing

Moves to
enham
rs of
ing)
leted
954

Eliot
Computer
installed

LCSA renamed
CESD Security
Dept.

CESG relocates
from Eastcote to
Cheltenham

Film on
Bletchley Pk
'The Imitation
Game' released

US Marines
moved in to
Block 1 at
Eastcote
(FMFEUR)

GPO
ace transfers to
LCSA at
at Eastcote

Remaining
Colossus
machines
destroyed at
Cheltenham

USAF Special
Investigations
Team at Eastcote

Eastcote site
sold for
housing

**2 Colossus
machines sent to
GCHQ Cheltenham
from Eastcote**

Post-War Activities at Eastcote varied. The site was in use until mid-1990's. Anti-spy intelligence
played a major role at Eastcote when it was GCHQ, and afterwards. More advanced machines
were brought in, and many key Bletchley Park personnel came to Eastcote post-war.

14

WRNS – EVOLUTION

The WRNS were sent a message of congratulations and thanks in May 1945 by the Board of Admiralty, for their contribution during the war. The WRNS became a permanent part of the Royal Navy on 1 February 1949. Sadly, they were disbanded in 1993 under MOD restructuring, personnel being absorbed into the Royal Navy, but now with equal opportunities. It is now possible for females in the Royal Navy to carry out roles and responsibilities which previously only men would be allowed to do; from handling advanced weaponry to repairing naval aircraft guidance systems, and becoming captain of the most advanced, high-tech warships, perhaps one day, even Admiral of the fleet.

This book concentrates on the WRNS, as the body of women who most influenced the operational codebreaking at outstations. However, the WAAF, ATS and others provided critical support roles to Bletchley Park and elsewhere, and are no less important.

Dame Vera Laughton Mathews, Director of the WRNS, was told initially when she wanted to apply to the Admiralty all those years ago that women were not allowed. She would have been proud today, had she still been alive, to see able, intelligent women operating in the Royal Navy and other armed forces, carrying out complex, dangerous, and highly skilled tasks. Their support role has developed into leading officers and management in the services.

The chart on page 119 illustrates the female personnel in outstations and Bletchley Park. It reveals the spread of ATS and WRNS. ATS personnel were also heavily used in various listening Y-stations up and down the country. Several photographs exist showing WRNS dispatch riders transferring information across the country from listening stations to Bletchley Park, and from Bletchley to codebreaking outstations. The bikes were reliable, they had to be, to cover the hundreds even thousands of miles travelled. A dispatch motorcycle is located at the museum of Bletchley Park in a glass case, situated in a barn, and in military colours.

There exists a black and white photograph of Wrens proudly marching down the High Street at Eastcote, past the shops and cheering civilians, after VE day, and the end of the war in Europe. Inspecting the online WRNS History listings of WRNS 1939-1945, it is apparent that many were allocated to Pembroke V (or Pembroke III), and to places such as Bletchley Park and Pembroke V (London).[84] Neither Eastcote nor Stanmore are specifically mentioned, relying on the more general 'Pembroke V' term.

It is fitting to mention Dorothy Killick (Née London), who worked her way up as a Wren, starting off as an ARP volunteer initially, to become a Wren Cipher officer, and who eventually worked on the intelligence cyphers of the Normandy Landings. Whilst she did not work at any of the main five codebreaking outstations, nor Bletchley Park, her achievements in the listings make fascinating reading.

Another was Barbara Linton (later Hyatt-Box), who was a trained cipher officer and attended the Yalta Conference with Prime Minister Winston Churchill in March 1945. There was tremendous trust and ability in the WRNS, and other female services. This degree of trust was reflected in the Bletchley Park management 'allowing' WRNS personnel to set up and operate

Bombes, Robinson, and Colossus machines. The WRNS proved themselves as professionals who would not let down their commanding officer, nor their country, and would do them proud.

Whilst training prior to allocation to outstations was often stated to be two weeks, the WRNS history mentions that three weeks training in most cases was the norm. The start of Special Duties 'X' linguist training was based in Wimbledon, South London. There are many references at the National Archives as to the logistics problem that Bletchley Park had to overcome, after the first three codebreaking outstations were established, of finding enough trained WRNS personnel and support staff to operate the Bombes. It was a serious resources problem for management.

The training stations at Wimbledon, Mill Hill, and elsewhere, would become sophisticated production lines to churn out uniformed, trained Wrens. Studying the range of skills that the different categories of WRNS were trained under, I am in awe at the range of specialisms and tasks that they took on: from cipher officer to aircraft radio maintenance, from mechanics to plotters, learning skills to disassemble torpedoes and depth charges, and to reassemble them competently.

Dame Vera Laughton Matthews retired in late 1946, having been appointed as Director of the WRNS in 1939. Many Wrens would be great achievers in their careers. A few individuals would go down in history. Some feel that their contribution during the Second World War under Special Duties 'X' was forgotten. When the declassification of certain information occurred in the 1970s some Wrens and others at Y-listening stations were able to talk about some of their wartime work. But it was often the case that by that time, their parents had passed away, and they would never learn what important roles their daughter had during the war.

When Colossi came to Eastcote after the war, Wrens operated those machines. One of the Wren's jobs was to ensure the photo-electric cell 'eye' was wiped clean frequently, to ensure the data on the tape with the dots and crosses could be seen and processed. Here were WRNS personnel using one of the first computers. They may not have understood how it worked, but in many ways they were pioneers of the computer age.

They would work closely with the technical personnel and engineers, who understood the workings of the machine. No one outside the design team would have had a clue about how to operate Colossus, or realise what it was capable of. Yet, today, we rely on computers to do almost everything for us.

The Wrens' thorough training of the 6812th US Signals personnel on the use and operation of ten allocated Bombes in early 1944, resulted in an increased intelligence output. The output of intelligence was far in excess what was expected at the time. The quality of that training was key to the success of the Americans.

Below is provided a list of the ranks of WRNS during wartime:[85]

Ordinary Wren
Wren
Leading Wren
Petty Officer Wren
Chief Wren
Third Officer   Equivalent Sub-Lieutenant
Second Officer   Equivalent Lieutenant
First Officer   Equivalent Lieutenant Commander
Chief Officer   Equivalent Commander
Superintendent   Equivalent Captain
Commandant   Equivalent Commodore
Chief Commandant   Equivalent Rear Admiral

The Wrens achieved in excess of 95% efficiency, averaging around 97%, together with U.S. Signals Division, in operating the Bombe codebreaking machines, during WW2. This was due to a combination of their training, determination and resilience.

15

INTERCEPT STATIONS

Y-Stations/listening stations were across the country, and abroad. They were effectively outstations, but did not possess codebreaking machines. They did have equipment to start the process of codebreaking, the radio receivers. Beaumanor, Chicksands, Flowerdown, Harpenden, Knockholt, and many others made up the listening teams. The name 'Y-stations' probably came from the phrase 'wireless interception'.

Around ninety locations in the UK and abroad would tune in to various frequencies, listen in for German and Italian radio or radio-teleprinter transmissions. It took extensive training before one would be permitted to be a Y-station listener, competent to take down the message and category of source. You would need a good understanding of Morse code, and later on, the special Morse which came from the teleprinter transmissions. The atmosphere or 'ether' would impact on the quality of information received, so fading of the signal was commonplace.

Shortwave radio can be transmitted over very large distances, and some were surprised that transmissions over in eastern Russia could be detected in the UK. Allied unoccupied countries would have listening stations too, and places like Malta in the Mediterranean would be extremely useful, picking up intelligence traffic from Sicily, Crete, Italy, North Africa, and the surrounding areas.

Malta would be under constant attack from the Luftwaffe, becoming famously 'the most bombed place on earth', but it was in a unique position to provide movements of shipping intelligence back to Bletchley Park and the UK. Its information would help to target Italian ships and German enemy supply ships, to slow the supply chain to Rommel in North Africa. This would help the Allies to mount effective counter-attacks, where Rommel would need to consider his diminishing fuel and supplies before advancing further.

Intelligence through Y-stations also proved invaluable during the Battle of Britain. German-speaking personnel at the stations would intercept information from German Luftwaffe bomber pilots and send it on to Bentley Priory at Stanmore, where the coordination of fighter groups was organised. Shortwave transmissions would

Malta, the most bombed place on earth. Smokescreens were used to confuse enemy aircraft.

form the basis of the intelligence intercepted, and help forewarn Spitfires and Hurricanes of the Luftwaffe intentions.

Some calculate that had the Allies not been in a position to collect and read the German intelligence 'Ultra', the war would have been extended by at least two more years. Bletchley Park relied 100% on the listening stations to intercept the coded messages as the first stage in the codebreaking process. No listening stations, no intelligence, no need for codebreaking machines or mathematicians.

If one Y-station was temporarily out of action, another would slot in, and take over quickly. Power supply problems would be efficiently sorted. Shift patterns could be adjusted at short notice. The resourcing and logistics of the outstations would have been a nightmare. Some personnel would need to speak and understand German. Some would become proficient in detecting different German Morse-key operators, and could read them like a book.

A typical Y-station for direction finding, or D/F, would have a small hut and four aerials as tall poles at ninety degrees to each other. Cables connected the aerials to the operator's hut. In the hut was a radio receiver capable of receiving shortwave frequencies. There would also be a goniometer, which helped identify bearings of the transmissions. There would be no GPS and of course no satellites to assist direction finding digitally. This analogue D/F process required experience, patience, and a large degree of skill and personal determination.

Beaumanor in Leicestershire is one of the better known wartime intercept stations. It was referred to in the feature film *Enigma*, and John Barry wrote a short piece of music with 'Beaumanor' in the title (*At Beaumanor*). Buildings were erected within the grounds and disguised as barns, pavilions, greenhouses, outhouses and stables. These had advanced radio receiving equipment within. Messages from German-occupied territories and Italian intercepts were recorded and passed onto Bletchley Park. Most of the listeners were ATS personnel, men and women.

The site was heavily guarded by Military Police, and even the Home Guard had their role to play there to prevent unauthorised entry or prying eyes. Many would have moved to Beaumanor from other Y-stations, such as Chicksands and Chatham in Kent. That could be considered as a promotion, due to the specialist nature of the work carried out there. Beaumanor would also specialise in German High Command 'Tunny' intercepts, these being of particular interest to Bletchley Park, which would by-pass most codebreaking outstations because the information was teleprinter-based.

Intercept stations sometimes had direction finding equipment, or D/F, to help pinpoint the enemy transmission source. This could prove to be as important as the information transmitted. Receiving operators would become familiar with various sources of transmissions, particularly in conventional Morse code. Encrypted transmissions would be sent to Bletchley Park. Non-encrypted messages would sometimes be studied in detail on the Y-station base, and then information distributed.

Communications receivers varied, but concentrated on valve-based shortwave receivers, with many of robust American manufacture. Some would be available after the war to the public and electronics trade as army surplus, and were bought up for their valves or components. Several thousand National HRO communications receivers were acquired by the British and used extensively at Y-stations across the country, and on ships and foreign bases too. The German Siemens company made a version, as did a rival electronics firm. Both sides were copying each other's better designed equipment.

To give an idea of the range of shortwave radio, an American wartime listening base (US Federal Communication Commission), in Providence, Rhode Island, was able to receive from the following locations in Africa, Europe and elsewhere:

Cairo:	8,767 km Distance
Berlin:	6,139 km Distance
Midway:	9,142 km Distance

The antenna used 85,000 feet of wire and cabling to achieve this, which was strung below the tree-line to keep it out of view. Of course, reception quality would vary tremendously due to atmospheric conditions. The National HRO receivers were extremely durable and well-built, with precision micrometer dials for tuning, and geared internally to allow fine-tuning adjustment by the operators. It would be crucial to selectively tune out interfering frequencies to obtain the best signal. The HRO had a slot in the front of the chassis where one could insert a removable coilset to cover a range of specific radio frequencies. If you needed to scan and search across a wide band of frequencies, you would need a wooden case full of coilsets to cover the complete range for the shortwave band.

There were multiple operators in most of the larger Y-stations, and they would be scanning for specific frequencies. eg 3.5 MHz-7 MHz, or 14 MHz-30 MHz, and so on. Thirteen sets of coils were available for later models. A large, precision tuning dial dominated the front of the machine.

The HR-05 Model came later in the war, and was very popular.[86] It weighed 22kg, but could just about be lifted and moved by one person. Not so for some of the competitor's receiver models, which were more of a two-man lifting operation. The HRO was designed for ease of maintenance with a top cover hinged lid to access the valves. The demand was such that many tens of thousands would be made. The receiver was designed by the National Radio Company in Massachusetts, but information indicates that some were built in England under licence. They were successfully used in Y-stations for direction finding (D/F), as well as in the field for mobile direction finding, to trace the source of radio transmissions from the enemy. Due to the large volume ordered by the British during the war, the HRO became the standard communications receiver for many Y-stations.[87] There was an external power supply and a speaker, although much of the listening would have been on headphones, particularly where multiple receivers and operators were located side by side.

Other models of receivers available included the Marconi CR100, a much heavier model than the HRO, the Marconi R1155, and the bulky American RCA AR88. Apart from the R1155, these were designed for ground-stations only, and not aircraft, due to their heavy weight. The AR 88 had very high reliability, and was also used to scan the shortwave radio frequencies at US coastal stations. It contained fourteen valves, and was highly sensitive in operation.

Most of the early AR88 production during the war came to Great Britain under Lend-Lease arrangements. The use of this wartime receiver was for a variety of different purposes in the UK, including the substantial Portsmouth Portsdown underground tunnel communication centre, which was a WRNS-operated wartime communications base.

Most of the Allied AR88s after the war had ended, had to be destroyed or dumped, a condition in the Lend-Lease agreement, as RCA, the manufacturers, did not want any used receivers returned to them. Some were even thrown down an abandoned well in considerable quantities by American servicemen, a terrible waste.

The consistency of having similar models of receiver in multiple listening stations made maintenance straightforward, as well as breeding familiarity with the controls and operation. A supply of spare valves was required to ensure that equipment was out of action for the shortest possible time when valves failed. Y-station staff also included some WAAF personnel. Some went to Chicksands and had only just finished school, being only seventeen. It must have been quite a challenge for them to fit in with the older, much more experienced receiver-operators. Sharing of facilities was far from ideal, until the accommodation blocks were expanded with more buildings.

Storms in Africa and the Far East would interfere with the reception, causing extensive, unpleasant crackling in the headphones. The headphones used during the war were not designed for comfort like today. The folding headband clip would sometimes trap your hair, and if you happened to be female, you would have to unravel the entwined mess, and be quick about it.

Listening in the tropics would be particularly uncomfortable in small rooms with high humidity, sweat running down you as you tried to write down crucial intelligence information. Lots of strange insects and even the odd snake to keep you company, and of course, mosquitoes; but at least you weren't freezing cold. Quinine tablets were a must, assuming you could get your supply.

Russian officers were permitted to come to Britain to observe the operational side of several Y-Stations. But they apparently were not allowed to access Bletchley Park. Too many questions would have been asked. Bletchley was a large site, but if they had wandered anywhere near the hut with the Bombes, or the specialist sections such as the Newmanry, or Testery, or to hut six, it would be extremely difficult to explain the the potential consequences to Churchill. The Russians had insecure cipher systems, and leaking of our processes to the Germans could have been disastrous.

Hanslope Park and Whaddon Hall were two locations which supported Bletchley Park in coordinating intelligence reception and listening. The Radio Security Service or RSS installed special radio masts at Hanslope Park to intercept and listen to the German Secret Service, the *Abwehr*. Knockholt, Y-station would be established following suspicious intercepts over the radio discovered at a listening station in a police station in Denmark Hill in South London, and would have a key role to play.[88] The special Y-station would be approved in August 1942 (known as Ivy Farm).

Correspondence from that time mentions communication with the Ministry of Works and Planning, and detailed reports of the local farmer ploughing the field where the Knockholt station was to be established. It would have been so tempting to tell him, 'Don't bother ploughing for a new crop, even though Britain needs the food badly, you'll soon be moving on elsewhere when we requisition your land, in a few week's time.' The War Ministry had to hold back, as they had to have feedback from 'The War Lands Department' before they could move on this. This was the sort of dilemma the Government departments faced. Formal notices headed 'D.R.50' were then served on the landowners to requisition the land for the new base in late September 1942.[89] A meeting would follow on the site, to discuss location and scale of the receiving towers for the aerials and the electrical supply, with an electrical engineer. Things had to move quickly. It was unlikely that any appeals against requisitioning land from landowners could be considered.

Knockholt was owned by the radio section of MI6, and its operators listening in would become very successful over time in collecting intercepted 'Tunny' or 'FISH' messages, based on teleprinter transmissions. It would would have very strong links with Bletchley Park, to enable processing the collected coded, intelligence in the 'Testery', a section at Bletchley set up by Ralph Tester. Tester coordinated his work with Max Newman, who managed the processing of intelligence via advanced 'Tunny' machines, the newer 'Robinsons', and the Colossus machines.

These machines would assist in stripping out a key part of German Lorenz and 'Secret Writer' machine enciphers, with information from the special 'Chi' wheel rotors. It was a sophisticated, top-secret production line, one section providing crucial information to the other, with the objective of reading the Nazi intelligence on strategic decisions, across numerous 'FISH' communication links across Europe and elsewhere.

Many of the early Y-station staff were amateur radio enthusiasts or radio 'hams' which clearly had a passion for the work. These would be the 'VI's or 'Voluntary Interceptors', enrolled for the secret work on behalf of the Y-stations. In the early years of the war, a whole network of amateur radio enthusiasts would be sought out by the Government agencies and Bletchley Park to secretly listen across Europe with their radio equipment. Sometimes, radio receivers would be allocated to them, and log books, but they would not be able to tell their friends or family what it was they were listening to, or who they were working for. If they had other duties after work, such as Home Guard or firewatching/ARP involvement, they would be advised that they should still keep that up to avoid questions. But the enthusiasts would put in two hours or so per night listening for Morse code messages during weekdays, usually after work. Many had built their own radios, or modified them, and understood the various electronic components such as valves, condensors, resistors, and what to do with them in an electrical circuit. Some had large antennae in their gardens or on the roof, and experimentation with antennae would be common to improve reception over the shortwave frequencies used. Many experienced 'ham' radio enthusiasts would be proficient at listening to Morse code from shipping or aircraft, and this was an extension of those skills put to good use. They would be able to detect automated Morse transmissions, due to the regular dots and dashes and spaces between them. A degree of consistency and regularity impossible to achieve by human hand on a Morse-key.

Those machine-Morse transmissions received were of particular interest to Bletchley Park. Some teleprinter-based messages from larger Y-stations would be sent to Bletchley Park by motor cycle couriers, and in some cases via GPO land lines. This enabled speedy processing and evaluation of intelligence at Headquarters. Admiral Donitz suggested radio transmissions of less than thirty seconds to limit detection of signals by the Allies, but he underestimated our radio signals personnel, and with experience they could identify the source of naval transmitted signals in just a few seconds. That indicates the level of expertise which our operators could achieve, with a lot of practice.

With the 'Voluntary Interceptors', all this additional intelligence written down by the amateurs onto the log sheets, together with information on direction/location where possible, was a head start in processing information. Add this to information from the military Y-stations being established, the French and Dutch resistance workers, agents in the occupied countries, and the picture began to build of what the enemy was doing and planning.

A proportion of those eligible amateur radio enthusiasts would be called up for military service, filtered as to their skills and abilities, and almost certainly put to good use at Y-stations, or in Signals sections of the armed services. It would be a good way to start your career in radio communications. If you could repair and maintain the receivers and transmitters, as many trained operators could, then you would be highly valued. Those who survived the war would often end up in radio and telecoms companies, or the Post Office, helping to design and develop new equipment. Some would end up teaching electronics in colleges and universities and writing research papers. The post-war period would always be looking out for talented, experienced, electronic engineers in the field of modern telecommunications. Television would soon be coming into every household and need engineers. Transistors would soon revolutionise electronics, replacing valves with semi-conductors. Hi-fidelity audio and PA systems would need designs for amplification. Telephone systems and exchanges would be greatly expanded.

Communication through radio and electronics would change the world in the nineteen-fifties and sixties. Satellite technology, still in its infancy in the late 1950s and 1960s, would be of interest to the most talented communications people. The groundwork as Y-station listeners would have been a sound basis, having to deal with atmospheric conditions, direction finding of sources, antennae, tuning of frequencies, Morse code, logging the intelligence transmissions, and for some, analysis of intelligence messages. But there would also be an important transition from valve technology of the 1940s and 1950s to transistors and semiconductors in the 1960s.

Today, in the armed services, Signals and Telecoms is a major career path in the Army, Navy and Air force. The equipment today may be a lot more advanced and sophisticated than in the 1940s, with GPS tracking, etc., but one still needs to be dedicated, professional, be able to problem-solve quickly under pressure, and to work as part of a team. The principles are still the same as in the world wars. To be one step ahead of the enemy, and to communicate effectively to men and women on the battlefield; and to detect the slightest changes in the enemy's radio and telecoms transmissions, which might indicate a change in position or other crucial information. Accuracy, precision, discipline and teamwork in intelligence gathering and communication procedures are as important today as they were in the Second World War.

16

BOMBES & NAMES

The numbering and naming of Bombe machines was necessary to ensure a degree of control, allocation to various bases, and tracking for modifications, maintenance and training purposes. The Bombe bays in each location were substantial physical areas, and would require space around each individual machine to access the front, rear and sides. The naming of machines had certain advantages. Although each machine was individually numbered in the register, numbers can become confusing. A name is more easily recalled from memory than a digit.

The names were grouped depending upon the allocated section, which were often countries in Europe and elsewhere, such as the French section, the Greek section, the Yugoslavian section, etc. The Bombes were then issued with names of cities and large towns within those countries. This made it relatively straightforward for officers to allocate the shifts of personnel, usually Wrens, to the section and machine that they would be responsible for during that shift. You would be in GREECE section tonight, and looking after OLYMPIA with Wren 'X'. You might be allocated more than one machine depending upon the workload and available resources.

Someone initially must have made a long list of countries and chosen towns and cities and plotted them on a map of the huts for that specific station.

The Wrens would come into the hut, have their instructions for the shift, and check with the Officer the part of the block they would be working in that shift, and the location of the Bombe or Bombes that they would work on. Some Bombes did not have names of cities or towns. 'VICTORY' was the first Bombe, so it had an excuse to be different from the rest. But what of 'SPITFIRE', 'HURRICANE', 'DEFIANT', 'HAVOC', 'MARATHON', 'SAVAGE', 'UNIQUE', 'FORTRESS', 'NELSON'? We do not know if these names were selected or proposed by a senior officer, by Hut 6 at Bletchley Park, or even by Churchill, but they could well have been. We have already commented upon the renaming of certain Bombes, some renamed up to five or six times, although that was rare.

It may be of interest to single out some Bombes which were special, and different, such as 'High Speed Keen' (HSK) versions. These included Bombe No. 139 originally 'LOUVRAIN', and renamed 'CORINTH' for the Greek section at Outstation Eastcote. It was a H.S.K. bombe. Bombe No. 142 'ZEEBRUGGE' was also a High Speed Keen at Eastcote. It was renamed 'THEBES', again for the Greek bay. Bombe No. 150 'WATERLOO' (H.S.K.) was renamed 'ATHENS' for the same Greek bay. Bombe No. 151 'OLYMPIA' (H.S.K.) (O.S.E.) was not renamed.

Once the Bombes were delivered to a base, how long was it before they were in operation? For most it was in about 4–5 days, and certainly within a week or so. Examples of actual Bombes becoming operational include 'ATLANTA' (USA Bay) O.S.E. Delivered 12/7/44 operational 17/7/44. Another might be 'SPARTA' O.S.E. Delivered 24/7/44. Operational 31/7/44. But some did have a larger gap between delivery and operation, perhaps because of technical problems, waiting for spares, etc., for example 'SPLIT' O.S.E. Delivered 15/9/44. Operational 6/10/44. This was certainly not the norm.

'Victory' Bombe Number 1 entry from the Bombe Register Volume 1. (The National Archives)

A Bombe might be moved around the same base, or to a different outstation altogether. When that happened it would be renamed, so as not to cause confusion. Each Bombe had a reference number, but the name might have changed, and one could track it in the Bombe register by looking at the reference number and reading the text showing the Bombe history. The Bombe Registers at time of writing are on loan to the National Archives at Kew.

Below are a small sample of Bombe names which were based at O.S.E. during the war:

ARNHEM
SAN FRANCISCO (USA Bombe Bay)
ATHENS (relocated later to O.S.S. renamed KANO)

MARATHON
SPARTA > relocated to O.S.S. renamed YOLA
WARSPITE > HAVRE
SPITFIRE > SPARTA > relocated to O.S.S. & renamed.
HURRICANE > NAVARINO > HOUSTON > OLYMPIA
    >relocated to O.S.S.
ROCHESTER (USA Bombe Bay)
JUMBO
OMAHA (USA Bombe Bay)
WANAKA > KANKOW > MOSCOW > BRUSSELS
WARSAW
NEWTON > DIEPPE > BOSTON (USA Bombe bay)
JAMAICA > CRACOW >ATHENS > LOUVRAIN >relocated to
    O.S.S.

The names in italic indicate Bombes that were on other sites prior to Stanmore. One assumes that when Bombe machines were relocated to different codebreaking outstations, eg Eastcote to Stanmore, the method of transport would have been similar to that when the machines were delivered from BTM in Letchworth: on the back of a lorry, with a tarpaulin cover, one driver, and no escort or security, to attract minimal attention. A crane or hoist of some type was needed to offload the one-ton machines at the receiving end. The offloading would need great care and precision. Damaging the Bombes would almost certainly have been a disciplinary offence.

Outstation Stanmore almost became a clearing-house for Bombes. It built up a high number of operational machines but many of these were renamed and sent onto Outstation Eastcote, which had the space available. One particular Bombe (number 41) started off at Stanmore, was sent to Eastcote and was returned later to Stanmore. If it was not for the renaming of machines there could have been much confusion.

17

BTM DEVELOPMENTS

In 1945 and 1946, after the end of the war, certificates/diplomas were issued by BTM management to certain staff who worked on project 'Cantab'. These incorporated a specially designed logo on the papers and the dinner menus, and were a 'thank you' to staff.

The British Tabulating Machine Company Ltd
    The Board of Directors of The British Tabulating Machine Company Limited wish to convey to you their sincere thanks for the valued assistance you have given in the fulfilment of the Cantab Contract.
    It will be gratifying to you to know that His Majesty's Lords Commissioners of the Admiralty have expressed their appreciation of the rapid and efficient production of the Cantab equipment which has materially assisted in the successful prosecution of the war.

Yours faithfully
R. Phillpotts, Esq.
The Chairman,
British Tabulating Machine Co. Ltd.,
New Icknield Way, Letchworth, Herts.[90]

Perhaps it was rather premature for the management to do this, bearing in mind the secrecy of the project and ongoing requirement to adhere to The Official Secrets Act. One wonders what the value might be in possessing one of those BTM 'Cantab' Diploma certificates, or perhaps a celebration dinner 'Cantab' Menu, today? A true piece of British history on a piece of paper, and probably quite rare.

After the war, the key players at BTM were given awards. Chairman Raleigh Phillpotts was given a knighthood. Harold 'Doc Keen was made an OBE, and his principal assistant H. Morton, given an MBE. They would not be allowed to divulge the reasons why they were given the award, at least not the details.

To give an idea of the success of BTM in early years of the company, from mid-1916 to 1919, BTM had sold 153 million cards for punched card operations, across industry, the British Government, the railways and foreign governments. That was the equivalent of 75 million cards per year. It would rent out their 'Hollerith' tabulating and punched card sorting machines, and make lots of money doing so. Data processing using punched cards was not a 1950s invention, even though many films and pictures around that era show 'modern' computers using punched cards prior to using tape. It was already developing on a big scale in the early part of the twentieth century, with the assistance of BTM in the UK and Hollerith in America.

The uses for punched cards for sorting and analysis was rapidly expanding, and the Government Census analysis would be one such important area, contracted to BTM. The Egyptian Government used up ten per cent of their overall sales of cards in just one census, indicating the importance of foreign governments as clients. Earlier, in 1911, a Hollerith three-bank counting machine had been used in the Census for England and Wales, and it was this link with the Government that helped to tie the knot with the codebreakers almost thirty years later. BTM became flexible in assisting clients in finding elegant solutions to their unique problems in counting and sorting.

BTM were used to dealing with both commercial organizations and governments, so had a track record here. They would use

Hollerith card reader in the Science Museum.

the inter-war years to build their knowledge, expertise, and workforce. The social changes in Britain during the First World War and afterwards would impact on BTM's status and increase its turnover and profits. More and more records were needed by HMSO and other government departments, and that involved mass-counting of data. National Insurance and unemployment needed monitoring on a large scale, and Hollerith machines would be used on such tasks. A major order to BTM came from the Milk Marketing Board in 1933. BTM did not have it all their own way, and there would be competitors such as Powers-Samas, who would wrest away some contracts from them.

In 1951 BTM became ambitious, and built a computer. It was the 'HEC' or Hollerith Electronic Computer. This used valves as digital switches, but the designer would not have had access to the valve-based 'Colossus' semi-programmable computer used for codebreaking Nazi cyphers, as most had been dismantled at Bletchley by then, and the remaining two machines at Eastcote were considered at the time to be top secret. An electronics and computer engineer, Tony Booth from Birkbeck College in London, assisted BTM with their computer design. Considering the links of BTM to IBM, perhaps this route was not considered that unusual. Here, their experience of punched card technology would pay dividends. Several more models of HEC were developed, some with a printer output.

BTM would grow and become ICT (International Computers and Tabulators), and later ICL (International Computers Limited.) It operated from 1968 up to 2002, when Fujitsu acquired it and it was rebranded under that name. Although at one point it became Fujitsu Siemens, it returned back to plain Fujitsu in 2009. How strange and ironic that Siemens would be part-owner of the British firm that effectively copied some of their excellent relays and electronic components during the war, to incorporate within the advanced Bombe codebreaking machines. ICT were formed in 1958 through negotiations between BTM and Powers-Samas, the key negotiator being Sir Arthur Humphreys, who headed the commercial arm of BTM. In the late 1960s he was made the Managing Director of ICL, and ensured that the firm was a market leader in modern computing technology, particularly for business machines. ICL would win major government and business contracts, such as for the Post Office.

So the British Government, following a contract for census work in 1911, later selected the same firm to assist them in making codebreaking machines, and that firm went on to supply British businesses with early computers in the 1950s. Few firms would have had the specialist manpower, engineers, skills, ability and management to put all this together and achieve what they did. BTM would be rare in this respect. Sadly, BTM has since disappeared from Letchworth, and no longer exists. The groundwork for a large part of modern business computing and technology was done at ICT and ICL, which had come about from the evolution of BTM and their highly skilled labour force.

The Bombe registers record that as the Bombes were dismantled after the war finished, parts were 'returned to Mr Keene for disposal'. One wonders whether any parts were retained by workers as souvenirs. How fortunate that the British Government were able to identify BTM's specialist expertise, and harness it to develop Alan Turing's Bombe machine. The link to early data-processing through Hollerith machines makes the history even more remarkable, as this was, arguably and effectively, the forerunner of Google and other search engines.

18

PEMBROKE

The name 'Pembroke' formed part of the reference name for assigning Naval WRNS personnel to Station 'X' duties. It has been previously explained that Pembroke V or HMS Pembroke V were not the official names of the codebreaking outstations from a Bletchley Park viewpoint. The outstations would be formally known as Outstation Wavendon, Outstation Stanmore, Outstation Eastcote, and abbreviated O.S.W., O.S.S., O.S.E., etc. Bletchley Park would be referred to in the Bombe Registers as O.S.P. Outstation 'Park', even though it was the hub.

At a stretch one might consider the actual hut where the Bombes were located as a separate 'Outstation', but that was not really the intention. Looking at from the naval viewpoint, if you were naval personnel, e.g. WRNS, you could be assigned to HMS Pembroke V or Pembroke V following training. But as even Bletchley Park could be referred to as PV or Pembroke V, you needed clarification as to which base you would be sent to. So, we can say that the codebreaking Outstations had dual names. At least there would be no confusion if one said 'Outstation Stanmore'. But Stanmore also had Bentley Priory, an RAF command and control base, and

Stanmore Park, also used for military purposes, so if you were unfamiliar with the area, you might need to check with someone first before arriving for duties in your smart uniform at the incorrect base.

HMS Pembroke V and HMS Pembroke III were two nominal depot ships used for pay and administration of all land-based Royal Naval personnel. Here we have the link between WRNS and Bletchley Park and GC & CS. All the Wrens at all the outstations and at Bletchley Park were listed under Pembroke V.

HMS *Pembroke* was one of several warships, the original going back to the sixteenth century. There have been eight *Pembrokes* historically. The ninth, current HMS *Pembroke* (M107), is a minesweeper with a hull and a superstructure built of advanced glass-reinforced-polyester. It is a 'Sandown Class' Minehunter. It has anti-magnetic properties for obvious reasons, being largely non-metallic. It has been on operations and exercises in the Gulf and elsewhere. HMS *Pembroke* uses the advanced 'Seafox' mine disposal system to detect and eliminate mines.

The most recent Pembroke warship prior to the modern variety was named in 1890 before being renamed some years later. No HMS *Pembroke* existed in the war. In the inter-war years, there were some HMS *Pembrokes* which had been renamed.

Chatham became HMS Pembroke, being a land-based barracks, and had Pembroke I, Pembroke II, and Pembroke IV names attached at different times. Pembroke 'X' was headquarters for Royal Navy Patrols at Lowestoft in 1939, but had no real link to the name of Pembroke used later at Chatham.

As regards 'Pembroke III', between 1942 and 1952 this was the name for some of the barracks for accounting purposes in London, and some outstations. Outstation Stanmore was sometimes referred to as HMS Pembroke III in reports. 'Pembroke V' was identified as the secret base for codebreaking at Bletchley Park 1941–1945 and codebreaking outstations supporting Bletchley. Between 1945 and 1946 it was allegedly also the name for WRNS personnel in London. Most reports and accounts by WRNS personnel refer to 'Pembroke V' when talking about Outstation Stanmore, Outstation Eastcote, Outstation Wavendon or Bletchley Park.

Post-war, the locals tended to call Eastcote 'RAF Lime Grove', and a few might have called it GCHQ until it was relocated, but GCHQ was not widely known about. The fact that the local Barclays Bank in Eastcote set the account name up in April 1946 as GCHQ indicates clearly there was no problem with this being known to the general public, providing one did not let on that the base had anything to do with intelligence work. That would have been a disciplinary offence.

The Royal Ensign would be flown on the quarterdeck on the bases. You had to raise the Ensign and lower it at the appropriate times, and salute it, as if you were saluting the top brass, or HM the King. The housing estate which has replaced the Eastcote base is now known as 'Pembroke Park', which is a well-chosen name, but maybe only a few of the residents of that estate understand why, unless they have studied the metal plaque tucked away behind a green-painted steel railing.

The plaque makes it clear, on the first line that the estate name came from the Second World War base there, 'HMS Pembroke V'. It mentions it was GCHQ after the war. It does not indicate on the plaque that it was also 'Eastcote Outstation' during wartime, or post-GCHQ was called 'RAF Lime Grove'

The local history society and the residents' association did well to arrange the plaque, even though few people will probably actually see it, in its current position, set back from a footpath. A circular wreath exists at time of writing, on the side of the angled brick plinth, a symbol of Remembrance Sunday, in November. If you wish to see the plaque, it can be located by a footpath, near the pedestrian crossing on Eastcote High Road, next to the Pembroke Park residential housing estate.

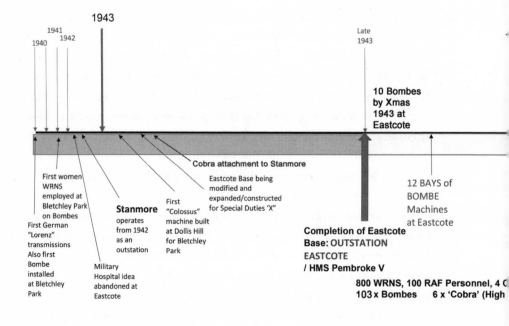

'OUTSTATION EASTCOTE' - Pembroke

1943

1941
1942
1940

Late
1943

10 Bombes
by Xmas
1943 at
Eastcote

Cobra attachment to Stanmore

First women
WRNS
employed at
Bletchley Park
on Bombes
First German
"Lorenz"
transmissions
Also first
Bombe
installed
at Bletchley
Park

Stanmore
operates
from 1942
as an
outstation

First
"Colossus"
machine built
at Dollis Hill
for Bletchley
Park

Eastcote Base being
modified and
expanded/constructed
for Special Duties 'X"

Military
Hospital idea
abandoned at
Eastcote

**Completion of Eastcote
Base:** OUTSTATION
**EASTCOTE
/ HMS Pembroke V**

12 BAYS of
BOMBE
Machines
at Eastcote

800 WRNS, 100 RAF Personnel, 4 O
103 x Bombes   6 x 'Cobra' (High

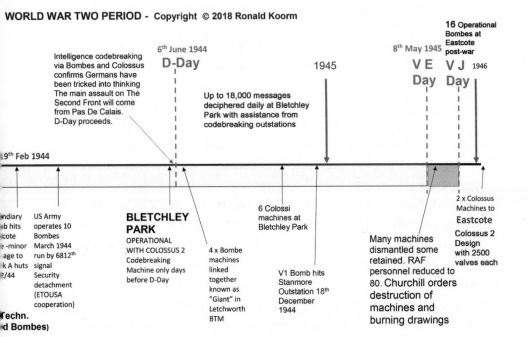

WORLD WAR TWO PERIOD - Copyright © 2018 Ronald Koorm

Intelligence codebreaking
via Bombes and Colossus
confirms Germans have
been tricked into thinking
The main assault on The
Second Front will come
from Pas De Calais.
D-Day proceeds.

6th June 1944
D-Day

Up to 18,000 messages
deciphered daily at Bletchley
Park with assistance from
codebreaking outstations

1945

8th May 1945
**V E
Day**

**V J
Day**
1946

16 Operational
Bombes at
Eastcote
post-war

l9th Feb 1944

ndiary
b hits
cote
e -minor
age to
k A huts
2/44

**Techn.
d Bombes)**

US Army
operates 10
Bombes
March 1944
run by 6812th
signal
Security
detachment
(ETOUSA
cooperation)

**BLETCHLEY
PARK**
OPERATIONAL
WITH COLOSSUS 2
Codebreaking
Machine only days
before D-Day

4 x Bombe
machines
linked
together
known as
"Giant" in
Letchworth
BTM

6 Colossi
machines at
Bletchley Park

V1 Bomb hits
Stanmore
Outstation 18th
December
1944

Many machines
dismantled some
retained. RAF
personnel reduced to
80. Churchill orders
destruction of
machines and
burning drawings

2 x Colossus
Machines to
Eastcote

Colossus 2
Design
with 2500
valves each

19

EASTCOTE AND SURROUNDINGS

Eastcote is within the London Borough of Hillingdon, one of the larger borough. It enjoys a substantial amount of green, open space.

Ruislip Lido, not far from the old outstation site, is a popular local attraction with a lake, beach, and extensive woods. In years gone by, the lake was popular for water-skiing and swimming. Both are now not permitted. A water-ski champion, David Nations, visited the Lido regularly to practise when water-skiing was still allowed in the 1950s and 1960s.

In the summer months, the beach gets very crowded with families,. A children's pirate ship dominates the large open, sandy beach. Cliff Richard's film *Summer Holiday* was filmed against the background of the sandy beach there, with the lake in the background. An upgrading programme by the local authority of new cafeterias, new car park, and other structures has been ongoing, and the trains have a new, smart engine shed.

A narrow-gauge railway takes children and their parents around the lake for a small charge, and is popular in summer and at Christmas. The woods around the lake are those which the US Army and other American personnel would have jogged and marched across when the base at Eastcote was operational post-war. Some recall American servicemen on the lido beach in the 1950s, listening to transistor radios, relaxing between military duties and shifts at the Eastcote base. This would have been when it was still GCHQ, or was transferring to Cheltenham. Donald Campbell's *Bluebird* went onto the Lake in 1959, and some residents at the time recall the ear-shattering noise of the engines. Several feature films were made at the lido site, including films with Kenneth More and Norman Wisdom.

During the war, anti-aircraft guns were hidden amongst the trees to discourage the Luftwaffe using the reservoir as a wayfinding point for the Northwood base. Over time the gun trenches were filled in as ponds.

There were three great houses in the area of Eastcote, being Eastcote House, Haydon Hall, and Highgrove House. Only the last remains, and that was rebuilt following a major fire in 1879.

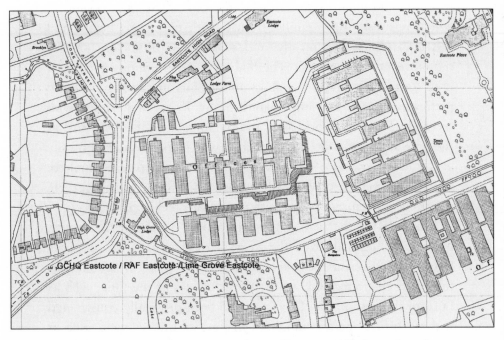

GCHQ Eastcote. (Original map courtesy of www.old-maps.co.uk/Ordnance Survey)

Eastcote House, half a mile or so north of the Outstation site, is sadly no longer in existence. That house was closed in 1962 and later demolished. It survived for almost five hundred years. A Lottery Fund grant enabled the Eastcote House Gardens, the Dovecote, Stables Block, and Walled Garden, to be upgraded some years ago.

The Stables originally went back to the early 17th century, and was later fronted with clay brickwork over the timber. Large structural cracks accentuated by tree root damage opened up the south-east gabled corner brickwork to alarming levels, allowing water penetration and further damage until it was rectified structurally at great cost. The author was involved with both measured and photographic surveys on this site, liaising with engineers, prior to the funding being confirmed, and co-ordinated with local Bat Conservation officers, in relation to the old buildings and physical features on the site. Repairs to the Stables block roofing had to be severely restricted and controlled, to ensure minimal disturbance of the bats. 'The Stables' Block, which is substantially timber-framed with enormous beams and rafters, attracts bats locally, and several bat boxes are around the Dovecote in the trees. The Stables is a community facility, is used for exhibitions, crafts, talks and events. In 2018 it displayed pictures, cuttings and information about locals at Eastcote who served in The First World War, and the impact on the local area at the time and post-war. The Dovecote, which was once structurally at risk to one corner of the building, has been structurally repaired, as have the perimeter walls of the large, attractive walled garden, which have been reinforced with structural steel in places.

The walls of the walled garden go back to the 17th century, but were modified over the years. The Dovecote at Eastcote House was given a retrospective licence in 1601 to be built, as they were restricted only to the upper classes at the time, such as Lord of the manor. The Dovecote had been originally constructed without official permission. The pigeons and doves were used as supplementary cattle feed.

Entrance to Pembroke Park showing the public footpath which divided the Outstation into two parts.

These gardens, both the walled gardens and surrounding landscaped and bordered areas, are very popular locally, and lovingly tended by local volunteer gardeners.

The High street at Eastcote lost its Barclay's Bank a few years ago, the same Bank Branch which set up the GCHQ account in April 1946. The public footpath, which now divides Pembroke Park residential estate, remains as the sole physical feature left after the demolition and redevelopment of the Eastcote base. The treelined path is a quarter of a mile long. There are several path junctions from the estate and surrounding residential roads feeding into the long main footpath. The plaque and plinth which commemorates the Outstation and GCHQ is on Eastcote High Road. Some aerial views of the commencement of the demolition of the old site are available online.

Highgrove House still stands a few metres away from the public footpath. There is no sign to indicate its history. It was an 18th-century house, destroyed by fire, and later rebuilt. There is a separate access road leading up to it and the lake. One can wander down a short path to come out to Kent Gardens, a cul-de sac of residential two-storey housing constructed some considerable time after Lime Grove. Following this around to the east, it leads via a small T-junction into Lime Grove, which terminates at the North end to become the south entrance to Pembroke Park estate. Nearby, the 'Siger's', nowadays a residential road, was once a farm and a nursery. It was to the south-east of the site.

The St Thomas More Roman Catholic church to the east of the outstation site, has since been rebuilt to a modern specification, and is accessed near the eastern end of the old footpath at the intersection with the Field End Road. The church was built in 1977 and consecrated in 1978. The Parish of Eastcote was founded in 1935. In 1939, the Parish had around 15,000 people as residents, and was growing. An older precast single-storey concrete building structure with a corrugated roof is nearby, but may not have been part of the post-war outstation.

The main shopping parade runs up to Eastcote station on the Piccadilly and Metropolitan lines. There is no sign of any of the cafes which the Wrens and personnel frequented during their breaks away from the Bombes. No sign remains of the café where the slip of paper from the outstation was found on the floor, indicating a careless security breach, and leading to various security talks to base personnel. At least one report mentions Kerswall's café during the war. Some of the public houses remain nearby, such as 'The Case is Altered', and are very popular in the summer months. The old cinema at Eastcote, the 'Ideal', was demolished many years ago.

The Eastcote Residents Association website has a section compiled by the RNELH Society, and refers to HMS Pembroke and its replacement by Pembroke Park housing estate, and the names of estate roads reflecting some of the history. Names include 'Wren Lane', 'Flowers Avenue', 'Blagrove', and 'Aitken Close' and 'Blagrove Crescent. Blocks of flats include Beaumanor House, Bletchley House, Flowerdown Court, Denmark Hill House and Alexander Court. Susan Toms of the local history society published a glossary of the road names and their relevance to the codebreaking activities.

Not all of the recommendations of proposed names were selected by the developer, but choices were made from the list provided by both the history society and the local residents' association. It is good to have Tommy Flowers surname as one of the longest avenues on the estate. The site is split into two, the north entrance of the residential estate is accessed via Eastcote High Road, and the south portion is accessed via Lime Grove. Lime Grove, of course, was one of the main entrances to the outstation, to Pembroke V and GCHQ over the years.

At Haydon Hall Park, shared with Eastcote cricket club, a nearby concrete single-storey low level building positioned near The Case is Altered pub (and adjacent directly to a nursery school), was built for the purpose of decontamination after nuclear attack. The date of construction is not entirely clear, but was probably the

Road names to the residential housing estate at Pembroke Park. (Pembroke Park Estate, photos Ronald Koorm)

early 1950s. It became a billiards club in February 2013. Haydon Hall house was demolished in 1964.

The Black Horse pub still exists on Eastcote High Road. Presently called 'Nico's', it is Eastcote's oldest pub, and is grade-two listed. The pub is in more 270 years old, and was the site of a murder many years ago.

Eastcote Library is at the upper end of Field End Road at the end of the Eastcote shopping parade. It is a few hundred yards from the outstation base, and the author gave his very first talk on 'Eastcote to GCHQ' there, in September 2018.[91] At the initial talk, some local Pembroke Park residents attended, who were pleased to learn something of the history of their site. Later on that day the author was introduced to a local resident who had worked with Tommy Flowers after the war. This resident worked with him at The Post Office Research Establishment at Dollis Hill, North London, the man who designed and built the world's first semi-programmable digital electronic computer. Some of the older local Eastcote residents remember clearly the post-war GCHQ/RAF Eastcote/Eastcote Lime Grove base as children growing up, and one or two worked there.

Not far away is Ruislip, the site of Manor Farm, a medieval heritage site with an old moat, and barn. The Old Barn dates back to the thirteenth century, and is one of the oldest in England. The original castle dates back to the ninth century. The area is steeped in history and is within a conservation area. Medieval jousting, demonstrations of old crafts, medieval costumes and armoured displays have proved popular during the summer months. The Manor at Ruislip is mentioned in Domesday Book.

Bombing took its toll in Eastcote, Ruislip and the surrounding area during the war, and some bomb maps are available for 1941, when some properties were damaged or destroyed. However, fortunately, the destruction was not on a large scale. Much of the housing was built in the 1930s and gives the area the character it possesses today.

The local authority community hall adjacent to The Manor Farm site is named Winston Churchill Hall. A fitting tribute to the man who studied at length detailed summaries of Bombe-decoded intercepts in Downing Street, which may well have originated at Eastcote; the same man who visited Highgrove House on his honeymoon in 1908, only a few yards away from the site of the future Outstation Eastcote.

Could we have preserved any of the buildings? If it was suggested that Westminster Abbey or The Royal Albert Hall be demolished for residential housing, there would be a public outcry. Not so with the Eastcote or Stanmore Outstations. But the comparison is of course absurd. The outstations were a combination of barracks, stores, galley kitchens, quite basic buildings. It is not so much the buildings themselves, but what was done in them, and how they interacted with Bletchley Park and other bases, which changed history.

The buildings were of basic construction, could not easily have been upgraded without concealing much of the external and internal structure and finishes, and what would you then use them for? A museum? But a museum has to be staffed, funded, maintained. It is one thing having it in an accessible place, like central London, or Manchester, or Birmingham, but the numbers of visitors in Eastcote would be minimal annually, and it would probably need to be heavily subsidised.

The islands of Jersey and Guernsey, within the Channel Islands, had a similar problem, but they have one enormous advantage over Eastcote and Stanmore. Those islands attract thousands of tourists from Britain and France annually, and the underground military hospitals, and the gun enplacements and mini-museums on the island do get visited by tourists and enthusiasts, so they keep going. They have numerous older concrete lined gun emplacements/ turrets and features built by slave labour under the Nazis. Some of them are left to the elements, the harsh winds and the corrosive sea air, causing corrosion of the steelwork over time. There are too many structures to preserve them all spread around the islands, many in inaccessible rocky places, difficult to access, and not really viable to be part of a museum. But even those unmanned structures can be photographed or painted.

The Channel Islands concentrate upon those WW2 features which are viable to open to the public, and some are kept going by volunteers to keep costs under control. The Channel Islands military Museum in St Ouen, on Jersey, is particularly interesting, and gives a flavour of what it must have been like to be in a German lookout post, defending the Island from Allied invasion forces. D-Day of course, by-passed the Channel Islands, much to the consternation of the locals, but probable relief to the occupiers, who would not have stood a chance against the scale of the D-Day force, had they included Jersey, Guernsey, Alderney and Sark. They were not seen as high priority by the Allies at the time, for good reason. The range and diversity of structures, including the German Underground Hospital, are a fascinating, historical insight into what it must have been like to be under German Occupation during the war, and the closest one we have.

So, we have to be practical in preserving wartime structures, buildings, and sites. If we are unable to retain such places as Eastcote, then perhaps we should consider a site elsewhere to rebuild Block 'B' as a replica, and make it part of a larger, more accessible site?

Ideally, such a proposition would be better suited to Bletchley Park, which already is a museum, and adds important features and exhibitions from time to time. But it could also be considered in London, more centrally, more accessible to people, subject to land costs and commercial viability. Or it could be a roving exhibition to be displayed at festivals, events, etc. It would make a good advertising base for recruiting women to the services, if handled in a sensitive way.

A modern alternative, to preserve the heritage of the codebreaking Outstations in some form, would to be to create a virtual digital site to show the layout, space, furniture and arrangements, much like an architect's modelling of a large building enables a 'walk-through' for the client, to experience the scale and layout of the building. Whilst not cheap to produce accurately, it would be much cheaper than reconstructing the blocks and codebreaking machines on real land. It has the added advantage of being more accessible to more people, and could easily form part of an educational experience at exhibitions and events. Food for thought.

As regards Outstation Eastcote and its further development after the war, the Blocks 'A' and 'B' referred to earlier in the text Block 'B' was to become Blocks 1, 2 and 4 and Block 'A' was later Block 3.

Block 1 housed the code construction section, administration and a cafeteria. Constructed *c.* April 1942

Block 2 was analytical machinery and later on, Colossus computers. Commenced late 1943.

Block 3 was mainly the operational part, northern part commenced late 1943.

Block 4 may have been stores and support section. This is listed by Historic England to have been erected in 1947 for GCHQ.

Map showed the the Block numbers written against the buildings on the site. The Official Monument code of the Eastcote site is 1400211, location TQ 10558 88313.[92]

Although not in the same borough as Eastcote, a few miles away to the north lies Stanmore (L.B. of Harrow) and Bentley Priory, which is now a refurbished RAF museum. The main site surrounding the base is a landscaped, gated residential estate, but the Grade II listed building itself, housing the museum, and which has had not one but two fires over the years, is quite magnificent architecturally. It contains a fine collection of RAF memorabilia.

This site was the headquarters of Fighter Command and worked closely with the RAF Uxbridge Battle of Britain bunker during the war. There was no codebreaking at these RAF bases, but there were sometimes female intelligence RAF personnel to help

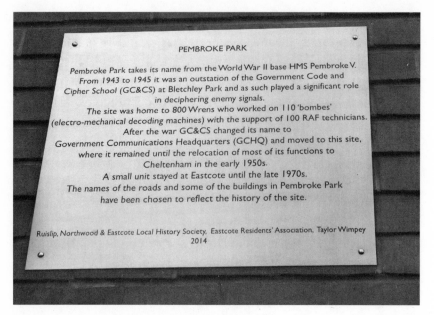

Plaque commemorating Outstation Eastcote/Pembroke V.

coordinate the information coming in from radar, observer corps and aircraft sightings. There was a runway on the site during the war in 1943 for a time, to aid communications and planning for D-Day. Churchill, Eisenhower, and King George VI visited Bentley Priory that day on 6 June 1944. It would have a key role in monitoring the D-Day landings progress in the underground bunker, along with other sites.

Bentley Priory had an important role to play post-war, during the Cold War period, and there was a nuclear underground bunker on the site in the 1980s, but is no longer accessible, being sealed up for reasons of health and safety. When Strike Command combined two arms of the RAF, both Bomber Command and Fighter Command in 1968, there were to be inevitable reductions in both manpower and equipment. It then became an administrative and training centre.

Coordination of air-defence eventually relocated to Wycombe and Northwood after the war, and the site was closed for some time, whilst the surrounding residential development was evaluated.

Bentley Priory houses a range of awarded medals such as the DFC and bar for bravery in the RAF. It has one extraordinary exhibit: a letter written to his parents by the chap who dropped Douglas Bader's artificial legs to him from a British bomber into a prisoner of war camp in Germany. That such a letter actually survived the war is quite astonishing.

Air Chief Marshal Hugh Dowding's office room is in this building, where he fought for fighter-support against several politicians and senior military officers, to shape the RAF strategy against the Luftwaffe. Churchill trusted him, and the British narrowly avoided allocating all valuable fighters to a doomed attempt to defend France. Dowding was close to retirement when he took on the challenge of coordinating air force and defence. He was the right man for the job, but it would be 'touch and go' as regards having sufficient resources at the time.

Whilst Bentley Priory thankfully survives, sadly, the Outstation Stanmore base down the road, along Watling Street/Elstree Road, is no longer in existence, built upon by much-needed housing. One wonders if the children of the residents in the housing on that estate know what went on there, during the war, and the part that Outstation Stanmore played?

20

COLOSSUS, MICHIE AND A.I.

After the war, two Colossus machines were just sent to Eastcote 'for mothballing.' While that might have been Bletchley Park's intention, the two Colossi were used post-war, and most probably not just for training purposes. However, the details of some of the uses may still be classified.

Several 'Robinson' machines went to Eastcote after the war, but it is not known if those were just stored away, or used for some purpose such as training. The 'Robinson' was the predecessor to Colossus, but nowhere near as advanced technically, or as reliable.

Robinson was built at three different locations, and required much close cooperation and coordination. It was complicated, not particularly reliable due to having to synchronise two large loops of punched tape at high speed. It did not have an adjustable wheel (according to some Wren operators), to tension the tape, so the tapes had to be pulled carefully onto the wheels before it could start operating, and paper tape breakages were common. This was partly also because of the perforations in the narrow paper weakening the paper and allowing tears.

It was not an elegant solution, as one had to spend a lot of time checking and synchronising lengthy tapes. If they were even

Robinson.

slightly out of synchronization, they would not give the results required. But Robinson served its purpose and bought the Allies a little time. Flowers did build part of it (a combination unit), and made later modifications, but was rather critical of its design. He had other, more ambitious ideas... Colossus. Colossus, in general terms, was designed to mechanize a statistical method of counting the frequency of the letter characters in an intelligence message. This was aided with optical readers of the high-speed punched tape, and of course the many valves as digital switches. It was semi-programmable via a plugboard panel.

GCHQ at Eastcote were provided with the Colossus Mark 2 versions which had approximately 2,400 valves each, and worked five times faster than the original models, at an astonishing 25,000 characters per second. There was no way that this rate of processing, or anywhere near it, could be achieved on a Robinson machine. It was too poor a design, by comparison with Colossus, and the paper tape would have ripped and broken at a fraction of those speeds. Perforated tape was substituted with non-punched tape and optical readers read the dots and ink coded markings.

As only ten Colossi were built during the war (an eleventh was partly built, but was stopped as the war ended), Eastcote then had access to 20% of the Colossi built.

Improvements were made by the team who had assembled them, or reassembled them. Dollis Hill sent staff down to Eastcote to assist. Did Tommy Flowers visit Eastcote GCHQ to help set up the Colossi? Most probably. At the time, there was very little specialist expertise on those machines around. This still was all top-secret, even after war's end, and there would have been very few people to assemble and connect it all together and to test it. It is highly likely that Tommy Flowers helped to set the machines up at Eastcote. The local history society appears to have some confirmation of this. The Colossi transferred to Eastcote were called 'RED' and 'BLUE'.

So much for following Winston Churchill's instructions to destroy all the machines after the war. Most were destroyed, but these two did remain, at least until sent eventually to Cheltenham.

There is a quite a difference between the monstrous scale of 'Colossus 2', and your smartphone, but there are most likely common elements in both. The process of development had to go through numerous stages, and it matters not that the origins of the smartphone might have by-passed Colossus due to imposed UK secrecy, post-war. The principles of digital processing are common to both. Colossus was not as adaptable as your smartphone to run countless programmes, or Apps. It didn't need to be. It had one key objective and that was to help decipher Lorenz intercepts. It could not decipher the entire message, it wasn't designed to do that. That is where the mathematicians and others at Bletchley came in.

When Flowers proposed the idea of Colossus to those at Bletchley Park, he had a mixed reaction. His proposal to use thousands of valves was looked upon as peculiar, wasteful of resources, and liable to failure. Flowers realized that if the valves were kept on for long periods, the chance of valve failure was minimal, and he was correct. Max Newman at Bletchley, a key codebreaker and head of the 'Newmanry', supported Flowers. Turing also did, and he had initially introduced Flowers to Newman.

The funding for Colossus was not confirmed for some time however, and time was not on their side. If Colossus had not been built, they would have been left with a half-hearted approach, through Robinson, a bit of this, a bit of that, rather 'Heath-Robinson' in fact. That, and manual methods of codebreaking Lorenz. Robinson was built at different sites, and was a forerunner to the much more advanced Colossus. But they needed speed to cope with the many messages coming through and being intercepted on the FISH intelligence links. These were links with fishy names such as 'Jellyfish', 'Bream', 'Stickleback', 'Sturgeon' and others. Jellyfish would be of particular interest to the Allies, being the Paris-Berlin encoded security link.

The importance of intercepting these links was not in dispute, they were providing key strategic information from the German High Command. Messages that could come from Hitler himself to his key Generals and Field Marshals. Yet, there is no statue or celebration of Tommy Flowers for his efforts that very possibly helped to change the war in the Allies' favour. Flowers continued to work for a time, after the war at Dollis Hill. His sailing dinghy was sometimes seen sailing on the Welsh Harp (In L.B. Brent), and was sometimes sailed for him by an Eastcote resident who worked with him post-war at Dollis Hill on radio telecoms.

When Churchill learnt of the potential of breaking into the *Geheimschreiber*/FISH intelligence, he ordered full steam ahead on the production of Colossus. Churchill may not have understood the technical construction or detail, but he knew that intercepting the German advanced encoding machines used for strategic intelligence would most probably save countless Allied lives. It might even shorten the war.

One of the codebreakers at Bletchley Park who was to make a significant contribution to the Colossus project, and who later on was to become a pioneer of Artificial Intelligence (AI), was a man called Donald Michie, later to become Professor Donald Michie.

He worked closely with Alan Turing at Bletchley, and they were jointly interested in having programmable machines. Michie made some last-minute important changes to Colossus 2, which was ready just in time for D-Day. These changes were to improve the semi-programmable part of the world's first electronic computer. In 1986 Professor Michie became head of the Turing Trust in Cambridge. He was doing advanced research work in machine learning, involving robotics and computer vision.

Back at Bletchley, Michie was introducing ground-breaking systems for automatic deciphering of German codes Working in the specialist section of the Bletchley Park 'Newmanry', and liaising with the 'Testery' section, he was a key player in the analysis of FISH encoded data, along with the rest of the 'team. His work with Colossus enabled the deciphering of the second wheel on the Lorenz German encoding machine. The innovation was tested by Michie and Jack Good. We might never know how significant these changes to Colossus 2 were, in the big picture of things, and processing German High Command intelligence, just before and after D-Day.

Colossus machine. (Courtesy of GCHQ)

Discussions were held with Michie and Turing about the possibility of building computer programs that would communicate and display intelligence, and to play the highly complex game of chess. They foresaw machine computation taking away the burden of calculation work from man, and pass it onto automatic computers. Turing had prior to the war developed mathematical systems of logic in digital computation. He was way ahead of his time. One can only wonder what difference it would have made to the development of modern computers in the UK after the war, if the veil of secrecy had been lifted much earlier, particularly with men such as Turing, Flowers, Michie, Tutte, Welchman, Newman and Ralph Tester on hand.

As it turned out, the Americans and others developed digital computers after the war at an advanced rate, and Britain was left behind, mainly due to the Official Secrets Act restrictions that applied to the Bletchley and outstation personnel. Destruction of the Bombes and Colossus on Churchill's instructions, and the burning of blueprints and drawings immediately after the war compounded this error. Gordon Welchman recalls the time when he put the codebreaking machine drawings into a furnace and watched them burn. A few machines survived, and some went onto Eastcote, and even Birmingham, contrary to Churchill's orders.

We tend to define these pioneers by their wartime codebreaking work. However, Michie went on to do further pioneering work, some of which affects all of us today, in the field of machine-learning and A.I. A.I. is becoming more important in our world as we develop driverless cars, advanced diagnostic medicine techniques, and an infinite range of other A.I. applications.

When working at GEC in the 1960s and 1970s in Wembley, an old schoolfriend of the author worked with Professor Michie, who was then based at Edinburgh University, on advanced medical systems. Professor Michie's obituary (1923–2007), indicated he made a great contribution in the challenging field of medical science, together with his wife.

He developed machines after the war to play noughts and crosses automatically (*Menace*), and was the editor of many books and papers on A.I. and machine learning. Restrictions on research funding limited his work somewhat, but he still managed to help prepare the ground for what the Japanese and others were developing in robotics, visual sensory robotics, and A.I. Both he and his wife, Dame Anne McLaren, became experts in the field of in-vitro-fertilization.

Professor Michie became chair of an Artificial Intelligence research unit in the early to mid-1960s, when very few had ever heard of it. He, like Turing, was ahead of his time. He became Director of the University of Edinburgh's Department of Machine Intelligence and Perception, linked to the University's science computer unit. Michie had also nurtured newbie codebreaker Roy Jenkins, at Bletchley Park, who was later to become Chancellor. Jenkins was too late for Enigma decoding but was to work in the 'Testery', joining in 1942, helping to hand-break Lorenz and Tunny intercepts. Jenkins worked on intelligence until the end of the war. No doubt his attention to detail at Bletchley Park helped his political career considerably.

The challenge of breaking FISH and Lorenz all those years ago was a stimulus to Michie, and his colleagues, whether they worked in the 'Newmanry' or 'Testery' at Bletchley, or in the Post Office Research Establishment at Dollis Hill, or elsewhere.

For Flowers, Michie and others to get Colossus 2 ready for D-Day was like designing and building the first rocket ship to go to the moon, with very limited testing before you press that firing button. But these people were committed, and knew what they were doing, led by Tommy Flowers. He was later awarded a prize for his work and a cheque for £1,000. Some prize for helping to save the UK and the Allies from Hitler.

It was mainly Flower's research manager, Radley, who, as director, supported him in the venture to construct Colossus initially. Colossus might not have been built if Flowers had not taken the initiative and progressed the task with Radley's blessing and initial funding, assembled a team of engineers, and got on with the job. Or, at best, the start of building Colossus might have been delayed by months. The nightmare scenario is that Hitler could have used that extra time to develop atomic weapons.

Max Newman had faith in Tommy Flowers, and they worked well together, but the start of the programme as regards organization and funding left a great deal to be desired. In hindsight, that was largely the fault of Bletchley Park. Newman, Radley, Flowers, overcame the indecision at Bletchley Park by having faith in the Colossus objective, even though this was at some risk to them if the project had failed.

The creation of Colossus relied principally on the Post Office Research Establishment at Dollis Hill. For Tommy Flowers to design and build them in the time, given their complexity and resourcing problems, was nothing short of a miracle. Flowers, was one of few who had experience with valve technology in other projects for the Post Office, and knew what they could achieve. He was up against many negative views, from Bletchley and elsewhere in going down this route. There was clearly an initial lack of commitment on the part of Bletchley Park. Otherwise, why would Flowers have to dig into his own pocket to fund certain materials? Turing did not develop 'Colossus', and took a back seat in this respect, but could perceive that Flowers had ability that Bletchley Park could benefit from.

Welchman did not get on with Flowers, however, and thought his use of valves in large numbers was a complete waste of resources. But Flowers was essentially an engineer, and a practical one at that. Turing, in comparison, a genius of a mathematician, needed guidance in practical conversion of his ideas to an end result. When a building is designed, there needs to be an architectural brief before it can be developed. The architect or designer often will prepare that brief with the client, and talk it through and fine-tune it before commencing drawings.

The brief for the Colossus was developed largely by Max Newman at Bletchley Park. Which parts of the Lorenz machine or 'Tunny' needed to be broken, so that the mathematicians and staff at Bletchley Park in the 'Newmanry' and 'Testery', could do their bit?

Newman and others had discussions with Flowers to see what was possible, but it was Flowers alone who had the vision for a valve-based processing machine to process the non-Morse teleprinter coded messages that came into Knockholt and Denmark Hill. It was one thing having developed solutions for the Post Office using valves, on exchanges and other equipment, but a completely different challenge to design and build a monstrosity of a machine using electronic valves on such a large scale; and to convince your team it would work, and admit that some of the ideas would need constant review during the process. This was quite a risk for Flowers. There were to be no second chances.

Colossus was never going to decipher the entire intelligence message, but was designed to eliminate certain settings on selected rotors on Lorenz. It was a process of elimination of millions of settings. One still needed humans to do the last stages to crack the code, but Colossus saved enormous amounts of time, and time was everything in war.

Unlike Robinson, Colossus used non-sprocketed paper tape so it was much stronger and was able to accelerate to very high speeds, almost sixty miles per hour before the tape would fail. There was only one tape, not two. The first model achieved 5000 characters per second, being read through a small photo-electric cell, which had to be kept clean by the Wrens and maintenance engineers. As Colossus was introduced, the accuracy of processing intelligence, and the speed, improved. It was ironic, that Robinson, built largely at Dollis Hill, was heavily criticised by Flowers, who worked in the same organisation that helped build it; perhaps an embarrassment for P.O.R.E., and for Bletchley Park too.

Flowers had quite a bit of experience of using valve technology in post-office telephone equipment, and was effectively scaling up, using thousands of thermionic valves. Of course, Colossus, being a specialist machine for a unique purpose of codebreaking, would not bear any resemblance to Post Office telephone exchange equipment. It would, however, contain many of the same components, for the purposes of both economy and speed of construction.

The setting up of the first Colossus after transporting it from Dollis Hill, amazed the team, as it worked on a test the first time, and on repeated tests also. It did what it was designed to do.

After the war, at the Post Office Research Establishment, Flowers was not given the opportunity to develop his knowledge and ability to any great degree, beyond making advanced telephone exchange equipment for the post office, but he was asked to develop 'ERNIE' (or Electronic Random Number Indicator Equipment) the premium bond random number generator. The key to fairness for the punter who wanted to gamble with premium bonds was the randomness of the numbers generated. Enigma was not generating random letters, there was a pattern to find. Lorenz, was not a truly random generator. Had Enigma been truly random in its mechanism and generation of letters, it would have been far more difficult to decode messages, maybe even impossible.

Codebreakers love patterns. Repeating patterns are the key to success. It seems that ERNIE (now in version 4), is probably as random as you can get, as it is based on thermal noise of transistors (i.e. voltage and heat fluctuations), and is tested by an independent actuary monthly, to see that it remains random, and no patterns are generated.

Their test or tests are applied to see if the results are *statistically* random. But we all know that you can present statistics in certain ways to give the answer you require. How random? To what degree? I doubt if Tommy Flowers lost sleep over this problem. He did his best, and came up with a system that was far more advanced than Enigma in generating random characters. But, then again, Arthur Scherbius, the Enigma designer, may have well decided that he had no intention of generating random letters, but needed just enough complexity in the design, semi-randomness if you like, to stop the enemy penetrating the cipher. He failed.

Perhaps he could not have foreseen the sloppiness and lazy approach of many of the German Enigma operators. He could not have predicted the resending of near identical encoded messages using the same settings, allowing the British to penetrate the cipher with cribs or clues arising directly from the poor procedures. The consequences of the operators failing to follow the Enigma protocol and rules, were cumulative and contributed to a series of Nazi and Italian failures that would help to bring their downfall. No one could accuse Scherbius of being responsible for the failure of Enigma operators to follow the correct procedures, but maybe he could have thought ahead, and built in various extra safety features to reduce the impact of incorrect procedures. But Scherbius needed to get his machine to market, and recover his manufacturing costs. 'Tweaking' the machine to improve security would come later.

There are many examples of aircraft accidents where the cause was down to a maintenance engineer who modified a small part, because it didn't fit the aperture or housing, sometimes because it was the incorrect part chosen. It is not easy to design out problems when operators and technicians effectively by-pass the operational rules entirely. This is what Scherbius was up against: human nature, boredom, wanting to take short cuts in operational procedures, would all contribute to mistakes and opportunities for the allied codebreakers, both with Enigma and Lorenz. One German operator would broadcast via Enigma that it was so very hot in Italy, and his mind was clearly not on operational procedures.

Flowers used a gas neon diode to produce 2000 random number per hour when his ERNIE machine was first developed. Later, in the twenty-first century, ERNIE 4 produced, a million random numbers per hour by comparison. It cannot be 'hacked' by outsiders as it is only connected to the electricity supply by a plug. Flowers did well to tackle a difficult and unique problem at the time. Software at present can only generate pseudo-random numbers; you could say that nature is more random than machines.

One of the tests for computers and software, therefore, is to devise a program and system that can generate truly random numbers. Humans have great difficulty generating random numbers themselves. Sooner or later a pattern emerges if you shout out random numbers, or write them down. Mankind has survived life with computers without truly random numbers, but nature has probably provided the randomness in the stars, universe, and beyond. Scientists, mathematicians, and philosophers will take this question further in future. In the meantime, we can say that Tommy Flowers started the ball rolling.

In January 2019, the BBC had a series of programmes outlining pioneers in the areas of culture, science, etc., called *Icons*. There were four contenders for the Science category; Albert Einstein, Marie Curie, the Chinese scientist, Tu Youyou, who discovered the key treatment for malaria, and Alan Turing. The BBC presenter called the Bombes 'Computers'. They were not computers. They were electro-mechanical machines. The presenter outlined some of the role and vision of Alan Turing and his various technical papers (including 'Computing machinery and Intelligence' published in 1950 in 'Mind'). He wrote numerous mathematical equations and papers over his career, outlining his vision for a computing machine.

Turing was adamant that there was out there a 'Universal Machine', which could be adaptable and used to calculate many different problems, but it would take some considerable expertise to bring it to fruition. Turing had Asperger's syndrome, and did not fit in well socially with others. He was a bit of a loner. But that enabled him to bury himself into his maths, logic and equations, and come up with the idea for the Bombe. But others had to convert his ideas into practical machines. Just having the idea alone is not enough. The design of the equipment needs to be developed to a practical level, otherwise it is just an idea. You can't easily patent an idea.

The key difference with Alan Turing, is that he saw the world in mathematical terms. Everything could be converted, or explained mathematically in his eyes and brain. But he would not get past his sketches without bringing in many experts to develop those ideas further. He may even have some difficulty explaining his concepts to some of them, as he was not an engineer, and may not have appreciated fully the limitations of what could be achieved in practice. But sometimes not knowing the boundaries and limitations may stimulate others into developing innovative practical solutions.

The development of the laser in the 1960s was a scientific milestone, and yet, scientists and others did not fully appreciate what a laser could be used for longer term at the time, the range of applications.[93] It took time to develop those applications, and now lasers are everywhere, in audio and video equipment, security scanners, medical equipment, survey measuring equipment, scanning objects, 3-D printing, gunsights, rangefinding, astronomical use, etc. Your 'Blu-Ray'™ disc is laser-based, as is the army's military tank rangefinders for their guns, the bricklayer's alignment tools to obtain a level line, and the surveyor's theodolite. Remove lasers from modern society and the public would quickly become aware of how influential that technology has been.

Fibre-optics was another ground-breaking technology which uses light and pulsed light to help our communications and links to computers. The first fibre-optics designed would have not achieved anywhere near the distances to send data that we can use today, as the materials had to be developed to obtain the best efficiency in sending pulsed wavelengths of light down very fine, small diameter tubes of glass, and synthetics. It would have been another case of developing a technology first, and then establishing what this could really do for us longer term. Today, fibre-optics is rapidly replacing copper-cabling for data transmissions. With special light-amplification equipment along the fibres, it enables us to transmit data over many kilometres.

If fibre-optics had been around in Turing's era, teleprinters and telephone landlines would have been much faster, connected by optical fibres (together with light amplifiers at strategic positions), compared with copper wires. The story of fibre-optics begins in Bell laboratories in the 1880s, when the 'Photophone' was invented. This permitted telephone conversations through the transmission of sound using light. In 2006, the data transmission rate achieved in optical fibres reached some 14 Tbit/s per second over 140 km. In 2011, the data transmission rate achieved was 101 Tbit/s. In 2018, the record for a single-cable data transmission rate was 159 Tbit/s. The next generation fibre optics will exceed this. There is a clear overlap of laser technology with that of advanced fibre-optics, which is transforming data transmissions and telecommunications. Your smartphone, the internet, military security, and many other systems and devices are now dependent upon it.

Turing was a visionary, and just needed the technology of the day to catch up with him. He could communicate his ideas to others sufficiently well to make progress with his Bombe machines. He worked constructively with his colleagues such as Gordon Welchman, and was a little put out that he himself had not come up with the idea of the diagonal board electrical circuit for the Bombe. It was such a logical idea, but he accepted his colleague's proposal and was pleased the Bombe could be made even more efficient than before.

Was it really the case that the Bombe, and Turing's visions and papers, gave rise to the smartphone' and all future computers? Certainly, Turing had the Universal-learning-machine vision, and made really significant progress in machine technology. But wasn't Tommy Flowers closer to starting the computer age in practical terms, in designing and building Colossus?

Turing won the BBC viewer's vote on 16 January, 2019 as the most significant icon in the field of science and in February 2019 he won out of all the categories, as the most influential person in the BBC *Icon* series. His vision and ability should not be overlooked. He helped to change the world in the direction it went to a significant degree. But then, so did many others, and some of those people had little or no recognition for their achievements.

Flowers was made an OBE, and awarded a prize of £1,000. That sum hardly reimbursed him for the money he had personally put into the Colossus-build. Flowers became quite frustrated after the war, when he wanted to work on advanced computers, but the GPO directed him to work on electronic telephone exchanges instead. After all, that was his job.

In 1936, Turing's paper on the Universal computing machine, was way ahead of his time. Turing worked on the design of the 'ACE' computer post-war, and had prepared a paper on an electronic calculator. But the Americans were farther ahead, and the restriction on the work at Bletchley Park severely limited developments in the UK, so Turing was at a significant disadvantage. Add to that his personal difficulties and persecution, and he became more frustrated over time. In 1948 Turing produced and published an essay called 'Intelligent Machinery'. This attempted to show how machines could be developed to act as the human brain did, with relevant logic circuits and processes. It was probing how intelligent machines might emulate human behaviour. This was a radical proposal at the time.

Another paper, 'Computing Machinery and Intelligence', went further still. The game of chess was considered by Turing, the choice of moves available, and planning strategy as a human might, looking several moves ahead, whilst obeying the rules of the game. His vision of artificial intelligence anticipated progress in the 1950s, linking hardware and software programming, using the human brain as an analogy. Turing would mentioned 'the unorganized machine', one which was perhaps several modules or sections, which were limited in use by themselves, but when combined with the appropriate instruction, to control and give structure, would become organised.

The idea of Artificial Intelligence was a distant dream at the time of the Second World War, but Turing had been playing around with ideas with Donald Michie on making machines work for man on a large scale, and using logic processing. It was not, at that stage, Artificial Intelligence, but learning machines certainly were discussed at some length. Colossus certainly wasn't A.I. After all it was only semi-programmable, and needed people to set it up (Engineers, and Wrens), and to monitor its output constantly. It was perhaps, a first stage on the long, complex road to A.I.

The author recalls being shown a plastic case full of miniature metal or synthetic 'rings' in the early 1960' by his older brother, who worked in electronics. Those rings were an early version of memory storage. It is not known if they were just experimental, or were actually used in an early computer. We have gone from manually setting hundreds of switches on early computers, to punched cards, to magnetic wires, to magnetic tapes, to magnetic drums, to spinning hard drives, to SSDs, all within a relatively short time. There is even research on using bacteria and micro-organic life in nature for possible memory storage. The processors and chips are increasing in capacity for processing data exponentially, but one needs to consider Moore's law when predicting future advances in this area.[92]

Turing's genius was dampened due to a combination of factors, but the largest impact was his persecution for being gay, and the medical treatment that was forcibly imposed upon him in exchange for avoiding a prison sentence. He never really recovered from that, and took his own life. If times had been different, he may have gone on to do greater things, working alongside other specialists and pioneers. He inspired Michie and others to carry out further research in A.I., and to aim higher than before in science and technology. Some individuals are 'driven' in their quest for achieving their objectives. Turing was like that. So were Welchman, Flowers, Michie, Lever. The environment they worked in would have a great impact on their achievements and recognition in history.

Marie Curie, by comparison, achieved considerable success in her important scientific discoveries despite being discriminated against to a large degree as a woman scientist, and yet this almost seemed to make her a stronger person. She had to overcome many difficulties at different stages in her life, but still had children, continued to develop portable X-ray equipment for the battlefield, and saved numerous lives. Curie discovered Radium and new elements purely due to her determination, drive and energy, and was eventually awarded the Nobel Prize after initially being overlooked. In current times, prejudice against women scientists may still exist in places, but we have moved forward significantly compared with years ago, and this should make for better understanding of A.I., with male and female scientists, programmers, and developers working more closely together.

China has announced the world's first female A.I. news anchor for TV[94] Her name is Xin Xiomeng. Is this the future? Very possibly. In time, we won't be able to tell the difference between a human, and an A.I. machine. Turing, Michie, and others laid the groundwork for all this. We still have some considerable way to go, but the rate of advancement in A.I. will be soon be exponential. It will completely change the way that we work, play, are entertained, socialize, have medical treatment, travel, educate ourselves and our children, and help defend our country from both physical attack and cyber-attack.

Michie later went on to develop and invent the process of 'Memoization', a specialist technique of computer optimization, which rapidly speeds up computer programmes and is still used today. He was still preparing papers in 2007 when he and his wife were tragically killed in a road accident on the way to London from Cambridge.

Alexa-type devices are not A.I. They are a converter of human speech into data, which then can be searched through various words, phrases in a vast electronic database, and pre-arranged phrases are announced. But ask it to determine a human problem involving and taking into account human emotions – the prognosis of a forthcoming medical operation, complex risk-based financial decision-making, involving complex life-choices and perhaps the impact of worldwide events on your decision – and it cannot answer. It may well have some information on a database, but it isn't structured to pull together all that information from so many different complex databases, or research the vast range of options, and to analyse, or process it in a meaningful way.

A human being could provide me with an answer, or at least appreciate how human beings think and arrive at decisions, but computers cannot do that, yet. That human answer may well be subjective, but most of us can appreciate what is subjective and what is factual, that which cannot be challenged.

To demonstrate how complex this area is, I might say 'This ball in front of me is black'. I consider this a fact. It is not white or any other colour, it is black. But, is it really black? How do you define its blackness or colour in comparison to other colours or shades? If you can do this with reflection or absorption of light values, then the computer or machine can cope with it, as it is measurable. But I might consider it to be black, and you see it more as a very dark grey. Now we are becoming subjective in our assessment. If I can say I am correct, because I can relate the ball in front of me to a known technical standard of measurement of 'black', then I can 'prove' I am correct, and it is no longer a subjective statement.

The A.I. machine, would then try and assess the colour of the ball against known technical standards, and to do that it needs to know something of the ambient lighting conditions in the room, ie both the colour temperature of the light source, and lux (lighting) levels measured at a certain distance, information on the material the ball is made of, and the properties of that material as regards light falling on the surface. Then it might have the data to determine if it meets those technical standards for the colour of black, or not. But as humans in conversation, we can understand that some might just 'see' a different colour than black. It might be because of a degree of colour-blindness in the individual, or it might be that in their lifetime experience, they saw similar balls to this one as dark grey, and have 'learnt' that in their brain, over time.

Humans accept subjectivity as part of being human. Whether we are arguing about politics, or how to approach climate-change, these are all subjective arguments. Sure, we can support some of the arguments with a financial business case, but not everything in life is valued by money or currency. Quality of life is a factor too, the condition of the environment, the health and well-being of our children, having empathy with others, being charitable towards others.

The database for an A.I. machine learning to participate constructively with humans on those and other subjective issues, would have to be extensive. It would need a virtual lifetime's experiences to provide meaningful arguments on the same level as humans. Subjectiveness would need to be somehow measurable, and converted into complex algorithms to be of any use to a machine. Pulling data from a database or several databases may well be the initial stage to provide an A.I response, but it needs to go much further, having a good understanding of say, mathematical probability algorithms and formulae, understanding the needs of human beings and human emotions.

A machine would have to understand concepts, such as race in society, racial discrimination, political issues, love and emotion, ambition, modesty, etc. These are learnt by man and woman as they reach adulthood and acquiring life-experiences and knowledge. Even then mistakes are made along the road of life by all of us, to varying degrees. Judgement, is a concept which is subjective again. We usually settle disputes by debating the subject matter, perhaps giving examples to support our case. An outside impartial listener, may be swayed by an initial argument, but change their mind when the other side of the case is put.

For a machine to really be A.I. enabled, it would need to be able to participate meaningfully in assessing which side had the best, overall argument, with supporting evidence. Even then, there can be stalemate. But stalemate in a negotiation is not necessarily failure.

Colossus, was far away from that level of sophistication, but the principle of eliminating certain data from the processing of coded intelligence was a useful start. Because, if we think of it logically, we would expect A.I. machines, if they are to think and learn like humans, to search its memory for information, and to eliminate all the irrelevant data, before coming up with an answer or a recommendation or suggestion. A.I. therefore, in basic terms, is nothing more than a sophisticated way of elimination of surplus and irrelevant data.

We do this process of data elimination instinctively, because of the way our brains are wired. Some humans may have their brains wired in a slightly different way to the average person, perhaps with conditions as autism and Asperger's Syndrome. They may think in a particular way, and analyse data, such that sometimes their response to a question might seem illogical to us. But sometimes, they may come up with a solution to a problem which is quite brilliant, and makes us wonder why we can't all be like them. Turing and others had this gift, but at times it could be a challenge, as social interaction with others was not always easy for him, or his colleagues and friends.

To process information in 'real time' improves our interaction with computers and devices. We don't like waiting whilst the computer searches for the information on multiple complex databases. Surveyors and building engineers find and report on a crack in a building for a client, and the client wants to know the reason behind the crack, whether it is serious, and the prognosis. They don't care that in most cases, to give a scientifically based answer, one needs to perhaps, test and analyse the soil conditions of the building, measure moisture content, check penetration with specialist tools, dig trial holes, check drainage locally, monitor the crack over several months or longer. There should be an analysis, a process, before one gives a recommendation and a prognosis. That sometimes takes time. The clients may not want to wait because they selling the property, and the engineer's report may well have serious consequences. One bit of information and data is going to affect another. Computers can deal with that. It is called 'programming'; multiple lines of computer code.

A modern car will easily contain 100 million lines of computer code in. No longer is a car just to get you from 'A' to 'B'. We now need an entertainment system, SatNav, aircon, Lane-assist, Cruise-control, proximity sensors, traffic signal recognition systems, auto-parking, security alarm system, power-sensing systems, power-sharing algorithms, fuel/mileage calculators, lumbar-support memory programs, etc. Facebook has approximately over 60 million lines of code. Society is becoming more and more impatient with social media and the world wide web.

The interface between man and machine is crucial. Delays in response from machines and computers can seem like an eternity, even though they may only be a few seconds. So, at present, we just have voice 'toys' on our kitchen table, and all it really demonstrates is that the designers have more or less cracked the 'speech to digital processing' part, but even certain human accents will still throw it a curveball.

Machines and computer programs can deal with different options with lots of sub-programs and algorithms, but perhaps not in the same way that a human approaches the day to day problems they experience in life. There are considerable challenges in computer experts and A.I. programmers arriving at programs which encourage the A.I. machine to learn in a way that is emulating humans. Some don't even think this is possible in practice, due to the complexity of the human brain.

The Internet was transformed by a technique called 'packet-switching' which is still used today. Developed at the National Physical Laboratory in Teddington, it was a giant leap forward in data communications. Without it, you might still be waiting to download that text or picture on Instagram sent by your friend sometime last week, due to the limitations of data transfer. It is the process of transferring data by the shortest route across complex data networks in bits, and then reassembling it at the other end to make the complete picture or text. It was a data revolution that was capitalized on by America and others, but it was Britain who invented the technique. One needs these major 'leaps' of technology to make progress.

During the Second World War, a German engineer, Helmut Schreyer, had the skill and ability to build an advanced electronic computer, based on an initial design of Konrad Zuse, but was turned down by the German High Command, based upon a directive given by Hitler. Hitler only wanted new technology to be supported where it advanced the war in modern weaponry, such as the V2 rockets and advanced jets. They could not see that a programmable machine could solve many different problems if you programmed it correctly, and that it could have advanced the German war machine significantly.

Zuse was a civil engineer, and wanted to have a machine capable of solving many complex equations together in civil engineering and building projects. Schreyer assisted him in the early war years. Schreyer, like Tommy Flowers, had seen the advantage of using valves and electronics in creating the design of a computer, as compared with relay switches, and this was Schreyer's major contribution to the electronic machine's design. It was 1936 when the concept of using valves for switches instead of electro-mechanical relays was tabled by Schreyer to his friend. Initially, this was poo-pooed by Zuse as a crazy idea, but later on accepted as a viable proposition. The offer by Zuse to the Nazis to build a computer for the Luftwaffe using 2000 valves was rejected. No one had built a machine with anything like this number of valves.

This was, of course, several years before Bletchley Park was established as GC & CS, but at a time when Turing was developing his own ideas about advanced machines and mathematics at university, prior to joining Bletchley. It would be 1958 before the first Zuse valve-based programmable electronic computer was ready. The bombing in the final years of the war made development and research almost impossible, made far worse by the wartime shortages of materials in Germany.

The Allies and Tommy Flowers got there first, although his Colossus machine was only considered to be semi-programmable. This demonstrates that many people on both sides of the war had similar ideas and aspirations, but very few had the backup and support or finance to develop those ideas into something practical at the time. The driving force for the British was clearly the defeat of the Third Reich. If it had not been wartime, Colossus would probably not have been built by the British. It was very costly in terms of quantities of valves, highly complex in design and construction, and some thought it was based upon suspect technology. There are those who say never mind that the Turing Bombe was not a computer, Colossus was not a true electronic computer either. It did not have a memory bank, it required constant attention and setting up. It was digital in operation, and there lies the link to computers. It could perform calculations other than breaking teleprinter-coded messages, though. It was far closer to being an electronic digital computer than the Bombe ever was.

On 21 June 1948, Max Newman managed to achieve the design and implementation of an operational stored-program, digital computer at the University of Manchester.[95] There would be later collaboration with the University and the Ferranti company to develop a mass-production computer. Many would say this was a computer, and not Colossus. After all, it is closer in principles of design to a laptop than Colossus. It had a stored program, so didn't require lots of people to press hundreds of switches.

After the war, the Colossus at Eastcote (GCHQ) was probably used to evaluate parcel logistics for the GPO. It had to be programmed to do that with setting of switches, but it was possible. The Bombe could not perform that function, as it was a one-problem machine. How strange that Universal machines and artificial intelligence were discussed between Donald Michie and Alan Turing all those years ago, when playing chess at lunchtimes at Bletchley. How incredible and fortunate that Donald Michie was to go on and specialize in this subject later on, after the war, and to write numerous papers, and be a true leader and eminent expert in this field. How ambitious and fortuitous, that he also studied anatomy, and contributed significantly to medical science too. Few people would link together anatomy and human life, and artificial intelligent machines.

Michie did later study advanced anatomy for the purpose of making robots, but the thought no doubt crossed his mind and stimulated his thoughts. The best designers today, will adapt elements of nature and the natural world into their technological and aesthetic designs.

How sad that Turing was not able to develop fully his true potential after the war, and came to a tragic end. Michie also died far too soon. Who knows what might have been, if he had lived on and further inspired young people to take risks in specialist areas of computer design and A.I. systems?

Colossus was a stage on the way to development of Artificial Intelligence, with people thinking differently, and applying their intellect in different ways. Michie was certainly involved in practical terms with Colossus, and added to its design and efficiency, but then Michie was a visionary as well, like Alan Turing, and in some ways achieved mor because he lived longer than Turing and was able to explore new areas over time.

When Turing was considering the concept of Universal Machines, he wanted to have a machine that could be used to deal with many different and varied problems. We see this now as commonplace, with our laptops, smartphones, iPads, etc. But would Turing and Michie and even Flowers have contemplated that designing such a machine would have serious consequences, in the long-term for society? It would most likely bring about mass redundancies, closures of factories and shops, eliminate the need for typewriting pools. Of course, there would be benefits too, the reduction of health problems by reducing the numbers in mines and pits, avoiding some of the heavy lifting by using robotic machines, carrying out automated manufacture with machines in environments much too dangerous and hazardous for humans.

The concept of machines taking work away from humans would have been very exciting in the 1940s, and Turing wanted to see this happen in practice, using his ideas. The release of humans from the drudgery of tasks would release them to do more interesting and inspirational things with their lives. One single machine to do all those things, all those calculations, a mathematician's dream. One could explore challenging problems which had vexed other mathematicians and philosophers over many decades and centuries, and press a button and out comes the answer, all from one machine.

We understand that our computer support in daily life is more a combination of specialist machines rather than one single, universal, super-computer. The factory with robots spray-painting cars with high quality precision; the automated machine making components to a high precision, and the work then measured by it, to ensure it falls within acceptable tolerances; the car which recognizes the speed and position of the car in front through use of sensors and programs. Ironically, the author's schoolfriend who worked with Donald Michie in the 1970s was almost run over in San Francisco by an early test self-driving automated car.

All these are generally, single use, or at best, limited use robots, not really A.I. They are sophisticated electronic data processing modules, sensors and components of an advanced machine which is for a specific purpose. But Turing probably wanted more. Turing would have been fascinated by the algorithms and programming which made these machines operate, how they avoided errors and mistakes, the statistics on operational failures, and how to overcome them. Both Turing and Michie could foresee the time when we had the technology to develop specially advanced machines, sometime in the future, and that this would completely transform society in the way we work, travel, shop, make choices, are educated, play, and have medical treatment. Turing knew it would all come down to mathematics, or numbers, and the application of those numbers.

If everything can be converted to numbers, then this forms the basis for the processing using algorithms in his Universal Machine. It's just a simple matter of getting the design correct, and the programming and algorithms checked out for errors and anomalies. But understanding how humans think, and how we analyse problems in practice, is a very big part of the equation. Copying that over to a 'Universal Machine' is not going to be simple. True A.I. is, however, probably not that far away. But it would have been that little bit closer, had Alan Turing and Donald Michie lived longer.

CONCLUSION

The purpose of this book has been to give the reader the bigger picture in respect of the integration of outstations with Bletchley Park and how it worked in practice. Other books may have elements of this to varying degrees, but do not demonstrate how reliant Bletchley Park was on the outstations with operational codebreaking machines, or the supporting infrastructure. The most useful and interesting descriptions and accounts seen by the author have been by Wrens in diaries, books and articles, who describe in some detail the working and living conditions on various bases.

This became an expanded, and growing army of specialist female individuals (not forgetting the ATS, WAAFs etc) spread mainly around the lower Midlands and south of England, supported by relatively few men,. This period was instrumental in demonstrating how women can apply themselves to a difficult and complex task, generally without complaint, and just get on with the job. Not only that, but some Wrens went on to become actual codebreakers such as many of 'Dilly's Girls', who cracked German Enigma codes. Then there were the Wrens and others who operated Robinson and Colossus/Colossus Mark 2 machines at

A 'Tunny' (Lorenz) decryption from Bletchley Park formed from parts of two messages to the German Army Group Courland (Kurland) on 14 February 1945. (Photo courtesy Dr David Hamer) the start of the electronic digital computer age, when few had ever heard the word 'computer', and would have no clue as to what such a machine could be used for.

After the war, several of these individuals were to form part of the new GCHQ and the basis of the modern intelligence service. The plaque at one of the entrances to Pembroke Park Estate at Eastcote is brief in both description, and content. Most people passing by on the Eastcote High Road will miss it.[95] Many of the locals who have lived in the area have never walked along the quarter mile long public footpath dividing the housing estate, and never knew what went on at Eastcote, Stanmore or beyond.

The declassification of the information has come in stages, commencing in the early 1970s, and Lorenz was only declassified in 2002. Some information is still classified. It is hoped that this book has sent the message to the reader that Bletchley Park and Alan Turing, for all their importance and coordination of the codebreaking period during the war, were reliant totally on the Y-stations, the codebreaking Bombe operational outstations, the manufacturing facilities at Letchworth, BTM, *Spirella*, Dollis Hill, TRE, the Wren dispatch riders delivering the messages, and certainly would have not been able to achieve a fraction of what they did without them. It truly was a team effort. Yet, at the time of writing, the outstations do not feature much at Bletchley Park.

The Imperial War Museum in Lambeth, London should be the key venue in the capital to educate and communicate on matters of codebreaking and military intelligence. Perhaps when the IWM has completed its refurbishment programme, it will give codebreaking intelligence during the war, by both military and civilian personnel, the importance and emphasis it deserves. When younger people visit museums and places like the IWM, it should be expected that they come away with a balanced view and understanding of the key issues that affected the development of wars and conflict. That appears to be lacking at present in some museums. Others are better in this respect. Not everyone can easily visit Bletchley Park due to its location in Buckinghamshire. Those visiting military museums need to be informed that intelligence was a key part of the Allies winning the Second World War, and has been developed further to help security in the present day, and is particularly relevant to armed forces.

The author was saddened to read of a Wren that mentioned the 'sub-stations' that she and others worked on during the war are now not mentioned, and have been largely forgotten about. They must never be forgotten. They were a crucial link in the chain of intelligence gathering and data processing. Some even applied their knowledge and experience to work on the 'Purple' machine and its decoding, which was used by the Japanese based on a special version of Enigma. Many Wrens and others were sent out to Colombo, Ceylon (now Sri-Lanka), and the Far East after VE day.

Bletchley Park emphasises that whilst the Enigma and Bombe machines were of critical importance in the Allies gathering intelligence before, and during the war, decoding of Enigma was about *tactical intelligence*, and only the more advanced encoding machines such as Lorenz and the T52s were of *strategic intelligence* importance. It was Robinson and Colossus that assisted us in decoding that strategic intelligence.

However, it would have been the case that strategic information would sometimes be sent or confirmed via Enigma, and intercepted by the Allies at Bletchley Park or via the codebreaking outstations. This might because a particular German officer was in a particular location in the battlefield, and had no choice but to use it to ask for urgent Panzer reinforcements, or to divert a division of Tiger tanks for a counter-attack, or even communicate the order of battle in a pocket of resistance which needed to be overcome. The order of Battle would have been crucial strategic intelligence.

It may have been the case that the message would then be retransmitted in a different form via Lorenz, and intercepted via Knockholt Y-station and broken via Robinson or Colossus as strategic information. It is highly likely that in the confusion of war, with mass artillery attacks, bombings, troop and tank movements, shortages of fuel, ammunition, ordnance, and supplies, Enigma would have been used by senior officers for communication of strategic decisions.

The only way we would know this for sure, is if some of those actual decoded Enigma messages were still around to see. Most will have been destroyed. It is important to understand that the codebreaking outstations were in no way inferior to Bletchley Park. Everyone had their role to play. Mistakes would be made, but the fact the Allies overcame the Nazis shows that the intelligence gathering worked, and on the whole, worked remarkably well. It was for the senior officers and generals to put the decoded pieces together, whether they came from Enigma, Lorenz, a T52 secret writer, or even from a carrier pigeon sent to a German agent in Britain.

Enemy intelligence could sometimes be intercepted via more than one route, and where it was particularly difficult or impractical to do so, such as intercepting via penetrating enemy landlines, the easier option would often be taken. Sometimes, intelligence might come via Tunny and be exposed via Colossus, only to be confirmed via another separate route via Enigma and decoded via the Bombes. Churchill, his generals and admirals did not care too much about which technical *system* was being used by Bletchley Park, to intercept and decode the Nazi intelligence. Although strategically important deciphers via Lorenz on the FISH links and 'Tunny' were considered the 'prize' for Bletchley Park, the Allied officers who had to attack the Germans in the battlefield, in the air or at sea, really didn't mind which source the information came from, if it gave them an advantage. Pieces from Enigma were all part of a complex jigsaw puzzle to be unravelled, but one had to filter out the trivia initially, and there would have been a lot of that, and much less trivia via Lorenz and the more advanced 'Tunny' intelligence. That made a difference in practical terms.

The challenge for many at Bletchley Park and elsewhere, would be to sort through and filter out that trivial information, and be aware that what might be seen as a piece of insignificant intelligence individually, when added together with other data, might form part of an important and bigger picture.

There is a famous account of a German operator of a Lorenz, or secret writer machine, who had sent a long message of 4,000 characters to a colleague, but received the reply back 'Did not receive, Please resend'. Resending the message, the operator forgot to change the machine settings, a security breach. Not only that, but he started making abbreviations such as for the word 'number', which then became the German equivalent of Nr. The British now had two near identical messages, but with very slight variations, and the resent message was several characters shorter than the original message. This, then opened up for the British the possibility of cracking that cipher, with the 'depth' of message and the cribs or clues provided. It was just like providing the Allies with the combination of a secure safe containing German military secrets

Of course, errors were made on both sides of the war. It was just that the Allies appeared to make fewer mistakes, and the Germans did not appreciate how exposed they were from an intelligence perspective due to the sloppiness of their Enigma and Lorenz operators breaching the rules.

It seems a bit of a paradox that the outcome of the Second World War was influenced significantly by the errors made on both sides, in dealing with their intelligence equipment, their operational efficiency, and organisation of both intelligence gathering and processing. Deception of the enemy was also a key intelligence-led area, and this was demonstrated by the effective use and application of 'Operation Bodyguard' and 'Fortitude South' deceptions, leading up to D-Day. Listening in to Enigma, and particularly to Lorenz/Secret Writer transmissions, it was possible to confirm whether the enemy were being deceived, leaving the Allies to exploit that intelligence to save numerous Allied lives, and to gain time in penetrating into occupied France before the Germans could respond in force.

The one item that makes an indelible impression upon the author is that Winston Churchill truly understood the importance of military intelligence. Churchill also appreciated that the Russians would be our next challenge, and that Britain needed to protect its specialist knowledge in codebreaking from them and others, even though his destruction of codebreaking equipment may have been a mistake. It was Churchill who wrote or stamped 'Action this day', on the request by three individuals at Bletchley Park for more resources to increase the Bombe processing capacity against Enigma. He could see that military intelligence was one thing that could make up for the imbalance in military forces, and that advance, accurate knowledge was key to success in battle. Another leader may not have put so much emphasis on Bletchley Park and codebreaking.

Churchill may not have visited the codebreaking outstations, but he was aware of their contribution, and saw daily decrypted messages from Stanmore, Eastcote, Wavendon, Gayhurst, Adstock and of course Bletchley, too. He did visit Dollis Hill, as at that site was an underground bunker containing wartime cabinet rooms next to the building where Tommy Flowers worked at the Research Establishment. Churchill only used the secret cabinet rooms infrequently, as they were damp and not particularly pleasant. He would use the London Cabinet war rooms, near Whitehall, for most of the war, and have special telecoms links via an American SIGALY speech scrambler to speak with Roosevelt and others, across the pond.

Tommy Flowers and his Colossus-building team, Donald Michie, Max Newman, Bill Tutte, Ralph Tester, Alan Turing, are just some of the people we need to be thankful for making this happen. Not forgetting the support personnel, the WRNS, ATS, WAAF's, RAF and Post Office engineers, and many others. We must also not forget those dedicated WRNS, engineers and personnel who operated the Bombes at Bletchley Park in Hut 11A. Although relatively few Bombes were present, between six to eight machines, they would have had the same issues as the outstations, except that communicating back the output of Bombes would be much less of a problem, as they were on the spot. Some of the Bombes were used for training purposes.

Bombe Registers at the National Archives indicate 'O.S.P' for a machine which went to Bletchley Park. It was a convenient way of referring to the Park, when machines were allocated or moved there. It is a pity that the Bletchley hut now contains full-sized card (?) replicas of Bombes on frames, with printed pictures to give the illusion of Bombe machines. It must come down to cost, but it would be wonderful if proper, working replica Bombes were in that hut. Maybe that might be for some future time.

The modern developments after the Bombe and Colossus in the field of computing makes for interesting reading. The acquisition of BTM's successor, ICL, by Fujitsu-Siemens in the late 1990s, might have made a few of the remaining BTM retired engineers and managers chuckle. It was Siemens that provided the inspiration to BTM engineers during wartime to improve relays and components to make the Bombe machine more efficient. Siemens design and technology would ironically help BTM, Bletchley Park and the codebreaking outstations to process and decode Nazi messages much more efficiently than before. And yet, we have come almost full circle, where a joint-venture involving Siemens acquired BTM's successor, ICL, then acquiring mainly the hardware part of the business. In peacetime, close relationships are made and business deals done, leaving history in the past, and perhaps, forgetting those ugly times years ago.

BTM worked efficiently, in the nation's interest during wartime and went on to innovate and build on the success of that company. They managed to do all their wartime work without slave labour of course, in what was a free society. They might have been situated in a small city some miles outside London, but they became a focal point, much like Bletchley Park, in being a key player in wartime. Failure at BTM would perhaps have meant allowing the Nazis to gain a foothold in

Britain. It wasn't just BTM, though. Those workers at *Spirella*, Irvin's, the Wrens at the outstations and Bletchley, the ATS, WAAF, GPO and RAF engineers, Royal Marines security guards – all of them played their respective roles and worked as a team to save Britain in wartime.

It is hoped that in reading this, one realises that intense stress was also a factor in the building and the operation of the codebreaking machines, whether they were Typex, Bombes, Robinson, Colossus, or others. The pressure on mathematicians and cryptographers to crack a message key, and save lives within given timescales, would mean many sleepless nights. Today, we are more aware of mental health issues, and there is often a mechanism to support personnel in difficult and challenging jobs and careers. Back in the 1940s that wasn't recognised, and there were mental breakdowns and illness, some of which may not manifest themselves for years afterwards. The fact that so many individuals were not permitted to talk about their work to their friends and relatives due to official secrecy meant that become like a wound-up spring needing release, but that release would not occur for many years, if at all.

In most jobs, menial or cerebral, one can see what one has achieved, and obtain feedback on it from others. It was rarely the case that the operators knew exactly what they had achieved when a message had been decoded. It was a multi-stage process, and that meant one often did not have a clue what was your achievement that day, despite spending a long eight-hour night shift in a smelly, hot, oily, poorly ventilated hut, with noisy machines requiring your attention. This why occasional talks on what codebreaking activities had achieved against the enemy offered at a few sites were welcomed by most, as there was less of a detachment, knowing that your work had helped sink a U boat or provided crucial intelligence for a counter-attack on a Panzer division. The problem here, was that there would always be a lengthy delay between the codebreaking part, and the eventual feedback talk at the outstation.

In the next few pages there are some timelines of key events. This should assist the reader in further understanding the sequence of discoveries, events and actions that enabled the Allies to win.

It is almost inconceivable that Signals Intelligence started back in 1914 in Room 40 at the Admiralty in London, expanded and developed via Bletchley Park, Eastcote, and with the help of other outstations and infrastructure, to become the modern GCHQ at Cheltenham. It has many thousands of staff in the UK and around the world. GCHQ was not in the public vocabulary until the early 1970s. It will continue to be the focal point for helping to guard the state from hackers, terrorists, and enemies.

In February 2019, H. M. The Queen unveiled a green plaque at Watergate House in London, commemorating 100 years of GCHQ, November 1919–2019. The plaque states that Bletchley Park was known as GC & CS. But it is accepted that this was really the beginning of GCHQ.

Note that it was only Eastcote that had the official title of Government Communications Headquarters (GCHQ) in 1946, some years before it relocated to Cheltenham. The occasional use of the name GCHQ at Bletchley Park prior to 1946 was probably unofficial as Bletchley had several different names. However, it had used 'GCHQ' since around 1939 at various times. The National Archives may, arguably, provide some evidence that Eastcote was the first official GCHQ. Eastcote is completely by-passed in many books and articles on intelligence, and this book wishes to redress that balance. It was an important stage in the development of GCHQ after the war, established modern procedures and protocols. One book refers to 'Bletchley Park's Outstation Eastcote' or 'Bletchley Park's Stanmore Outstation'. Neither of these outstations were owned by Bletchley Park, and they acted as semi-independent units, but of course, constantly liaised with and communicated with Bletchley on a daily basis. We had the rather strange scenario whereby the outstations were onshore naval bases, but ran by the Government with naval management, and RAF managers too, with a smattering of post office engineers. Bletchley Park went from being a leading HQ during the war, to being abruptly wound down in spring 1946. All eyes were then on Eastcote, as it took on the developed, modern GCHQ role, absorbed many Bletchley and other specialists, and developed further as a multi-functional base, supporting the US Army and US Navy.

As far as can be reasonably ascertained, the following key personnel visited Eastcote:

Alan Turing
Tommy Flowers
Commander Edward Travis
Mavis Batey (Nee Lever)
Joan Clarke
Margaret Rock
Hugh Alexander
Hugh Foss
Hugh Denham
Josh Cooper
James Aitken
Leslie Yoxall
James Ellis
Ruth Bourne
Bernard Rafferty
Bobs Brooke Taylor (Nee Kirby)
Mary Moore (Nee Davis)
Rosemary Podd (Nee Williams)
Winifred Roberts

This is not intended to be a complete list, but is only a small sample of persons that had a link with Outstation Eastcote, or of Eastcote when it was GCHQ. Several more names can be found, particularly for the GCHQ period, elsewhere.[96] Margaret Rock is one, someone who most people have never heard of. She was a trained mathematician who worked initially at Bletchley Park in April 1940 before coming to work at GCHQ after the war. Rock was one of 'Dilly's Girls', who achieved so much in that team of cryptographic, codebreaking pioneers. She was considered to be one of the best codebreakers in his team by her boss, Dilwyn Knox, working on German *Abwehr* intelligence. She would continue breaking German ciphers and codes after Knox's death.

The name of Tommy Flowers has been included, based on the high probability of him visiting the site, although no specific paperwork confirms this. However, The local history society (RNELHS) does mention that former staff on the base can recollect him working at Eastcote.[97] 'Flowers Avenue' now dominates the north part of the residential housing estate at Pembroke Park. The relocation of the two Colossus computers to Eastcote after the war would have required setting up by specialists, and few would have been able to do this, so the logic is that Flowers directed that part of the work on site, or at least some of it. These were very complex and unique, specialist machines. Few would have been familiar with their design, construction or operation. The inventor/designer would be the perfect person to set up the machine and calibrate it prior to operational use.

The chapter on Colossus, Michie and A.I. was prepared to demonstrate how something quite complex in some ways (i.e. valves, switches, photo-electronic tape readers, etc) but also considered quite basic in our view of modern technology in the 21st century can be a stepping stone to greater things, such as A.I. Flowers, Michie and others provided the building blocks of technology, for others to develop further. The chapter also tries to convey to the reader that randomness and subjectiveness are but two concepts which will need a lot of thought and effort to incorporate within advanced machines.

At the end of this book is a section on how educationalists and teachers can appreciate the relevance of this subject to informing children and students about what happened in the past. The author has listed a series of topics related and relevant to intelligence and codebreaking, and how with a structured programme, students can learn mathematics, history, geography, business learning, logistics, and other subjects taking elements from this story.[98] The social aspects of the story are as considered equally as important as the technical side, if not more so.

Cyber-attack is now considered perhaps our greatest threat, and earlier intelligence gathering, codebreaking and computers make for a sound base to confront it.

Surprisingly, even H. R. H. Prince William has taken an interest in the role of GCHQ and spent some time there, learning about the challenges in protecting us from cyber-attack and terrorism. A future monarch needs to be aware of modern technology and security issues.

Finally, I do hope that Bletchley Park, now an important museum, and The Imperial War Museum, exhibit much more information and displays on the Outstations.[98] As regards GCHQ at Eastcote, there should be a proper recognition of its input in progressing intelligence operations post-war, to protect Britain and its post-WW2 allies, and not just a small metal plaque tucked away behind steel railings.

TIMELINE

1908	Churchill visits Highgrove House in Eastcote on his honeymoon with his new wife, Clementine
1914	UK Signals Intelligence Room 40 Admiralty London
1918	Arthur Scherbius files patent for Enigma machine
1919	1 November, GC & CS Established in London
1923	Enigma machine for sale to the general public commercially
1926	Enigma machines in use extensively
1927	Enigma patents applied for in Britain and obtained
1929	Arthur Scherbius dies at the age of 50 in a horse and carriage accident
1930s	The Poles break Enigma Code
1938	Poles use Bomba codebreaking machine
1939	Bletchley Park established. Alan Turing joins
1939	Govt. Code & Cipher School at Bletchley Park (First wave of GC & CS moved there on 15/8/39)
1939	BTM approached in Letchworth by Bletchley Park
1940	First German Lorenz transmissions
1940	First Bombe Installed in Bletchley Park, 'Victory'

1941	First WRNS women employed at Bletchley Park on Bombe machines
1942	November, Outstation Stanmore operational
1942	Cobra attachment for Bombe machines
1942	Gayhurst established with five machines
1942	*Spirella* at Letchworth moves corset production to London, to enable Bombe components to be made at Letchworth
1942	Bill Tutte at Bletchley Park works out Lorenz/Tunny structure
1943	September, commencement of work on Eastcote
1943	Completion of Outstation Eastcote/Pembroke V
1943	First prototype of 'Robinson' machine delivered to Bletchley Park
1943	February, commencement on Colossus at Post Office Research Establishment at Dollis Hill, with Tommy Flowers
1943	First Colossus machine built at Dollis Hill
1943	SIGSALY American Speech-encryption-machine developed by Bell laboratories in US and used in London
1944	January, Outstation Eastcote obtains Siemen's relays Bombes
1944	US Army 6812th Signals comes to Eastcote to operate Ten Bombe machines under ETOUSA agreement
1944	February, incendiary bomb hits Block 'A' at Eastcote but does not explode
1944	January, Outstation Wavendon closes
1944	June, BTM at Letchworth build 'GIANT' Bombe, four standard Bombes connected together
1944	Colossus Mark 2 ready at Bletchley Park on 1 June 1944 in time for D-Day intelligence
1944	6 June, D-Day. Mobile Y-listening stations in France
1944	September, V1 flying bomb explodes close to perimeter of Outstation Stanmore, no casualties

1945	May 8, Victory in Europe Day
1945	May, instructions by Churchill to dismantle the codebreaking machines and burn all drawings
1945	Signals Intelligence Centre with 1017 personnel Bletchley Park
1945	Alan Turing visits GCHQ as a consultant
1946	March, Bletchley Park moves intelligence department down to Eastcote
1946	April 1, GCHQ established at Eastcote
1946	Hugh Alexander comes to Eastcote
1947	Crown Estate purchases the Eastcote site
1947	GCHQ at Eastcote involved in intelligence on 'Venona' anti-spy project, which used data from 1942 to 1948
1948–52	GCHQ Eastcote intercepts East German/Russian intelligence transmissions during start of the Cold War
1948	Rebuilding of Colossus 'RED' at GCHQ Eastcote
1948	June 21, First stored-programme digital electronic computer in Manchester
1950	Significant reduction in 'Venona' Eastcote personnel, down to ten
1952	Start of relocating main part of GCHQ from Eastcote to Cheltenham, stage by stage
1952	Travis replaced as Director of GCHQ following relocation of GCHQ from Eastcote
1953–54	Security Section Intelligence of GCHQ remains at Eastcote until 1954
1954	GCHQ at Cheltenham completed February
1956	GPO transfers to LCSA at Eastcote
1956	Two Colossus machines from Eastcote sent to Cheltenham with other equipment
1958	Elliot 405 Computer at Eastcote
1959	One of the two Colossi dismantled at Cheltenham
1960	Final Colossus dismantled at Cheltenham
1965	LCSA renamed CESD Security Dept

1964–69	Work on the base remains secret
1974	US Marines moved into Block 1 at Eastcote
1977	CESG relocates from Eastcote to Cheltenham
1978	GCHQ support at Northwood Hills, the Services Communication Development Unit (SCDU), closes to move to Cheltenham
1984/85	US Navy contingent to RAF Eastcote
1990s	Plans for multimillion pound GCHQ at Cheltenham
1993–2008	Tony Sale rebuilds Colossus replica
2006	Last occupants (US Navy) prepare to leave Eastcote
2007	Eastcote site sold for housing
2007–08	Demolition commences of the Eastcote site
2014	Pembroke Park Estate Memorial Plaque for HMS Pembroke V at Eastcote, ceremony with Mayor and RAF represented
2014	Film *The Imitation Game* released
2019	February, Alan Turing voted as winner of BBC *Icons* as most influential individual of 20th century
2019	February, H. M. The Queen unveils GCHQ plaque at Watergate House in London, to mark 100 years of GCHQ

ABBREVIATIONS

ASDIC Anti-Submarine Division (Sonar)
AFSA Armed Forces Security Agency
BTM British Tabulating Machine Company
CESD Communications Electronic Security Group
CESG Communications Electronic Security Department
COMINT Communications Intelligence
CSO Composite Signals Organisation
ELINT Electronic Intelligence
GC & CS Government Code & Cipher School
GCHQ Government Communications Headquarters
JSRU Joint Speech Research Unit
JTLS Joint Technical Language Service
LCSA London Communication Security Agency
LSIC London Signals Intelligence Centre
NATO North Atlantic Treaty Organisation
NCSC National Cyber Security Centre
NKVD The People's Commissariat for Internal Affairs (Interior
Ministry of the Soviet Union)
SIS Signals Intelligence Service
SCAG Special Cryptologic Advisory Group
SCDU Services Communications Development Unit
SLU Special Liaison Unit
TICOM Target Intelligence Committee

APPENDIX – SOME FINAL THOUGHTS

The author is unaware of any personnel still alive who worked at Eastcote or Stanmore during the Second World War. However, there are a few isolated individuals who are alive and worked at the Eastcote base during post-war activities. Few of these people will disclose their duties and what they did at the base.

Some chapters, such as on Stanmore may be out of time sequence, but that is because the previous chapters revolve largely around Outstation Eastcote. The text has been written by the author, taking into account a considerable number of other books, descriptions, articles, online articles, photographs, meetings with people, inspection of maps and layouts, visits to the Eastcote and Stanmore sites, visits to Bletchley Park, Letchworth, the *Spirella* site, Uxbridge, Dollis Hill, Watergate House, Bentley Priory, Northwood, Ruislip, and elsewhere.

The author has emailed and had telephone conversations with several collection officers, librarians, archivists, journalists, local people to the site, and a very few who had worked with icons of their time, who in turn worked with, or knew Alan Turing, Donald Michie, Tommy Flowers or similar persons. It was clear to the author before he commenced this book, that others have also either previously provided detailed historical articles in history journals, or written books on aspects of the subject. However, this volume tries to bring together both technical aspects, as well as some of the social aspects of the period, and provides a framework which gives the reader an overview of the interaction of the bases and outstations involved. It avoids very detailed technical descriptions for the most part, as many other books and publications provide that degree of specialism, should it be required.

Letchworth History

The author has clarified some information re the production of codebreaking Bombes and relevance to Bombe Registers for the Collections officer at the Garden City Collection, Letchworth, to add to their information and resource. The author has studied relevant maps and information which were pertinent to *Spirella*, BTM and other sites, and visited the *Spirella* building. Many thanks to the Collections Officer for the information via telephone and emails and for the permission to publish certain photographs from the Garden City Collection. By the time this book is published, the writer will have given a talk on this subject to members of the local history society in Letchworth. There may be more relevant information arising from that talk and feedback from the audience.

Bombing at Eastcote/Ruislip

Residents have advised there was bombing at Eastcote during the war, and this has been confirmed with various maps of bombing at Eastcote, Ruislip and surrounding areas. However, such bombing was not targeting the Outstation, as the Germans had no idea of the relevance of Outstation Eastcote or Outstation Stanmore, or indeed any of the outstations during the war. The bombing was general, and not specific to the bases. The V1 doodlebug which hit the perimeter wall of Outstation Stanmore would have been targeted generally at London and the suburbs. There are detailed maps available at Headstone Museum, Harrow, of the bombing of the London Borough of Harrow.

Bombing at Stanmore, Middlesex

From studying local maps it transpired that there was considerable general bombing around the Stanmore area. Part of this might have been attracted by Bentley Priory, and Fighter Command. However, there was evidence of V1s and V2s near Bentley Priory and Outstation Stanmore, as well as a crashed plane near the Command base. A V2 rocket almost hit Bentley Priory in late January 1945 at 03:55 hours, slightly to the south. A V1 rocket landed to the east of Outstation Stanmore on 18 December 1944 at 04:14 hours. These were lucky escapes, particularly the V2 impact. General bombing came very close to the outstation, but was not specifically targeted as far as we know.

Communications with Bletchley Park

The outstations would need to have communicated regularly with Bletchley Park and vice versa. This would have been via telephone, and scrambler telephone where key information was communicated. Some bases may have had direct landline links back to Bletchley. Eg Drayton Parslow.

H. M. The Queen, commented at the unveiling of the hundred year anniversary plaque of GCHQ in 2019, that during the war the King had problems using the complex scrambler telephone at Buckingham Palace, and did not get on with it. There are also several reports of Wrens having to be trained for teleprinter operations.

The National Museum of Computing at Bletchley Park (TNMOC) had a representative member attend three of my talks and was very knowledgeable on the Colossus, Lorenz, and Bombe machines. The Computer Museum is an extremely important one, on the site of Bletchley Park, but it is run as a separate enterprise to the Bletchley Park Trust. It is important that schools and young people learn about this subject, and how it shaped their lives, and the lives of our wider society. A visit to Bletchley Park Museum, also to TNMOC/ Bletchley, is recommended to learn more.

German Codebreaking and Intelligence

The Germans were able to break British codes and cyphers both before and during the war. They had particular success with breaking our naval codes. Their U-boats were able to intercept instructions relayed to Allied convoys, and locate them easily. While some of these weaknesses were plugged over time, there were many mistakes made by the British. However, overall, the British were far better at breaking German codes and ciphers than the Germans were of breaking theirs, and the German cryptography units were not well structured in comparison. The false hope that Enigma, and later Lorenz, were totally secure, gave them a false sense of security. The advanced later 'secret writers' (eg Siemens T52 and T43), developed by the Germans to keep us guessing could not be produced in the vast numbers required, and Enigma was still the main encoding machine across the armed services. Had they done so, and produced the specialist machines en masse, Colossus and its cryptographic support teams may not have been able to cope with the volume and scale of German intelligence. The war probably would have been much extended beyond May 1945. The use of advanced machines on German landlines was also a worry, as penetrating and intercepting them would be problematical as compared with interception of radio Morse and non-Morse transmissions. Further information on German codebreaking can be found in the excellent book: *The Third Reich is Listening (Inside German Codebreaking 1939-45)* by Christian Jennings (ISBN 978-1-4728-2950-4).

Visiting the Eastcote Site

Those who wish to visit the remnants of the Eastcote site, should appreciate that the housing estate, Pembroke Park, either side of the public footpath is private property. However, the visitor is encouraged to walk the length of the public footpath, and even the surrounding roads such as Kent Gardens, Lime Grove, The Sigers, etc., also to visit The Case is Altered pub, and the public houses nearby. Note that The Black Horse public house has since been renamed. Highgrove House is currently private property, and is directly adjacent to the site. The plaque commemorating the Outstation and GCHQ is located near Eastcote High Road, near the pedestrian crossing. Nearby, it is worth visiting both Manor Farm Ruislip, and Eastcote House Gardens. The walled garden is particularly pleasant in spring and summer. The nearest public library is Eastcote Library, which is fairly small, and Manor Farm Library is not that far away, situated on an important Heritage site, and has one of the oldest barns in England. That site also has a museum.

Family Connections

The research for this book has sometimes opened wounds in respect of family history, particularly the Russian and Nazi impact on the Baltic States, and elsewhere in Europe. Indeed, there were new facts emerging from speaking to relatives that the author was unaware of prior to starting the research. The information received on some historical wartime issues was far too traumatic to put into the text. The lesson is that when one commences on the journey for information on a project, one may well come across unpleasant and even shocking aspects of history, which brings one down to earth rather quickly.

My late mother was originally born in Estonia, in the same year that Winston Churchill celebrated his honeymoon in Eastcote. She attended the 1936 Berlin Olympic Games, when Adolf Hitler was running the show. I remember her telling me, as a young boy, that she despised both him and the Nazis, but attended the Olympics purely for the sport. My late step-uncle Max was probably in the German armed forces during the war, and was a leading boxer in Germany, winning many titles. My aunt, Laura, told me when I was staying with her in Hamburg in 1967 of the terrible RAF and American bombing raids during the war that she and other German citizens endured. Hamburg was, of course, flattened by the Allied bombing, along with other cities. It is quite alarming to think that one human being, could have caused so much distress and suffering across the world.

Russian Affairs

Russian security forces history is probably for another place and other publications, but I set out the basic organization transitions from 1917:

CHEKA > OGPU > NKVD > KGB

The last one should be familiar to readers, even if the previous ones may be unfamiliar. The 'Venona' project period is probably more relevant to the early part of the formation of the KGB, although some older intelligence intercepts which were studied by the British and Americans, may have arisen out of earlier organizations before the KGB was formally established, such as the NKVD, which was originally formed in 1918.

Collecting Stories

Some people that I have met in this process of talks and discussions have told me that they have special information and experiences after the war that only they know about and would like to tell me about them. Some of these accounts go well beyond the war, and are unrelated to the codebreaking sites or GCHQ, but may be of interest to others. What we need is a mechanism to capture these stories, about intelligence, spying, political intrigue. There is an opportunity for others to research these areas and collect accounts from individuals who may have limited time to tell them. The author has met journalists who are keen to speak to those who worked at Eastcote or have links to the Eastcote base, as they will be writing an article on the site, at some time in the future.

Other Encoding Machines

In case the reader thinks that I have completely ignored other encoding machines, I mention here 'SIGABA', the USA encoder, which according to reports was never broken by anyone. It apparently had fifteen wheels in its design. There was more of a pseudo-randomness in the operation compared to Enigma, based on the movement of the rotor wheels. It was very complex but nowhere near as portable as Enigma machines. There were others of course, and the reader is hereby referred to www. *Cryptomuseum*, the excellent online database of codebreaking and encoding equipment, which sets out all the different models.

As mentioned in the text, one of the sub-basements of Selfridges, a famous department store in London, contained a Bell-laboratories American 'SIGSALY' encryption encoder for voice transmissions of messages, and was used by Churchill to communicate by telephone with President Roosevelt, from 1943, with encrypted voice messages, via Churchill's cabinet war rooms some distance away, near Whitehall. This was operated by US army technicians, forming a small, specialist, cryptographic unit to scramble telephone and telecoms messages at high level command. The equipment was huge, in several cabinets, underground and secure. However, there are reports it was bombed, and a guard killed.

Detailed Description of Bombe Operations and Checking Machines

The reader who wishes to know more on the detail of Bombe machines and the menus and checking process as used at Outstation Eastcote and Outstation Stanmore, and elsewhere, is directed to the website www.codes&ciphers.org.uk, The British Bombe. The 6812th Signal Security Detachment US Army, who had men operating Bombe machines at Outstation Eastcote, and who are also mentioned in some detail in this book, produced a detailed report in June 1945 of the operational side of the way the Bombe menus worked, the checking process and technical details of the cryptography logic, with many diagrams. Some of the checking sheets illustrated in the article are on Bombes which were actually held at Outstation Eastcote, and were under the direction of the Americans. The specific details contained in the pdf download which was arranged via the late Tony Sale, go beyond the scope of this book, but may be of interest for those who are mathematically minded. There are also many other excellent detailed publications out there on the workings of the Bombes, Enigma, Lorenz, and many others.

Development of Computing Post-war and Collectors

There will be those readers out there who are particularly interested in development of computers post-war, and vintage computer equipment. That is not the author's field or area of expertise. However, there are many such sources of information, and of course the Museum of Computing at Bletchley Park is a good place to start. Some collectors have acquired enormous quantities of important vintage equipment, and some are contactable online.

Up and down the country, there will be collectors of vintage equipment of all sorts, radios, receivers, aerials, codebreaking machines. As time elapses and people become older, it is more of a challenge for those people to manage their collections, and indeed to part with them. The collections become part of their lives. There is no easy answer to this. Some are more than happy to donate the collection or part of it to a museum, others will want to pass it onto their grandchildren. Others will want to retain their collection to the end, even if they have no remaining relatives or children. There needs to be better coordination with charities, museums, history societies and others, to enable the choices to be there for the collectors. Volunteers are important to help sort and catalogue equipment, to provide research notes, to find new locations and venues for displaying and exhibiting the items, to go to visit collectors, and assist them in making choices, without forcing decisions on them.

Bombe Quantities

If the reader is confused on the Bombe machine quantities mentioned in this book, then join the club! The counting of machines is problematical as so many machines were renamed, moved, sent back to the works at BTM for repair or modification, and transferred to different sites. Some could end up at several sites, and if one counted all those, the figures exceed the 211 built.

I set out below, for clarity, the quantities that ended up at the various sites, and these will add up exactly to the 211 Bombes manufactured, based on the entries in the Bombe Registers:

O.S.E.	103 Bombes	(Eastcote)
O.S.S.	76 Bombes	(Stanmore)
O.S.A.	5 Bombes	(Adstock)
O.S.P.	8 Bombes	(Bletchley Pk)
O.S.G	19 Bombes*	(Gayhurst Manor)
O.S.W.	See note below*	(Wavendon)

---

* O.S.G. and Wavendon had Bombes which would have exceeded these figures (about 32 Bombes), however, many were relocated to other sites and therefore not shown here. When inspecting charts and diagrams to illustrate this book, please take this into account.

GCHQ Cheltenham

The Cheltenham 'doughnut' shaped building has been controversial as regards cost, and also the level and nature of intelligence gathered. That is, do we know if any of it breaches our human rights or not? The cost, as understood by the author, was around one third of a billion pounds, but that is probably not the final cost. In comparison, Outstation Eastcote, Outstations Stanmore, Wavendon, Adstock and Gayhurst were exceptionally good value. Yes, Bletchley Park had an overall headquarters role, and there would have been substantial costs to reflect the thousands of men and women engaged on the site, the machines, the equipment, telephone communications, liaison with Y-stations and outstations. I expect the wartime costs and post-war costs of GCHQ to the time when it relocated to Cheltenham are not available, but if it meant our freedom was protected, there are those that say the price of freedom is never too high. The initial GCHQ was split mainly into two main parts, CSO and NCSC. The Composite Signals Organisation (CSO) was responsible for gathering information and intelligence. The National Cyber Security Centre (NCSC) was responsible for the UK's security of its communications. Finally, the JTLS, or Joint Technical Language Service provided technical support and translation.

The GCHQ museum has confirmed that a support base was in existence until 1978 in nearby Northwood Hills (up the road from GCHQ Eastcote) until 1978, when most of GCHQ had already relocated to Cheltenham. This would have been the Services Communications Development Unit (SCDU). Rented offices were used at the junction of Tolcarne Drive and Chamberlain Way. Modern housing now occupies the site.

Educational Opportunities

There is a potential here for communicating the history and science of the earlier codebreaking era, prior to and during the war to young people, in a way that should be both interesting and stimulating, and encourage further research and investigation. The range of sub-topics involved in this subject suits educational projects particularly well. One can look at mathematics (Enigma, sequencing, and mathematical probabilities), social aspects (Wrens and women in industry, and in a war setting, mixing of social classes in wartime), geography (location of outstations and listening stations, etc., Poland, UK, Europe, USA, Canada, Commonwealth countries), computers and I.T. (Colossus, use of valve technology as switches, development of computers, menus for programming, photo-electric cell development), electronics (valve technology, relays, logic diagrams, diagonal board circuit), History of course (the war, military leaders, Churchill, Stalin, Roosevelt, Hitler, post-war activities, Cold war, Britain in the 1950s), Materials Technology (Electrical contact materials such as with wire brushes, 'Cobra' cables and wiring, valves, conduction and properties of materials), Physics (speed and velocity of 'Robinson' and 'Colossus' wheels guiding punched tape, Data transmission rates via teleprinter, Bombe cable connectors and resistance, photo-electric cell technology), Radio Telecommunications ('Y' listening stations, frequencies of transmissions, aerials, headphones, Morse keys, teleprinters, radio equipment of the time, Morse code), codes and ciphers (Enigma methodology, Lorenz and T52 differences, Morse Code, Non-Morse Baudot vernam code, breaking of codes, Bletchley Park, codebreaking outstations, historical development of codes and ciphers), manufacturing and production (*Spirella*, BTM, Post Office Research Establishment, TRE, etc), people (Turing, Welchman, Batey, Michie, Newman, Tutte, Tiltman, Rock, Flowers, Freeborn, Clarke, Tester, Churchill, Denniston, Alexander, Travis, Scherbius, Koch, Keen, Hitler, Kesselring, Truman, Roosevelt, and many others.), buildings and architecture (Bletchley Park, The Manor House at Bletchley Park, Watergate House, Room 40 Whitehall, Beaumanor, Woburn Abbey, Gayhurst Manor, Adstock, Wavendon House, Highgrove House, Outstation Eastcote, Outstation Stanmore, BTM Factory, *Spirella* factory, Chicksands, Knockholt, London, P.O.R.E. Building at Dollis Hill, Denmark Hill, Mill Hill, etc.), laws (homosexuality laws, Official Secrets Act, Tolerance in society, changing attitudes leading to changes in the law), women in work (WRNS/Wrens, ATS/WAAF, prejudice against women carrying out 'male' roles in the 1940s and beyond, achievements and military awards for women, varied tasks and categories of WRNS during WW2, development of equality over time), spying and intelligence (Venona, famous spies in Britain, Ian Fleming, use of radio and equipment in transmitting messages during the war).

There is certainly enough here to support teachers and educationalists for a long time, in inspiring their pupils and students to learn about not just codebreaking, but many other aspects, such as social history, which was annexed to codebreaking, and to keep the subject matter alive for future generations. Using examples from history can bring a subject 'alive' to younger generations, and inspire them to carry out their own further research.

SOURCES OF RESEARCH/ BIBLIOGRAPHY

The National Archives at Kew
Bletchley Park Heritage Trust
The National Museum of Computing, Bletchley Park
The National Cryptologic Museum, Maryland, USA
The Wren Association
The Royal Navy
The Association of Estonians in Great Britain
LB Hillingdon, Uxbridge Reference Library
Pembroke Park Estate and Public Footpath –LB Hillingdon
Letchworth Tourist Information Office
Letchworth Garden City Collection www.gardencitycollection.com
Heritage foundation Letchworth Garden City
The Imperial War Museum, London
Bentley Priory Museum, Stanmore
Historic England
Ruislip Northwood Eastcote Local History Society
Eastcote Resident's Association
Headstone Manor and Museum, L. B. Harrow
BBC and BBC News – online sources
WinstonChurchill.org
Bletchley Park – David Kenyon, Research Historian
Bletchley Park – Guy Revell, Museum Archivist

Bletchley Park – Outstations, A Brief History
WRNS *Wren History 1939-1945* online source

Printed Works
Agar, John, *Turing and the Universal Machine* (London: Icon Books Ltd. 2001)
Agar, John, *The Government Machine: A Revolutionary History of the Computer* (Cambridge/London: MIT Press. 2003)
Aldrich Richard James. *GCHQ* (London: Harper Press, 2010)
Avarez, David, *Allied & Axis Signals & Intelligence in World War II* (London: Routledge, 1999)
Batey, Mavis. *Dilly: The Man who broke Enigmas* (London, Biteback Publishing, 2017)
Buttar, Prit, *Between Giants: The Battle for the Baltics in World War II* (Oxford: Osprey Publishing, 2013)
Campbell Kelly, Martin, *ICL: A Business and Technical History* (Oxford: Oxford University Press/Clarendon Press,1990)
Cawthorne, Nigel, *Alan Turing: The Enigma Man* (London: Arcturus Publishing Ltd, 2014)
Corera, Gordon, *Intercept: The Secret History of Computers and Spies* (London: Weidenfeld and Nicolson/Orion 2016)
Cox, Colleen A. *A Quiet and Secluded Spot: Ruislip, Northwood, and Eastcote* (London: Ruislip, Northwood and Eastcote Local History Society, 1991)
Dunlop, Tessa, *The Bletchley Girls* (London: Hodder & Stoughton Ltd, 2015)
Erskine Ralph & Smith, Michael, *The Bletchley Park Codebreakers* (London: Biteback Publishing, 2011)
Gannon, Paul, *Colossus: Bletchley Park's Greatest Secret* (London: Atlantic Books, 2006)
Gladwin, Lee A. Article: 'Alan Turing, Enigma, and the Breaking of German Ciphers in World War II' (Archives, gov., 1997)
Greenberg Joel, *Alastair Denniston* (Barnsley: Frontline Books, 2017)
Greenberg, Joel, *Gordon Welchman* (London: Frontline Books, 2016)
Hinsley F. & Stripp, A., *CodeBreakers-The Inside Story of Bletchley Park* (Oxford: Oxford University Press, 2001)
Jennings, Christian, *The Third Reich is Listening: Inside German Codebreaking 1939-45* (Oxford: Osprey Publishing, 2018)

Kasekamp, Andres, *A History of the Baltic States* (London: Red Globe Press, 2018)

Kerrigan, Michael, *ENIGMA: How Breaking the Code Helped Win World War II* (London, Amber Books, 2018)

Levine Joshua, *Operation Fortitude* (London: Harper Collins, 2012)

Macintyre, Ben, *Double Cross* (London: Bloomsbury Publishing, 2012)

Matthews, Peter, *SIGINT* (Stroud: The History Press, 2018)

McKay, Sinclair, *The Lost World of Bletchley Park* (London: Aurum Press Ltd, 2013)

McKay, Sinclair, *The Secret Life of Bletchley Park* (London: Aurum Press Ltd, 2011)

McKay, Sinclair, *The Secret Listeners* (London: Aurum Press Ltd, 2013)

McKay, Sinclair, The Spies of Winter (London: Aurum Press Ltd, 2016)

Messenger, Charles, *The D-Day Atlas* (London: Thames & Hudson, 2014)

Miller, Russell, *Codename Tricycle* (London: Pimlico, 2005)

Montefiore, Hugh Sebag, *ENIGMA-The Battle for the Code* (London: Weidenfeld and Nicolson/Orion 2011)

Page, Gwendoline, *We Kept the Secret* (Norfolk. Geo. R. Reeve Ltd, 2008)

Paterson, Michael, *Voices of the Codebreakers* (Barnsley: Greenhill Books, 2018)

Pearson, Joss, *Bletchley Park's Secret Room* (Stroud, Amberley Publishing, 2015)

RNELHS, *The Home Front Ruislip, Northwood and Eastcote in Wartime* (London: Ruislip, Northwood and Eastcote Local History Society, 2007)

Roberts, Captain Jerry, *Lorenz* (Stroud: The History Press, 2018)

Smith, Michael, *Bletchley Park: The Code-Breakers of Station X* (Oxford: Shire Publications, 2014)

Smith, Michael, *The Debs of Bletchley Park* (London: Aurum Press Ltd, 2015)

Storey, Neil R., *WRNS: The Women's Royal Naval Service* (Oxford: Shire Books/Osprey Publishing, 2017)

Taylor, Neil, *Estonia: A Modern History* (London: Hurst & Company Publishers, 2018)

The Rutherford Journal –The Turing Bombe (Online)

Tidy Josh, *Letchworth Garden City Through Time* (Stroud, Amberley Publishing Ltd, 2015)

Tidy, Josh, *Letchworth Garden City in Old Photographs* (Letchworth: Heritage Foundation Letchworth Garden City, 2016)

Toms, Susan (RN&E LHS) *The History Behind the Road Names for Pembroke Park, Eastcote*

Toms, Susan (RNELHS), papers and articles from The Ruislip, Northwood, Eastcote Local History Society, Codebreakers at Eastcote

Turing Dermot, *Prof: Alan Turing Decoded* (Stroud: The History Press, 2016)

Turing, Dermot *XY & Z: The Real Story of How Enigma was Broken* (Stroud: The History Press, 2018)

Welchman, Gordon, *The Hut Six Story* (Kidderminster, M&M Baldwin, 2018)

Weller, A. *Secret Eastcote* (London: Friends of Eastcote House Gardens Community Archive Publication)

Other Sources of Information

After the Battle Issue 37 (Historical society)

Bombe Registers on Loan to The National Archives at Kew.

Bombe Types, Bombe.org.uk

Cryptomuseum (Netherlands)

Discussion with ex B Telecom engineer who trained at Bletchley Park after the war.

Discussions or emails with individuals who worked on the base at Eastcote or had family members who had links with the base or Y-stations.

Discussions with a Bletchley Park Voluntary Guide at Northwood Hills Library in 2018.

Discussions with a member of the National Museum of Computing at both Northwood Hills Library and at Ruislip Manor Libraries in 2018.

Discussions with individuals who have had some knowledge of the Eastcote Outstation, mainly post-war.

Examination of local maps of the Eastcote and surrounding areas sourced at Uxbridge Reference library and elsewhere.

Extracts from Microsoft™ Powerpoint Presentation (R.Koorm
FRICS) on Eastcote to GCHQ (copyright 2018)
Helpful assistance from The Media and Publications manager at
The Bletchley Park Trust, and kind permission to use certain
selected photographs courtesy of The Bletchley Park Trust
Hertsmemories.org.uk (BTM webpage)
John Edmonds, Eastcote Resident
Maps, photographs and information via The Collections Officer
at The Garden City Collection, Letchworth, and the kind
offer of allowing several photographs and a city map from the
Garden City collection to be reproduced here, following detailed
discussions with the Collections Officer.
Pastscape, Drayton Parslow
Radio Boulevard, Western Historic Radio Museum
Ruislip Online, Online source
Tony Sale, Menus
Various TICOM reports: TICOM Secret Intelligence in Nazi
Germany, Fish and the Jellyfish Convoy
www.codes and ciphers.org.uk (The British Bombe, 6812th
Signal Security Detachment (Prov) APO 413 US Army via
Tony Sale)

Some of the National Archives reference documents researched are
listed as follows, but this is not a complete list, only some of the
most relevant:

HW 25/19, HW 25/20 (Vols 1 and 2 Bombe registers)
HW 14/57, HW 14/48, HW 14/43, HW 14/56 (cover story for
Stanmore and WRNS staff recruitment)
HW 14/48, HW 64/65, HW 14/51, HW 14/60, HW 34/17, HW
34/21, HW 47/1, HW 64/25, HW 14/164
HW 64/63, HW 64/25, HW64/45, HW 64/68, HW 64/76, HW
14/164, HW 14/62
FO 366/2221 (Financial arrangements GC & CS Eastcote)

ACKNOWLEDGEMENTS

The author thanks the many individuals who have provided guidance, information, direction and assistance in helping me collect relevant data for this book. In particular, my special thanks to The Collections officer at The Garden City Collection in Letchworth, Hertfordshire, who has been incredibly helpful dealing with my questions and enquiries, and arranging the permissions/licence for reproducing certain historical images and photos from the collection. Also, The Tourist Information Office in Letchworth, The National Archives at Kew, Uxbridge reference library, Doctor Rachel Abbiss (Military curator at Battle of Britain Bunker, Uxbridge), volunteer guides who attended my talks from Bletchley Park, members of The National Computer Museum at Bletchley Park who have attended my talks, and countless others.

My thanks to The Bletchley Park Trust who have allowed me permission to use certain photographs in this book, particularly of the Enigma in their excellent museum, the Typex machine, and the front cover picture in one of their huts. My thanks to the Museum Curator of GCHQ, Cheltenham, who has provided certain photographs for inclusion in this book.

Thanks to the librarians at L.B. of Hillingdon, who have been so welcoming and helpful in publicising and arranging my talks for local residents and others, of coordinating the dates with other libraries in the borough, arranging posters, and providing feedback on the response to the talks.

My thanks to Headstone Manor Museum and heritage site in L.B. of Harrow, and to Emily Thomas, Community Engagement Officer, regarding assisting the author in arranging a talk on the Codebreaking outstations on that site. Also, inspection of the excellent detailed bombing map of Harrow and other maps related to Stanmore and surrounding area.

My particular thanks goes to Toomas Ojasoo, Chairman of The Association of Estonians in Great Britain, who responded to my questions and email so promptly. His comments, and confirmation of some of the incidents that took place during the Second World War in Estonia, as well as that of the overall impression (as seen from the eyes of the Baltic states) between the Russians and the Germans, given the Baltic's geographical area's turbulent political and wartime history.

My brother, Taivo, who clarified several points relating to 1945 and beyond for me, regarding Estonia and Germany, and for some specific detailed information which is not generally available elsewhere. Also, his specialist knowledge of vintage radio receiving equipment, he having owned various equipment over the years, which proved to be an education both for him and his colleagues at the BBC and elsewhere. Only a relatively small part of the (family-sourced) information was included in this book, as the subject matter relates to family history, and was considered inappropriate to be shared. My brother has been an inspiration to me on the subject of Enigma, and he has read widely on the subject, and on Colossus too. Taivo also has a claim to fame in having demonstrated the first BBC Electronic news camera to H. R. H. Prince Charles some years ago, and for appearing on the front cover of *Wireless World* in the 1960s. There is not much he doesn't know about vintage radio equipment, valves, television cameras and televisions, vintage electric clocks, pianolas, and many other subjects.

I am indebted to Mr E. A. Schubert for confirming some aspects of the American wartime base in Ruislip. I consider him something of an expert on specific aspects of military history as regards the Second World War, with an excellent understanding and knowledge of military equipment, particularly German tanks, armaments and soldiers, also of Polish military history during the war. Ed is my oldest friend, also an experienced and is talented model maker of military items. We both share a passion for military history.

My thanks to my good friend, David Plummer, who has attended many of my talks, and says he learns something new each time. I am grateful to those people who come up to speak with me after one of my talks to share their experiences. Without you, David, those talks would not have happened, and this book would never have been written.

Many thanks to the Hillingdon librarians who have accommodated me within local library venues for talks and presentations on this subject, and who have been most welcoming and helpful in coordinating the events and making bookings. My thanks to the many history societies who have contacted me, for arranging talks at their venues. It is always interesting for me to be asked questions on this subject, and whilst I don't always know the answer, I usually have a contact and know someone who can assist the enquirer.

My schoolfriend and long-term friend Malcolm Pordes, who lives in San Francisco, who I email from time to time, and who advised me that he once worked with Donald Michie, gave me the inspiration to research Michie in some depth, and the significant contribution he made to the wartime and post-war periods. If it wasn't for you, Malcolm, I would probably have missed out an important part of this book, so thank you for that. Michie was such a unique individual, and few books mention him at all.

My thanks to Isobel, Alex, Rebecca, and her colleagues, trainee journalists at Brunel, who are intending to write an article on the codebreaking background to Eastcote, and have demonstrated their enthusiasm and passion on this subject. I hope I have assisted in steering them in the right direction on this topic, and wish them well in their ongoing research and future careers. It is encouraging that younger people are taking an interest here, to communicate the story of the outstations, and of Eastcote. If I have been able to raise the profile of this subject on codebreaking outstations and relevant aspects of them, I will have achieved my objective.

NOTES

1. Warner Brothers.
2. Patent filed for his machine by Koch in 1919 Amsterdam.
3. Additional rotors, different keyboards and other changes may have increased the versions further.
4. The British had nine months of failing to crack the Naval Shark codes in 1942 before some captured German codebooks changed the situation.
5. Connection via Churchill's mother.
6. Codenamed 'Purple'.
7. The 'Bomba' is supposed to have been named after a local ice cream but the machine bore no resemblance in design to the later Bombe of Alan Turing.
8. 26 x 26 x 26 letters.
9. 8 x 7 x 6 = 336.
10. 5 x 4 x 3 = 60.
11. 'Secret Writer' machines.
12. The Turing Bombe, Ellsbury.
13. 'Dilly' Knox had a team of talented females to assist with codebreaking, with considerable success.
14. GCHQ plaque at Watergate House was unveiled in February 2019 by H. M. The Queen, for the centenary of GCHQ.
15. Both sailors, a first lieutenant and an Able Seaman, were posthumously awarded medals for their bravery.

16. Kursk, July and August 1943, German name Operation *Zitadelle* (Citadel).
17. Association of Estonians in Great Britain – T Ojasoo (2019).
18. *Estonia – A Modern History*, Taylor.
19. Camps in Germany for Refugees from the Baltic Countries. 1944-1951, Estonia- Displaced Persons from the Baltic States.
20. Association of Estonians in GB – Chairman T.Ojasoo.
21. See Glossary of abbreviations.
22a. Churchill and Roosevelt agreed not to interfere with Stalin's intervention in the Baltics, which would then have serious consequences for the Baltic people.
22. 27-2-2019 email to Author via T Ojasoo – Association of Estonians in GB. Other credible sources give the same indication.
23. Possibly called 'Longfellow' by the British, after an American mathematician.
24. Approx 26% of the population.
25. Garden City Collection, Letchworth.
26. The National Archives Bombe Registers indicate the Bombe numbers and history of the Bombes. Bletchley Park has also confirmed this point separately.
27. *Spirella* Company.
28. Bombe Number 1, 'Victory'.
29. The name was changed twice, and ended up as 'LONDON' according to the Bombe Register Volume 1 at the National Archives.
30. TRE based in Malvern, and was involved in Radar research work.
31. Fifteen different Enigma ciphers are estimated to have been known about.
32. The National Archives Bombe registers confirm this.
33. Post-war, Britain would offer several updated Enigmas to the Swiss, who would acquire them. Britain was then in a strong position to decode their intelligence.
34. From 'VICTORY' to 'LEO' to 'LONDON', relocated to O.S.E. in 1943.
35. The National Archives HW/56.
36. The National Archives.
37. Later on, further expansion to Eastcote, destined to become the largest codebreaking outstation.
38. Volume I and Volume II.
39. GCHQ Eastcote would receive two Colossus Mark 2 machines, some Robinsons, and Tunny machines after the war.
40. Some have reported 5′ 6″ but there are more accounts of the 5′ 8″ height requirement.

41. Photograph of a Bombe room with checker machines shows this clearly to be the case.
42. Some reports say 'Job's up'. Both may have been used in practice.
43. It is not clear how common this restriction was, ie at other codebreaking outstations, it may be the case that there was less formality and flexibility.
44. 4pm–midnight would be the shift most hated as it affected social activities.
45. 6812th US Signals.
46. Triple checking the connections is mentioned in several accounts.
47. Several reports of nervous breakdowns, fatigue and excess tiredness, across several bases, resulting in sick bay rest for some. Monotony of the work added to this fatigue and stress.
48. The Bletchley Girls, T. Dunlop.
49. Bobs Brooke-Taylor Née Kirby 1943.
50. There were reports of a few exceptions to this, where a choice was given to some.
51. Bombe 269 for example, at OSE with six names (The National Archives Bombe Register Volume 2).
52. Wynn-Williamson worked at TRE in Malvern.
53. 211-total – 8 at Bletchley Park = 203 Bombe machines for the outstations.
54. Reproduction Bombes can be seen at Bletchley Park.
55. HW 25/19 & HW 25/20.
56. Plan of Town Area, spring 1936, Estate Office Letchworth, Herts.
57. HW/64/63 BTM & GC &CS Period of 1 June 1942–Sept 30 1943.
58. Now Existing as Flats off Brook Road as Chartwell Court, Dollis Hill NW2.
59. Historic England mentions Military Hospital Base.
60. Signage indicates 'Pembroke Park' at the entrance road to the estate.
61. Two weeks was average but some attended for three weeks across the training bases.
62. WRNS Dorothy Jewell 29/12/44–4/45.
63. See Chapter on Siemens.
64. Based on information from The National Archives.
65. Date of exact arrival of Colossi at Eastcote is not known, as these would not appear in the Bombe Registers, and were top secret.
66. The National Archives HW14/164.
67. The author has evidence of this via family connections, as well as Baltic States history.

68. Gordon Welchman comments in The Hut Six Story that he personally burnt the drawings and put them in the incinerator on instructions.
69. Thirty-three solutions reported.
70. The National Archives Bombe Register.
71. Siemens website makes the history and acknowledgement clear.
72. Siemens 2018 Annual Report.
73. Historic England Record. Monument No 1535542.
74. Anecdotal comments from one Wren who was based at Stanmore for a time.
75. National Archives HW 14/56.
76. The National Archives – letter written from the Intelligence Division of the Admiralty to Travis by a senior officer.
77. The National Archives – The Commander in Chief, The Nore 26-10-1942.
78. Headstone Manor Museum in Harrow has old maps showing the hospital.
79. However, the museum does have a fine collection of medals, prints and paintings of Second World War RAF history on a beautifully landscaped site.
80. Usually in the Assembly Block near Lime Grove
81. Headstone Manor and Museum, L.B.H.
82. Split from Post Office in 1980 to form British Telecom.
83. Thought to be along Victoria Road in South Ruislip.
84. www.unithistories.com WRNS Officers 1939–1935.
85. WRNS: The Women's Royal Naval Service, Storey.
86. See www.Cryptomuseum
87. The author's brother apparently owned one of these magnificent machines after the war. There are plenty about as they made so many of them.
88. Non-Morse teleprinter encoded messages.
89. The National Archives.
90. Garden City Collection, Letchworth.
91. Due to popular demand a return visit has been booked by the library.
92. Historic England – Register of monuments, online.
93. LASER – Light Amplification by Stimulated Emission of Radiation.
94. February 2019 commencing presentations in March 2019.
95. The Plaque commemorating Outstation Eastcote and GCHQ is behind railings in line with the pedestrian crossing on Eastcote High Road, north of Highgrove House.
96. The Ruislip, Northwood, Eastcote, Local History Society.

INDEX